Painting Constitutional Law

Legal History Library

Series Editors

C.H. (Remco) van Rhee, *Maastricht University*
Dirk Heirbaut, *Ghent University*
Matthew C. Mirow, *Florida International University*

Editorial Board

Hamilton Bryson, *University of Richmond*
Thomas P. Gallanis, *University of Iowa*
James Gordley, *Tulane University*
Richard Helmholz, *University of Chicago*
Michael Hoeflich, *University of Kansas*
Neil Jones, *University of Cambridge*
Hector MacQueen, *University of Edinburgh*
Paul Oberhammer, *University of Vienna*
Marko Petrak, *University of Zagreb*
Jacques du Plessis, *University of Stellenbosch*
Mathias Reimann, *University of Michigan*
Jan M. Smits, *Maastricht University*
Alain Wijffels, *Université Catholique de Louvain, Leiden University,* CNRS
Reinhard Zimmermann, *Max-Planck-Institut für ausländisches und internationales Privatrecht, Hamburg*

VOLUME 46

The titles published in this series are listed at *brill.com/lhl*

Painting Constitutional Law

Xavier Cortada's Images of Constitutional Rights

Edited by

M.C. Mirow and Howard M. Wasserman

BRILL
NIJHOFF

LEIDEN | BOSTON

Cover illustration: *Gideon v. Wainwright*, 372 U.S. 335 (1963). Miami, 2004. Painting by Xavier Cortada. Photo by Zenaida Pirri, Miami, Florida.

Library of Congress Cataloging-in-Publication Data

Names: Mirow, Matthew C. (Matthew Campbell), 1962- editor, author. | Wasserman, Howard M., editor, author.
Title: Painting constitutional law : Xavier Cortada's images of constitutional rights / edited by M. C. Mirow and Howard M. Wasserman.
Description: Leiden, The Netherlands : Koninklijke Brill NV, [2021] | Series: Legal history library, 1874-1793 ; volume 46 | Includes index. |
Identifiers: LCCN 2020046873 (print) | LCCN 2020046874 (ebook) | ISBN 9789004364301 (hardback) | ISBN 9789004445598 (ebook)
Subjects: LCSH: Constitutional law–United States. | Civil rights–United States. | Constitutional law–United States–Cases. | United States. Supreme Court–Decision making. | Cortada, Xavier. Classification: LCC KF4550 .P35 2021 (print) | LCC KF4550 (ebook) | DDC 342.73–dc23
LC record available at https://lccn.loc.gov/2020046873
LC ebook record available at https://lccn.loc.gov/2020046874

Typeface for the Latin, Greek, and Cyrillic scripts: "Brill". See and download: brill.com/brill-typeface.

ISSN 1874-1793
ISBN 978-90-04-36430-1 (hardback)
ISBN 978-90-04-44559-8 (e-book)

Copyright 2021 by Koninklijke Brill NV, Leiden, The Netherlands.
Koninklijke Brill NV incorporates the imprints Brill, Brill Hes & De Graaf, Brill Nijhoff, Brill Rodopi, Brill Sense, Hotei Publishing, mentis Verlag, Verlag Ferdinand Schöningh and Wilhelm Fink Verlag.
All rights reserved. No part of this publication may be reproduced, translated, stored in a retrieval system, or transmitted in any form or by any means, electronic, mechanical, photocopying, recording or otherwise, without prior written permission from the publisher. Requests for re-use and/or translations must be addressed to Koninklijke Brill NV via brill.com or copyright.com.

This book is printed on acid-free paper and produced in a sustainable manner.

To Angela Beatriz
M.C.M.

...

To Jennifer and Lily
H.M.W.

Contents

    Acknowledgments   XI
    List of Figures   XII
    Notes on Contributors   XIII

1   *May It Please the Court*
    Of Florida, from Florida, for Florida   1
      Howard M. Wasserman

2   Legal Iconography and *Painting Constitutional Law*   10
    M.C. Mirow

3   Xavier Cortada
    Socially Engaged Activist Artist   27
      Renée D. Ater

Gideon v. Wainwright, 372 U.S. 335 (1963)   45
    Xavier Cortada

4   *Gideon v. Wainwright*
    The Surprising Power of a Prisoner Petition   48
      Paul Marcus and Mary Sue Backus

Williams v. Florida, 399 U.S. 78 (1970)   59
    Xavier Cortada

5   *Williams v. Florida*
    What's in a Number? Jury Function and Jury Numbers   62
      Jenny E. Carroll

Miami Herald Publishing Company v. Tornillo, 418 U.S. 241 (1974)   75
    Xavier Cortada

6   *Miami Herald Publishing Company v. Tornillo*
    Freedom of Speech for Whom?   78
      Leslie C. Kendrick

Proffitt v. Florida, 428 U.S. 242 (1976)   95
    Xavier Cortada

7   *Proffitt v. Florida*
    Distorting Death   98
        Corinna Barrett Lain

Palmore v. Sidoti, 466 U.S. 429 (1984)   119
    Xavier Cortada

8   *Palmore v. Sidoti*
    The Troubling Effects of 'Private Biases'   122
        Linda C. McClain

Church of the Lukumi Babalu Aye, Inc. v. City of Hialeah, 508 U.S. 520 (1993)   141
    Xavier Cortada

9   *Church of the Lukumi Babalu Aye, Inc. v. City of Hialeah*
    The Meaning of Free Exercise: Equality and Beyond   144
        Kathleen A. Brady

Seminole Tribe of Florida v. Florida, 517 U.S. 44 (1996)   167
    Xavier Cortada

10   *Seminole Tribe of Florida v. Florida*
    Sovereignty and the Eleventh Amendment Imag(in)ed   170
        James E. Pfander

Bush v. Gore, 531 U.S. 98 (2000)   189
    Xavier Cortada

11   *Bush v. Gore*
    Haste Makes Mistakes   192
        Erwin Chemerinsky

Stop the Beach Renourishment, Inc. v. Florida Department of Environmental Protection, 560 U.S. 702 (2010)   211
    Xavier Cortada

12 *Stop the Beach Renourishment, Inc. v. Florida Department of Environmental Protection*
    On Art, Law, and the Power of the Sea 214
        Laura S. Underkuffler

Florida v. Jardines, 569 U.S. 1 (2013)   231
        Xavier Cortada

13 *Florida v. Jardines*
    The Distortions of Implied Artistic License   234
        Andrew Guthrie Ferguson

    Index   251

Acknowledgments

The editors thank Xavier Cortada for his delightful and warm cooperation in this project and for arranging the rights to reproduce images of his art. His paintings inspired what follows in these pages. *May It Please the Court* was displayed at the Supreme Court of Florida and is on loan by the artist to Florida International University College of Law, Miami.

We thank Dean Antony Page of FIU College of Law for supporting and encouraging this work. We also thank our colleagues Thomas E. Baker, Stanley Fish, and John F. Stack, Jr. for their thoughts and suggestions on this project. Kimberly Wittman, an FIU law student with substantial skills in humanities publication and production, assisted with the editing and preparation of the manuscript. We thank her for her careful work.

We thank Zenaida Pirri for her photographs of Cortada's works. The Des Moines Art Center, Des Moines, Iowa, granted permission to reproduce Francis Bacon's *Study after Velázquez's Portrait of Pope Innocent X* (1953), and we thank Rich Sanders for his photograph of this work.

Figures

4.1 Xavier Cortada, *Gideon v. Wainwright*, 372 U.S. 335 (1963), 48" × 36", oil on canvas, 2004. Photo: Zenaida Pirri, Miami, Florida   47

5.1 Xavier Cortada, *Williams v. Florida*, 399 U.S. 78 (1970), oil on canvas, 2004. Photo: Zenaida Pirri, Miami, Florida   61

6.1 Xavier Cortada, *Miami Herald Publishing Company v. Tornillo*, 418 U.S. 241 (1974), 48" × 36", oil on canvas, 2004. Photo: Zenaida Pirri, Miami, Florida   77

7.1 Xavier Cortada, *Proffitt v. Florida*, 428 U.S. 242 (1976), 48" × 36", acrylic on canvas, 2004. Photo: Zenaida Pirri, Miami, Florida   97

7.2 Francis Bacon, Study after Velázquez's Portrait of Pope Innocent X. 1953. Des Moines Art Center, Des Moines, Iowa. Photo: Rich Sanders, Des Moines, Iowa   109

8.1 Xavier Cortada, *Palmore v. Sidoti*, 466 U.S. 429 (1984), 48" × 36", acrylic on canvas, 2004. Photo: Zenaida Pirri, Miami, Florida   121

9.1 Xavier Cortada, *Church of the Lukumi Babalu Aye, Inc. v. City of Hialeah*, 508 U.S. 520 (1993), 48" × 36", acrylic on canvas, 2004. Photo: Zenaida Pirri, Miami, Florida   143

10.1 Xavier Cortada, *Seminole Tribe of Florida v. Florida,* 517 U.S. 44 (1996), 48" × 36", acrylic on canvas, 2004. Photo: Zenaida Pirri, Miami, Florida   169

11.1 Xavier Cortada, *Bush v. Gore*, 531 U.S. 98 (2000), 48" × 36", acrylic on canvas, 2017. Photo: Zenaida Pirri, Miami, Florida   191

12.1 Xavier Cortada, *Stop the Beach Renourishment, Inc. v. Florida Department of Environmental Protection*, 560 U.S. 702 (2010), 48" × 36", acrylic, sand and mixed media on canvas, 2017. Photo: Zenaida Pirri, Miami, Florida   213

13.1 Xavier Cortada, *Florida v. Jardines*, 569 U.S. 1 (2013), 48" × 36", acrylic on canvas, 2017. Photo: Zenaida Pirri, Miami, Florida   233

Notes on Contributors

Renée D. Ater
is Associate Professor of American Art Emeritus at the University of Maryland. She holds a Ph.D. from the University of Maryland and has written many works on the relationship among art, race, gender, national identity, and public culture. She is the author of *Remaking Race and History: The Sculpture of Met Warrick Fuller* (2011) and co-author of a study on Xavier Cortada, 'Art in the Anthropocene,' published in *American Art* (2014).

Mary Sue Backus
is Robert Glenn Rapp Foundation Presidential Professor at the University of Oklahoma. She holds a J.D. from the College of William and Mary and has published widely on criminal law and the right to counsel.

Kathleen A. Brady
is Senior Fellow at the Center for the Study of Law and Religion at Emory University. She holds a Master of Arts in Religion and J.D. from Yale University. She is the author of *The Distinctiveness of Religion in American Law: Rethinking Religion Clause Jurisprudence* (2015).

Jenny E. Carroll
is Wiggins, Childs, Quinn, and Pantazis Professor of Law at the University of Alabama. She holds a J.D. from the University of Texas and an LL.M. from Georgetown University. She has published widely on juries in the criminal-justice system, including articles in *Georgetown Law Journal* and book chapters for Cambridge University Press.

Erwin Chemerinsky
is the Dean of the University of California, Berkeley School of Law. He holds a J.D. from Harvard University and is one of the most frequently cited legal scholars in the country. He is the author of numerous books on constitutional law, most recently *Closing the Courthouse Door: How the Supreme Court Has Made Your Rights Unenforceable* (2017).

Xavier Cortada
is Professor of Practice at the University of Miami Department of Art and Art History. He grew up in Miami and holds degrees from the University of Miami College of Arts and Sciences, School of Law, and Graduate School of Business. His work merges art with other disciplines, including law, science, and politics.

Andrew Guthrie Ferguson
is Professor of Law at Washington College of Law, American University. He hold an LL.M. from Georgetown University and a J.D. from the University of Pennsylvania. He is the author of *Why Jury Duty Matters: A Citizen's Guide to Constitutional Action* (2012).

Leslie C. Kendrick
is Albert Clarke Tate, Jr. Professor of Law at the University of Virginia. She holds a D.Phil. from Oxford University where she was a Rhodes Scholar and a J.D. from the University of Virginia. A former clerk to Justice David Souter of the Supreme Court of the United States, she has published extensively on the freedom of speech in journals such as *Harvard Law Review*, *Columbia Law Review*, and the *Supreme Court Review*.

Corinna Barrett Lain
is S.D. Roberts and Sandra Moore Professor of Law at the University of Richmond. She holds a J.D. from the University of Virginia. She has published on the death penalty in UCLA *Law Review*, *Georgetown Law Journal*, and *Duke Law Journal*.

Paul Marcus
is Haynes Professor of Law at the Marshall-Wythe School of Law at the College of William & Mary. He hold a J.D. from the University of California, Los Angeles. A recognized expert in criminal law, he is the co-author of several national casebooks on criminal law, criminal procedure, and criminal defenses. He was recently president of the American Association of Law Schools.

Linda C. McClain
is Professor of Law and the Paul M. Siskind Research Scholar at Boston University. She holds a J.D. from Georgetown University and an LL.M. from NYU, and has held fellowships at Harvard and Princeton Universities. She is the author or co-author of numerous books and articles on family, gender, and law, including *The Place of Families: Fostering Capacity, Equality, and Responsibility* (2006).

M.C. Mirow
is Professor of Law at Florida International University. He holds a J.D. from Cornell University and Ph.D.s from Cambridge and Leiden Universities. He is the author of *Latin American Constitutions* (2015) and *Florida's First Constitution* (2012).

James E. Pfander

is Owen L. Coon Professor of Law at Northwestern University. He holds a J.D. from the University of Virginia. He is the author of numerous books and articles on the federal courts including *Constitutional Torts and the War on Terror* (2017) and *One Supreme Court: Supremacy, Inferiority, and the Judicial Power of the United States* (2009).

Laura S. Underkuffler

is J. DuPratt White Professor of Law at Cornell University. She holds a J.D. from William Mitchell College of Law and a J.S.D. from Yale University. She is the author of numerous articles on property and constitutional law and of the book *The Idea of Property: its Meaning and Power* (2003).

Howard M. Wasserman

is Professor of Law and Associate Dean for Research and Faculty Development at Florida International University. He holds a J.D. from Northwestern University and has published on the First Amendment and civil rights, including *Understanding Civil Rights Litigation* (2018).

CHAPTER 1

May It Please the Court
Of Florida, from Florida, for Florida

Howard M. Wasserman

Two themes unite the Supreme Court cases Xavier Cortada captures in the ten paintings in *May It Please the Court*—the Constitution of the United States and the State of Florida.

Cortada is a law-trained artist raised and educated in Miami. *May It Please the Court* premiered as a 2004 solo exhibit in the rotunda of the Supreme Court of Florida and has been on display in the halls of Florida International University College of Law since 2011. The original series consisted of seven paintings portraying significant constitutional decisions from the Supreme Court of the United States, the latest from 1996; all cases arose from Florida events, persons, and places and all but one originated in the Florida courts and passed through the Supreme Court of Florida. When the editors approached the artist about this volume, he added three new paintings depicting three post-2001 cases.[1] Given his connections to Florida, it is unsurprising that Cortada would aim his artistic eye and his unique artistic style at that state's specific contributions to American constitutional law.

But it would be misleading to describe Cortada's series, the underlying cases, or the essays in this volume as being 'about' Florida. The Supreme Court decisions he depicts interpreted broad constitutional provisions and announced broad constitutional principles and ideals, on matters ranging from criminal procedure to freedom of the press to free exercise of religion to property rights to state sovereign immunity. Those principles are national in scope—as applicable in Florida as any state. As were the laws and government actions challenged in those cases. *Proffitt v. Florida* reaffirmed Florida's capital-punishment procedures the same day the Court approved identical procedures in Georgia.[2] Florida was not unique in utilizing, or attempting

---

1 Following the convention of constitutional law scholars in the United States, the Supreme Court of the United States is often referred to as the 'Court' with a capital initial letter. Similarly, 'Justice,' with a capital initial letter, refers to a judge of the Court.
2 *Gregg v. Georgia*, 428 U.S. 153 (1976).

to utilize, criminal juries of fewer than twelve persons[3] or in not providing counsel to indigent defendants.[4]

Cortada's series is, however, 'of' Florida. The paintings and their corresponding essays reflect instances in which Florida people, places, and events influenced other states and the rest of the nation, but from starting points special to that state.

Because Florida is a weird place full of weird people doing weird things.

Journalist Craig Pittman, a native Floridian whose family traces its roots in the state to 1850, writes that a 'combination of beauty and the bizarro makes Florida the most fascinating state of the fifty.' Florida 'is a place where tragedy often wears the mask of comedy.'[5] It is 'the Land of a Thousand Chances, the place where people go who have screwed up elsewhere and need to start over.'[6] And it is a place in which 'it can be hard to tell the good guys from the bad guys,' for sometimes 'they switch sides.'[7] The internet personifies this weirdness in 'Florida Man,' a meme invented around 2013 describing 'the world's worst super-hero' who engages in all manner of bizarre behavior, good and bad, in the state.[8]

But Pittman warns against turning 'the Sunshine State into the Punch Line State.' It would be a mistake not to take Florida seriously—'[n]o matter how hard you may laugh at Florida, the fact is it's constantly influencing all the other states. They just don't notice it.'[9]

In *May It Please the Court*, Cortada pictures how Florida has influenced constitutional law and the application of the Constitution to all other states. The essays in this volume complement those pictures with words describing Florida's influence.

Consider the quintessentially 'Florida' features of the events and actors giving rise to some of the cases that Cortada paints and that the contributors to this volume describe.

---

[3] *Ballew v. Georgia*, 435 U.S. 223 (1978).
[4] *Gideon v. Wainwright*, 372 U.S. 335 (1963).
[5] Craig Pittman, *Oh, Florida! How America's Weirdest State Influences the Rest of the Country* (New York: St. Martin's Press, 2016), 3.
[6] Ibid., 4.
[7] Ibid., 5.
[8] Logan Hill, 'Is It Okay to laugh at Florida Man?' Washington Post Magazine, July 15, 2019; Bob Norman, 'Who is Florida Man?' Columbia Journalism Review, May 30, 2019.
[9] Pittman, *Oh, Florida!*, 5.

1   *Gideon v. Wainwright*

Gideon famously established the right to court-appointed counsel in criminal proceedings,[10] which everyone knows from TV procedurals as one of the litany of rights that police must read to arrestees.

But the legal principle is bound to the legend of Floridian Clarence Earl Gideon. His handwritten petition to the Supreme Court represents the ideal that the poorest and least powerful can capture the attention of the Supreme Court of the United States and create fundamental change in constitutional law. All were depicted in *Gideon's Trumpet*, Anthony Lewis's book and the movie starring Henry Fonda as Gideon.[11]

Pittman highlights Gideon's forgotten Florida legal assistance, unmentioned in Lewis's book. The 'real brain' behind Gideon's success was fellow prisoner Joseph A. Peel, Jr., who advised Gideon in drafting his appeal. Peel was a corrupt former municipal court judge convicted and sentenced for being an accomplice to the murder of another judge and that judge's wife when they threatened to expose Peel's corruption.[12]

Before the Supreme Court, Gideon was represented by attorney (and future Associate Justice of the Supreme Court) Abe Fortas.[13] Fortas had his own unfortunate connections to Florida corruption. He resigned from the Court in 1969, in part because the press reported that, while on the Court, Fortas received a $ 200,000 retainer from a Florida corporate raider facing securities-fraud charges.[14] Fortas's seat was one of four that Richard Nixon filled in his first term, ending the liberal heyday of the 'Warren Court'[15] and precipitating a rightward move on the Supreme Court that continues to the present.

The respondent in the case was Louis L. Wainwright, who served as Secretary of the Florida Division of Corrections for 25 years, from 1962–1987. In that position, he was the named respondent in every federal habeas corpus petition filed by every Florida prisoner. His name appears in the Supreme Court data base hundreds of times, and he was party to dozens of significant decisions,

---

10   *Gideon v. Wainwright*, 372 U.S. 335 (1963).
11   Anthony Lewis, *Gideon's Trumpet* (New York: Random House, 1964); *Gideon's Trumpet* (CBS Television Broadcast April 30, 1980).
12   Pittman, *Oh, Florida!*, 144–45.
13   Lewis, *Gideon's Trumpet*, 48–56.
14   Pittman, *Oh, Florida!*, 146.
15   Lucas A. Powe, Jr., *The Warren Court and American Politics* (Cambridge: Belknap Press, 2000), 303–04.

including several in the 1970s and 1980s in which the Court narrowed the scope of habeas relief.[16]

2 *Miami Herald v. Tornillo*

The constitutional issue in *Miami Herald v. Tornillo* was the validity of a state 'right of reply' statute, requiring newspapers to provide political candidates with the opportunity and equal space to respond to negative editorials and criticisms. The Court declared that the statute violated the First Amendment, by compelling the newspaper to publish content it did not want to publish.[17] The case resonates today, as courts struggle with new questions of compelled expression.[18]

On the ground, the case was about Pasquale 'Pat' Tornillo, 'one of Florida's larger-than-life figures' and a 'classic power-broker' in the state. Tornillo was the head of the United Teachers of Dade for more than 40 years, wielding influence in South Florida and in the state capital.[19]

Tornillo invoked the right-of-reply statute in seeking to respond to a series of editorials in the *Miami Herald* opposing his candidacy for state legislature and criticizing his actions as union head. The newspaper referred to him as a 'czar' and 'Glorious Leader' who led an illegal teacher strike that harmed the children of Florida and who engaged in 'shakedown statesmanship.'[20]

After running afoul of the First Amendment in his efforts to respond to his critics in the pages of the *Herald*, Tornillo ran afoul of the law. He pleaded guilty to federal fraud charges in 2003 and served 27 months in prison for embezzling more than $ 3 million from union coffers. The government's evidence described lavish spending on travel, hotels, Caribbean vacation homes, and personal items, all while he excoriated state education officials for low teacher pay.[21] Ironically, Tornillo reached the *Herald's* pages upon his release from prison in 2005, publishing a letter of apology to the 'union members who

---

16   E.g. *Darden v. Wainwright*, 477 U.S. 168 (1986); *Wainwright v. Sykes*, 433 U.S. 72 (1977).
17   *Miami Herald v. Tornillo*, 418 U.S. 241 (1974).
18   *Janus v. American Federation of State, County, and Mun. Employees*, 138 S. Ct. 2448, 2463 (2018); *National Institute of Family and Life Advocate v. Becerra*, 138 S. Ct. 2361, 2371 (2018); *Masterpiece Cakeshop, Ltd. v. Colorado Civil Rights Com'n*, 138 S. Ct. 1719, 1745 (2018).
19   Vaishali Honowar, 'Disgraced Union Leader Pat Tornillo Dies' Education Week, June 27, 2007; 'The Rise and Fall of Pat Tornillo' The Ledger, August 30, 2003.
20   *Miami Herald*, 418 U.S. at 244–45 n.1.
21   Honowar, 'Disgraced'; 'The Rise and Fall.'

believed in me and stood with me through demonstrations and rallies and civil disobedience as we fought for collective bargaining and teacher rights.'[22]

3 *Palmore v. Sidoti*

The Court in *Palmore* held that a family-court judge could not consider negative societal attitudes about inter-racial relationships and families or strip a white mother of custody of her daughter because the mother was in a relationship with an African American man and community members may oppose such a union.[23]

This case highlights Florida's complicated racial history and its position in and as part of 'The South.'[24] Florida has uniquely multi-cultural origins. The long-standing perception is that Florida's northern areas are southern and its southern areas northern.[25] It thus may surprise readers that a major precedent tackling old-fashioned racial prejudice would originate in Florida rather than Mississippi or Alabama.

But Florida prior to the 1970s was as Southern as any state in the region. It had the highest lynching rate against African Americans in the South between 1890 and 1930.[26] It had poll taxes, segregated schools, and monuments to Confederate leaders. The same Civil Rights Era activism integrated buses, beaches, schools, and places of public accommodation in Florida as in other Southern states.[27]

Historian Gary Mormino argues that Florida is unique among Southern states because it changed quickly, beginning with the 'Big Bang' of migration in the 1950s that brought new residents to Florida from other parts of the United States and from Central and South America.[28] Florida also was the most urbanized state in the South.[29] The result of these demographic shifts, Mormino argues, is that 'Florida's connection to the South, long a tenuous relationship, cracked and loosened visibly after 1950.'[30] But Jim Crow practices and

---

22 Honowar, 'Disgraced.'
23 *Palmore v. Sidoti*, 466 U.S. 429, 434 (1984).
24 James C. Clark, *A Concise History of Florida* (Mount Pleasant: The History Press, 2014), 220; Gary R. Mormino, *Land of Sunshine, State of Dreams: A Social History of Modern Florida* (Gainesville: University Presses of Florida, 2005), 6–7, 15; Pittman, *Oh Florida!*, 249.
25 Mormino, *Land of Sunshine*, 6.
26 Ibid., 7.
27 Clark, *A Concise History*, 220; Mormino, *Land of Sunshine*, 15–16; Pittman, *Oh, Florida!*, 249.
28 Mormino, *Land of Sunshine*, 16–17.
29 Ibid., 17–18.
30 Ibid., 19.

biracialism co-existed in Florida, so it is unsurprising that vestiges of those racial attitudes remained in the late 1970s and early 1980s, the time of the *Palmore* controversy.

4   *Church of the Lukumi Babalu Aye, Inc. v. City of Hialeah*

If *Palmore* arises from an act of quintessential Southern racism, *Church of the Lukumi Bablu Aye*[31] is the quintessential Florida religion case, given the wide range of religious belief systems that Florida hosts. Santería occupies a special place in South Florida culture, with its large population of Caribbean immigrants. Pittman describes the 'Voodoo Squad' on the maintenance crews in the Miami-Dade County Courthouse, charged with cleaning up the sacrifices left outside the building by hopeful litigants.[32]

While lawyers and other actors in the system remained blasé about these practices, one city refused to remain so—the City of Hialeah passed an ordinance forbidding animal sacrifice in a targeted effort to prevent a Santería church from locating in the city.[33] The Church prevailed before a unanimous Supreme Court, which stated that the exceptions in the ordinance showed that the city's purpose was to single out this minority, uniquely Florida religious group for disfavored treatment.[34]

5   *Seminole Tribe of Florida v. Florida*

The Seminole Nation settled in South Florida in the 1830s, defeating the U.S. Army on several occasions and remaining the only tribe never to surrender. But it took the Seminole—with another Florida-based tribe, the Miccosukee—another century to build the mechanisms for financial stability.[35]

Success began in the 1920s with construction of the Tamiami Trail, a road cutting across the Everglades's 'River of Grass.' While the road killed animals and destroyed habitats and the ecosystem, it increased the flow of travelers moving past the reservations, which the tribes populated with gift shops, alligator-wrestling pits, airboat rides, and cheap cigarettes, all designed to lure

---

31   508 U.S. 520 (1993).
32   Pittman, *Oh, Florida!*, 239.
33   Ibid.; *Church of Lukumi*, 508 U.S. at 526–28.
34   *Church of Lukumi*, 508 U.S. at 524.
35   Pittman, *Oh, Florida!*, 191–92.

drivers to stop and look around.³⁶ Alligator wrestling evolved into high-stakes bingo halls and then casinos, ushering the nationwide Indian gaming industry and making the Seminoles one of the wealthiest and most successful gaming tribes.³⁷

The Court in *Seminole Tribe* was concerned with state sovereign immunity and congressional power to abrogate that immunity and subject states to suit by tribes under a federal law regulating casinos on reservations.³⁸ Indian gaming, and its unique Florida origins, provides the historical foundation.

6   *Stop the Beach Renourishment, Inc. v. Florida Department of Environmental Protection*

Florida is famous for its beaches, for constructing houses and other buildings on those beaches, and for determining on the fly how to keep those buildings from falling into the ocean.³⁹ In Florida, the natural laws of beach erosion 'collide violently with elementary laws of economics and politics.'⁴⁰

*Stop the Beach Renourishment*⁴¹ arose from this cycle. For years, Floridians have built on the sand, then sought federal and public funding for 'renourishment' projects to pump sand back onto the beach to protect those buildings from erosion.⁴² As of 2016, Florida had benefitted from more than 140 federal projects to restore the sandy shoreline, affecting more than half of Florida counties. Between 1969 and 2005, Florida received more than $1 billion in federal funds to pump sand onto eroding beaches.⁴³

The litigation Cortada pictures arose when several property owners, having benefitted from past renourishment projects that saved their homes from falling into the sea, argued against new projects that would permit public access on renourished portion of the coastline. They argued that their loss of a private

---

36   Ibid., 192; Mormino, *Land of Sunshine*, 280–81.
37   Ibid., 280–81; Pittman, *Oh, Florida!*, 192–95; Matthew L. M. Fletcher, 'The Seminole Tribe and the Origins of Indian Gaming' (2014) 9 Florida International University Law Review 255.
38   *Seminole Tribe of Florida v. Florida*, 517 U.S. 44, 47 (1996).
39   Pittman, *Oh, Florida!*, 74.
40   Mormino, *Land of Sunshine*, 346.
41   *Stop the Beach Renourishment v. Florida Dept. of Environmental Protection*, 560 U.S. 702 (2010).
42   Mormino, *Land of Sunshine*, 346; Pittman, *Oh, Florida!*, 74–75.
43   Mormino, *Land of Sunshine*, 348; Pittman, *Oh, Florida!*, 74.

beach, even one that saved their buildings, was a taking of property requiring compensation.

7   *Bush v. Gore*

This is the most infamously Floridian case in Cortada's series, because it announced that Florida's weirdness affects the rest of the nation and the world.[44] Weird Florida single-handedly decided the most consequential political question of who would be President of the United States in 2000.

Two Florida elements stand out. One is what Pittman calls the 'quintessential Florida Woman' (the distaff counterpart to Florida Man) in Secretary of State Katherine Harris, who became 'a living symbol of Florida's cuckoo elections.' While charged with supervising the elections and certifying the results, Harris served as honorary Florida chair of Republican candidate George W. Bush's campaign, while forever seeming not to understand Florida election law, her job responsibilities, or the obvious conflicts of interest.[45] The other element is the 'butterfly ballot,' the confusing ballot design used in Palm Beach County. It caused thousands of voters to invalidate their ballots by double-voting. It caused thousands of other voters, many of them Jewish and elderly, to vote not for their intended candidate, Democrat Al Gore (and his Jewish running mate, Joseph Lieberman), but for independent Pat Buchanan, who had a reputation (fair or unfair) as anti-Semitic. As an editorial in the *Palm Beach Post* lamented after the controversy ended, the 'world would come to know us as the baffling center of a baffling state, helplessly unprepared to overcome the dual limitations of our old technology and casual citizenship, which was expressed in tens of thousands of undecipherable votes.'[46]

...

That the cases featured in *May It Please the Court* originated in Florida, given what Florida Man represents, adds a layer of absurdity to the underlying tales. But Cortada, and the ten legal scholars in this volume, tell a serious and universal story in pictures and in words. While Cortada's Florida connections inspired

---

44   Pitman, *Oh, Florida!*, 3–4.
45   Ibid., 112–15.
46   Frank Cerabino, 'A Place Forever Changed by Indecision 2000' (The Palm Beach Post, December 14, 2000), in *Bush v. Gore: The Court Cases and the Commentary*, eds E.J. Dionne Jr. & William Kristol (Washington D.C.: Brookings Institution Press, 2010).

his choice of cases to paint, it is no accident that none of the authors is from Florida; we chose them for their expertise on the particular cases and constitutional issues that Cortada depicts. We gave authors a platform from which to speak about general constitutional ideals and principles that the Court could have identified and established in cases originating anywhere—were another state willing to do what Florida is willing to do in prohibiting animal sacrifice, attempting to preserve its natural resources, requiring newspapers to offer space to those it criticizes, or making hash of the electoral process.

Twelve chapters follow this introduction. M.C. Mirow contextualizes this book's approach with a discussion of the rise of legal iconography since the 1980s; this study builds on advances made by legal historians, cultural historians, and theorists who have sought greater insight into the relationship between art and law, a relationship Cortada reveals in painting ten constitutional cases. Renée Ater, an art historian, provides an overview of the work of Xavier Cortada, his artistic style, practices and motifs, and how he connects the artistic, the political, and the legal.

Ten chapters follow, each by a legal scholar analyzing one case and its accompanying painting. Readers will see a range of styles and approaches in these essays. We imposed few structural, organizational, or stylistic rules. We gave them freedom to make the paintings and the essays their own and to experiment—to approach familiar subjects (constitutional law) in an uncommon way and to connect unfamiliar subjects (analysis and interpretation of art) to the Constitution and the law. Each author undertook that challenge in a different way, particularly in the degree of exploration of the details and nuances of the painting. But the shared endeavor of combining art and constitutional law unites these efforts.

Recommended Reading

Clark, J.C. *A Concise History of Florida.* Mount Pleasant: The History Press, 2014.
Gannon, Michael, ed. *The History of Florida.* Gainesville: University Press of Florida, 2013.
Mormino, G.R. *Land of Sunshine, State of Dreams: A Social History of Modern Florida.* Gainesville: University Press of Florida, 2005.
Pittman, C., *Oh, Florida! How America's Weirdest State Influences the Rest of the Country.* New York: St. Martin's Press, 2016.

CHAPTER 2

Legal Iconography and *Painting Constitutional Law*

M.C. Mirow

For decades, European legal historians, cultural historians, and art historians have examined graphic sources of law and depictions of related concepts such as justice. A breakthrough moment was the five hundredth anniversary of the German Imperial Court in 1995, with the exhibition and publication of a large collection of images from the western legal tradition in *Frieden durch Recht: Das Reichskammergericht von 1495 bis 1806*.[1] The book was mostly dedicated to images and objects related to German law and the Imperial Court, but included essays, display labels, and descriptions of works of the same period from England (J.H. Baker), France (Serge Dauchy), Mechelen of the Low Countries (Alain Wijffels), and Italy (Mario Ascheri), among others.[2] The work remains a primary source of images on western law from the fifteenth to the nineteenth centuries.

This path-breaking exhibit had antecedents showing long-standing interest in the iconography of law. Samuel Edgerton's monumental study of criminal justice and image in Renaissance Florence was published in the United States in 1985.[3] Two years later, Dennis Curtis and Judith Resnik published an essay on the depiction of Justice in the *Yale Law Journal*.[4] In 1989, Margariet Becker-Moelands presented the work of her Centre for the Documentation of Legal History and Legal Iconography in Amsterdam, and A.H. Manchester announced efforts to collect graphic materials from England and Wales.[5] Manchester was influenced by John Langbein, who incorporated visual sources in articles in the early 1980s.[6] Langbein's approach bore fruit in 2009 in his

---

1   *Frieden durch Recht: Das Reichskammergericht von 1495 bis 1806*, ed. Ingrid Scheurmann (Mainz: Verlag Philipp von Zabern, 1994).
2   *Frieden durch Recht*, 347–364, 365–373, 374–382, 428–434.
3   Samuel Y. Edgerton, Jr., *Pictures and Punishment: Art and Criminal Prosecution during the Florentine Renaissance* (Ithaca: Cornell University Press, 1985).
4   Dennis E. Curtis & Judith Resnik, 'Images of Justice' (1987) 96 Yale Law Journal 1727–1772.
5   A.H. Manchester, 'An Introduction to Iconographical Studies of Legal History: England and Wales' in *Legal History in the Making: Proceedings of the Ninth British Legal History Conference: Glasgow 1989*, eds W.M. Gordon and T.D. Fergus (London: The Hambledon Press, 1991), 85.
6   John H. Langbein, 'Shaping the Eighteenth Century Criminal Trial: A View from the Ryder Sources' (1983) 50 University of Chicago Law Review 1–136.

richly illustrated textbook and treatise co-authored with Renée Lettow Lerner and Bruce Smith, *The History of the Common Law*, a set of teaching materials thoughtfully and beautifully unlike anything else available in U.S. law school classrooms.[7] Manchester wrote in 1989 that historians of Anglo-American law were behind in their work when compared with the significant advances already accomplished in Europe.[8] An early American foray into the field is Nancy Illman Meyers's brief essay describing her painting *Naked Restrains of Trade* depicting the important anti-competition case *United States v. Addyston Pipe & Steel Co.* and exploring the relationship of art and law generally.[9]

Interest in this field has picked up substantially since these path-breaking works thirty or so years ago. The exhibition *The Art of Law: Three Centuries of Justice Depicted* at the Groeningemuseum in Bruges from October 2016 to 2017 was a substantial contribution. Covering the period 1450 to 1750, this exhibit thematically presented European artworks related to the distinctions between divine justice and worldly justice, *exempla jusititiae* (instances of justice as instructional allegories, such as the Judgment of Solomon), the Judgment of Cambyses, representations of the practice of justice, and the image of Lady Justice.[10] The catalogue is a masterful collection of essays and images.[11]

There is nothing surprising about analyzing legal images. For centuries, Christian religious ideas of judgment, Heaven, Hell, justice, punishment, and mercy flowed from the brushes of master artists on altarpieces and church paintings for the consumption of the literate and illiterate.[12] Artistic or pictorial

---

7 John H. Langbein, Renée Lettow Lerner, and Bruce P. Smith, *History of the Common Law: The Development of Anglo-American Legal Institutions* (New York: Wolters Kluwer, 2009).

8 Manchester, 'An Introduction', 86.

9 Nancy Illman Meyers, 'Painting the Law' (1996) 14 Cardozo Arts and Entertainment Law Journal 397–406.

10 Vanessa Paumen, '*The Exhibition* The Art of Law. Three Centuries of Justice Depicted' in *The Art of Law: Artistic Representations of Law and Justice in Context, from the Middle Ages to the First World War*, eds Stefan Huyebaert, Georges Martyn, Vanessa Paumen, Eric Bousmar, and Xavier Rousseaux (Cham: Springer, 2018) 25–41; Rus Verstegen, 'The Judgment of Cambyses: A Rich Iconographical Topic with Multiple Sources and a Long Tradition' in *The Art of Law: Artistic Representations*, 125–147.

11 *The Art of Law: Three Centuries of Justice Depicted*, eds Stefan Huygebaert, Georges Martyn, Vanessa Paumen, and Tine Van Poucke (Tielt: Lannoo, 2016).

12 Mia Korpiola, 'Medieval Iconography of Justice in a European Periphery: The Case of Sweden, ca. 1250–1555' in *The Art of Law: Artistic Representations of Law and Justice in Context, from the Middle Ages to the First World War*, eds Stefan Huyebaert, Georges Martyn, Vanessa Paumen, Eric Bousmar, and Xavier Rousseaux (Cham: Springer, 2018), 89–110; Clare Sandford-Couch, 'Changes in Late-Medieval Artistic Representations of Hell in the *Last Judgment* in North Central Italy, ca. 1300–1400: A Visual Trick?' in *The Art of Law: Artistic Representations*, 63–87.

representations of divine judgment's secular corollary, the civil or criminal trial, could also be presented in sculpted or painted form. If Jesus, Mary, and the Last Judgment could be imaged, then depictions of secular Justice and kingly Mercy could be formed, analyzed, read, and parsed.[13] And, of course, works might incorporate both aspects of justice, such as Hans Fries's *Kleiner Johannes Altar* depicting John the Evangelist's trial on Ephesus.[14] The legitimacy of worldly judges might be substantially bolstered by their connection to divine powers displayed in dress, architecture, and surrounding artwork.[15] Visual representations might also serve more secular purposes such as establishing legal lineage for royal succession, noble status, and entitlements to property.[16]

The past two decades have witnessed a substantial increase in academic treatments of art and law, particularly in Europe and particularly focused on art from the medieval period to the nineteenth century.[17] Scholars now have numerous studies in the field from Europe and the Americas. Common law efforts, however, have been varied and less intensive. Contemporaneous with the Bruges exhibit, Mike Widener, the Rare Books' Librarian at Yale Law School, created an exhibit on illustrations in law books.[18] This exhibit led to a remarkable online resource for legal images entitle entitled *Illustrated Law*.[19] Because of Yale Law Library's extensive holdings, it included images from civil law sources and the common law world.

This book expands on these approaches. Cortada's *May It Please the Court* forms the central collection of works explored for the content of their images and what they say about law. Constitutional lawyers and historians view, read, consider, and analyze Cortada's work in relationship to the important principles these cases represent. Placing these studies into the broader field, this chapter provides a brief overview of recent approaches and contributions to legal iconography. The first part of this chapter examines the visual

---

13   Guy Delmarcel, 'Justicia, Examples and Allegories of Justice, and Courts in Flemish Tapestry, 1450–1550' in *The Art of Law: Artistic Representations*, 111–123.
14   Tamara Golan, '"*ut experiri et scire posset*": Pictorial Evidence and Judicial Inquiry in Hans Fries' *Kleiner Johannes Altar*' in *The Art of Law: Artistic Representations*, 319–336.
15   Georges Martyn, 'Divine Judgement, Worldly Justice' in *The Art of Law: Three Centuries*, 15.
16   Joan A. Holladay, *Genealogy and the Politics of Representation in the High and Late Middle Ages* (Cambridge: Cambridge University Press, 2019).
17   Georges Martyn and Stefan Huygebaert, 'Twenty New Contributions to the Upcoming Research Field of Historical Legal Iconology' in *The Art of Law: Artistic Representations*, 7–11.
18   Michael Widener and Mark S. Weiner, *Law's Picture Books: The Yale Law Library Collection* (Clark, NJ: Talbot Publishing, 2017).
19   Yale Law School, Lillian Goldman Law Library, Illustrated Law, https://library.law.yale.edu/illustrated-law.

representation of abstract ideas related to law, particular instructive examples of justice, the use of images as critique, and recent expansions of the field. The second part of this chapter turns to Cortada's *May It Please the Court*.

1 Legal Iconography

1.1 *Abstract Ideas*

Legal historians have availed themselves of surviving sculptures and images personifying abstract principles of law, such as Justice or Mercy. There are images of Justice blindfolded, Justice sighted, Justice with two faces, Justice with various animals, and even Justice decapitated; scholars have examined these for meaning, expression, and forensic function.[20] As Ann-Kathrin Hubrich reminds us,

> In early modern Europe, courtrooms were often equipped with a wide range of artworks: paintings, sculpture, and furniture as artistic mediums as well as the architecture itself all served to express a certain idea of how

---

20 Carolin Behrmann, 'The Mirror Axiom: Legal Iconology and the Lure of Reflection' in *The Art of Law: Artistic Representations*, 43–60. Bennett Capers, 'On Justicia, Race, Gender, and Blindness' (2006) 12 Michigan Journal of Race and Law 203–233; Curtis & Resnik, 'Image of Justice'; Peter Goodrich, 'The evidence of things not seen' in *Genealogies of Legal Vision*, eds Peter Goodrich and Valérie Hayaert (London: Routledge, 2015), 53–78; Martin Jay, 'Must Justice be Blind?' in *Law and the Image: The Authority of Art and the Aesthetics of Law*, eds Costas Douzinas and Lynda Nead (Chicago: University of Chicago Press, 1999), 19–35; Valérie Hayaert, 'The Paradoxes of Lady Justice's Blindfold' in *The Art of Law: Artistic Representations*, 201–222; Stefan Huygebaert, 'Justitia, The Cardinal Virtue that Became a Political Ideal' in *The Art of Law: Three Centuries*, 139–153; Desmond Manderson and Cristina S. Martinez, 'Justice and Art, Face to Face', (2016) 28 Yale Journal of Law & the Humanities 241–263 (discussing Sir Joshua Reynolds's *Justice* (1779)); Judith Resnik and Dennis Curtis, *Representing Justice: Invention, Controversy, and Rights in City-States and Democratic Courtrooms* (New Haven: Yale University Press, 2011), 1–17, 62–133; Judith Resnik and Dennis Curtis, 'Epistemological doubt and visual puzzles of sight, knowledge and judgment: reflections on clear-sighted and blindfolded Justice' in *Genealogies of Legal Vision*, 201–242; Ruth Weisberg, 'The Art of Memory and the Allegorical Personification of Justice' (2012) 24 Yale Journal of Law & the Humanities 259–270; Alain Wijffels, 'Justice and Good Governance' in *The Art of Law: Three Centuries*, 154–157.

For headless justice see, for example, the printer's mark for Ius Deco Publications, Leiden, with the motto "sub effigie justitiae decollatae" and Pierio Valeriano's *Astaeea/Justicia* (an 'acephal Justicia') in Valérie Hayaert, 'The Paradoxes', 222.

For a demonic, world upside-down depiction of the World mimicking Justice from the late sixteenth and early seventeenth centuries, see Stefan Huygebaert, 'A World off Balance …' in *The Art of Law: Three Centuries*, 187–189.

justice has been understood or how it was supposed to be communicated to the public.[21]

There was also a continuing tie to religion: 'Two particular Christian scenes are featured in virtually every courtroom of the *ancien régime*: Christ on the cross and the Last Judgment.'[22] The latter was a frequent decoration for the deliberation rooms where judges decided cases in conference.[23] And judges were to judge according to their Christian faith and with the judgment of God ever present in their work.[24] All in the courtroom were reminded to conduct themselves honestly. In analyzing depictions of the Last Judgment, Vanessa Paumen remarks on its cautionary nature: 'The judge is God's representative on earth. Equally explicit is the warning: allow yourself to be seduced by the devil in the courtroom, make a false oath or accept a bribe, and you will find yourself standing in front of the gates of Hell.'[25] Use of allegorical and symbolic artwork in the courtroom continued into the twentieth century.[26]

Physical representations of Justice or Mercy attempted to capture abstract notions only related generally to law and its application, often created for public display and consumption in town halls and courtrooms.[27] Statues of Justice

---

21 Ann-Kathrin Hubrich, 'Multi-layered Functions of Early Modern Courtroon Equipment: Lüneburg for Example' in *The Art of Law: Artistic Representations*,149–164. For architecture, see, for example, Barbara A. Perry, 'The Israeli and United States Supreme Courts: A Comparative Reflection on their Symbols, Images, and Function' (2001) 63 *The Review of Politics* 317–339; Latherine Fisher Tayor, 'The Festival of Justice, Paris, 1849' in Douzinas and Nead, *Law and the Image*, 137–177; Resnik and Curtis, *Representing Justice*, 134–377; Douglas P. Woodlock, 'Communities and the Courthouses They Deserve. And Vice Versa' (2012) 24 Yale Journal of Law & the Humanities 271–285.
22 Georges Martyn, 'Divine Judgement, Worldly Justice', 22.
23 Ibid.; Resnik and Curtis, *Representing Justice*, 33–37 (the Last Judgment in town halls).
24 Anne van Oosterwijk, 'Divine Judgement, Mortal Judges' in *The Art of Law: Three Centuries*, 29–30; Vanessa Paumen, 'Judging by Example of the Divine Judge' in *The Art of Law*, 31–34.
25 Vanessa Paumen, 'Judging by Example', 34.
26 Gaëlle Dubois and Amamdine De Burchgraeve, 'Experiencing Justice in the *Cour d'assise* of Brabant (1893–1913): A Place of Education and Entertainment' in *The Art of Law: Artistic Representations*, 385–405; Stefan Huygebaert, 'Legal Imagery on the Edge of Symbolism: The Decoration Projects for the Belgian Cour de Cassation' in *Law and the Visual: Representations, Technologies, and Critique*, ed. Desmond Manderson (Toronto: University of Toronto Press, 2018), 122–140; Stefan Huygebaert, 'The Judge, the Artist, and the (Legal) Historian: Théophile Smekens, Pieter Van der Ouderaa, Pieter Génard and the Antwerp *cour d'assises*' in *The Art of Law: Artistic Representations*, 407–432.
27 Martyn and Huygebaert, 'Twenty New Contributions', 17–20; Resnik and Curtis, *Representing Justice*.

reminded judges how to judge and reminded parties that their cases were handled with fairness and equality. Some depicted classic themes to remind judges to be just, such as the story of Mesopotamian King Cambyses who ordered a corrupt judge flayed alive.[28] Depictions of lawyers and judges and group portraits of lawyers and judges upheld continuity of institutions and the social role of individuals and groups.[29]

Artists might also depict justice in action as social commentary and critique. In Bruegel's *Justicia* (original version 1558–9, engraving by Philips Galle 1560), Lady Justice is surrounded by lawyers, judicially imposed torture, crowds, soldiers, and a multitude of executions in the background. Desmond Manderson skillfully deconstructed and explained the work.[30]

1.2   Instructive Examples

Other images related to law and justice appeared inside and outside the courtroom. These depicted well-known narratives from classical literature, the Bible, and western mythology. Referred to as *exempla justiciae* by legal iconologists and historians, they were found in paintings, engravings, stained glass in public and private buildings, and illuminated manuscripts.[31] These stories continue to be recognized because of their scriptural basis – Judgment of Solomon, Susanna the Chaste, and Esther and Judith.[32] Less well-known stories include Cambyses and the flayed dishonest judge; Zaleucus, who offered one of his eyes to mitigate his son's required loss of two eyes for the crime of adultery; Trajan, who beheaded a careless soldier whose horse trampled a widow's son; and Tomrys, Queen of Massagetae, who avenged Persian King Cyrus's invasion, triggered by her refusing his marriage proposal, by decapitating him and placing his head in bag of blood.[33] These are rich stories fit for graphic representation.

---

28   Martyn and Huygebaert, 'Twenty New Contributions', 7–11; Resnik and Curtis, *Representing Justice*, 38–43.
29   Martyn and Huygebaert, 'Twenty New Contributions', 14.
30   Desmond Manderson, 'Blindness Visible: Law, Time, and Bruegel's Justice' in *Law and the Visual*, 23–50; Resnik and Curtis, *Representing Justice*, 70–72.
31   Venessa Paumen, 'An Illuminated Example' in *The Art of Law: Three Centuries*, 93–96; Vanessa Paumen and Matias Desmet, 'Translucent Exempla' in *The Art of Law: Three Centuries*, 71–77.
32   Georges Martyn, 'Exempla Iusticiae: Inspiring Examples' in *The Art of Law: Three Centuries*, 39–45.
33   Matias Desmet, 'Tomyris' Bloody Revenge' in *The Art of Law: Three Centuries*, 64–67; Martyn, 'Exempla Iusticiae', 46–50; Vanessa Paumen, 'The Skin of the Judge: The Judgement of Cambyses' in *The Art of Law: Three Centuries*, 81–91; Vanessa Paumen, 'The

Criminal law and procedure offered another group of subjects. Joos de Damhouder's *Enchiridion Rerum Criminalium* (1554) contained 57 woodcuts illustrating criminal procedure and various forms of criminal activity.[34] And capital punishment and public executions offered unique artistic opportunities.[35] As Georges Martyn notes, to accomplish retribution to the criminal and deterrence in the populus, 'A harsh sentence, preferably executed on a scaffold in the heart of the community, was considered of great importance.'[36] Punishment as spectacle in legal images continues.[37]

Emblems and collections of emblems in bound volumes also attempted to encapsulate legal principles in no less abstract forms than sculptures or paintings. Beginning in the sixteenth century, authors summarized principles and aphorisms of law for private audiences of lawyers, state advisers, and princes. Even general collections of emblems, such as the mid-sixteenth- century edition of Alciatus's *Emblemata*, included not only depictions of general virtues such as faith[38] or concord,[39] but also legal principles such as that justice always triumphs,[40] just punishment,[41] respect within marriage,[42] and others related to justice.[43]

Collections with similar mixes of moral allegories and particular references to the law and its proper function include the *Thronus Iusticiae* (1605–1606)

Popularity of the Father's Skin: Cambyses after Gerard David' in *The Art of Law: Three Centuries*, 97–103.

34 Felix Jäger, 'Framing the Law: Joos de Damhouder and the Legal Iconography of the Grotesque' in *The Art of Law: Artistic Representations*, 223–244; Harald Maihold, 'Praxis rerum criminalium' in *The Formation and Transmission of Western Legal Culture: 150 Books that Made the Law in the Age of Printing*, eds Serge Dauchy, Georges Martyn, Anthony Musson, Heikki Pihlajamäki, and Alain Wijffels (Cham: Springer, 2016), 99–102; Jos Monballyu, 'Joos de Damhouder, an Internationally Influential Jurist from Bruge' in *The Art of Law: Three Centuries*, 107–119; Resnik and Curtis, *Representing Justice*, 38–61.

35 Jérôme de Brouwer and Xavier Rousseaux, 'A Ghostly Corpse in the City? Spatial Configurations and Iconographic Representations of Capital Punishment in the 'Belgian' Space (16th – 20th C.)' in *The Art of Law: Artistic Representations*, 337–368.

36 Martyn, 'Divine Judgement', 21.

37 Connal Parsley, 'The Exeptional Image: Torture Photographs from Guantánamo Bay and Abu Ghraid as Foucault's Spectacle of Punishment' in *Law and the Visual*, 229–247.

38 André Alciat, *Emblemata: Les Emblèmes: Fac-similé de l'édition lyonnaise Macé Bonhomme de 1551* (Paris: Les Belles Lettres, 2016), 15.

39 Ibid., 45–47.

40 Ibid., 35.

41 Ibid., 186.

42 Ibid., 206.

43 Ibid., 34–39.

and the *Emblemas morales* (1610) of Sebastían de Covarrubias.⁴⁴ Juan Solórzano Pereira, one of seventeenth-century Spain's most illustrious lawyers and crown officials, published a set of emblems that has been under-studied compared with his other work.⁴⁵ Legal emblems are also found throughout some editions of the *corpus iuris civilis*.⁴⁶

Peter Goodrich's richly illustrated exploration of legal emblems tackles the field by linking emblems to governance.⁴⁷ Explaining his project, Goodrich writes, 'The power of the image lay in its ability to carry and apply the abstract rule, the prosaic letter of governance to a terrain that law in its positive scriptural expression would never reach.'⁴⁸ In keeping with other legal iconographers, he observes that the images of law are too-often neglected; 'the most obvious and manifest dimension of law, its physical and visible forms – the architecture, the costumes, the inscriptions, the murals and paintings, the trials, the libraries, the books, the tomb-like tomes – are so familiar, so structural, and thence natural that they get overlooked.'⁴⁹

1.3 Critique

In addition to reminding viewers of justice, mercy, and the fair administration of the law, art graphically critiqued practices and exposed injustice. Images offered trenchant criticism of the abuse of litigation, greed, and dissension within the legal profession and in its interaction with society.⁵⁰ After discussing images of justice, Manchester reported of his work on the iconography of English law,

---

44 William Egginton, 'Crime shows: CSI in Hapsburg Spain' in *Genealogies of Legal Vision*, 243–258; Elissa Watters, 'Thronus Iusticiae: Divine Justice on Earth' in *The Art of Law: Three Centuries*, 57–60.

45 Juan Solórzano Pereira, *Emblemata centum, regio politica in centuriam unam redacta* (Madrid: Garcia Morras, 1653; reprint Madrid: Tuero, 1987). See, M.C. Mirow, 'Juan Solórzano Pereira' in *Great Christian Jurists in Spanish History*, eds Rafael Domingo and Javier Martínez-Torrón (Cambridge: Cambridge University Press, 2018), 239–257; Ditlev Tamm, 'Emblemata de Solórzano de Pereira', XX Congreso del Instituto Internacional de Historia del Derecho Indiano, La Rábida, Huelva, Spain, 17 September 2019.

46 Valérie Hayaert, 'The Gordian knot of emblemata: from the *Labyrinthus absconditus* to the affirmation of the *Prisca Jurisprudentia*' in *Genealogies of Legal Vision*, 17–52.

47 Peter Goodrich, *Legal Emblems and the Art of Law:* Obiter depicta *as the Vision of Governance* (Cambridge, Cambridge University Press, 2014).

48 Ibid., 85.

49 Ibid., 23.

50 Georges Martyn, 'Greedy Lawyers and Courtroom Monsters' in *The Art of Law: Three Centuries*, 133–135; Alain Wijffels, 'Lawyers and Litigants: The Corrupting Appeal and Effects of Civil Litigation in Hendrick Goltzius' *Litis Abusus*' in *The Art of Law: Artistic Representations*, 181–199.

Then we come to the Devil. I am sorry to have to report that, in the prints which are of interest to us as legal historians, the Devil and the Lawyer are often portrayed as being on the friendliest of terms: indeed, the one may be seen as the agent of the other.[51]

Resnik and Curtis note depictions of judges as fools.[52] Similarly, William Hogarth's illustrations and paintings offer rich and often critical views of legal life and practice of eighteenth-century England.[53] And in the 1790s, Pierre Goetsbloets reversed iconic images to create subversive interpretations during the French Revolution.[54] Indeed, the French Revolution inspired many forms of artistic expression defining the meaning of the Revolution and its aftermath.[55]

1.4 An Expanding Field

The field of legal iconography is not just the realm of European legal historians.[56] Social and cultural historians and theorists have taken up the field. Manderson traces this branch of legal iconography, or 'imaginal law' as he prefers, to a collection of essays published in 1999, *Law and the Image: The Authority of Art and the Aesthetics of Law* by legal theorist Costas Douzinas and art historian Lynda Nead. Manderson observed the growth of the field through the works of Dennis Curtis, Peter Goodrich, Judith Resnik, Richard Sherwin, and Alison Young, as having transformed legal iconography in recent years.[57]

Because of this school's theoretical tack, it cautions against 'dilettantism' while recognizing that the 'very best work in this exciting new field has shown

---

51 Manchester, 'An Introduction', 85.
52 Resnik and Curtis, *Representing Justice*, 67–69.
53 Langbein, Lerner, and Smith, *History of the Common Law*, 356 (*The Marriage Contract*, 1743), 684–685, 785; Christina S. Martinez, 'An Emblematic Representation of Law: Hogarth and the Engarvers' Act' in *Law and the Visual*, 75–100.
54 Brecht Deseure, '*Liberté, égalité, fraternité ou la mort*. The Iconography of Injustice in the Work of Pierre Goetsbloets' in *The Art of Law: Artistic Representations*, 273–295.
55 Morgan Thomas, 'Law and the Revolutionary Motif after Jacques-Louis David' in *Law and the Visual*, 101–121; Christina Schröer, 'Symbolic Politics and the Visualization of the Constitutional Order in the First French Republic, 1792–1799' in *Constitutional Cultures: On the Concept and Representation of Constitutions in the Atlantic World*, eds Silke Hensel, Ulrike Bock, Katrin Dircksen and Hans-Ulrich Thamer (Newcastle upon Tyne: Cambridge Scholars Publishing, 2012) 163–188.
56 I do not enter the debate over iconology vs. iconography. See, Desmond Manderson, 'Introduction: Imaginal Law' in *Law and the Visual*, 3–4; Martyn and Huygebaert, 'Twenty New Contributions', 4–5.
57 Manderson, 'Introduction: Imaginal Law', 6–7. See Recommended Reading for works by these authors.

an impressive willingness to deploy highly detailed analyses of images, works of art, and visual media.'[58] Manderson's foray into the field was an edited volume in which the contributors studied specific laws from various times and places.[59] Similarly, Mexican legal historian José Ramón Narváez wrote in 2010 about using images to interpret law and legal iconography while reminding us that law has been historically perceived as an art.[60]

Other recent studies have explored the visual representation of a wide range of legal topics. Visual representations of constitutions in the Atlantic world have been addressed in a useful collection of essays.[61] This includes studies of depictions of the United States Constitution and constitutions in Southern Germany.[62] A separate study examined The Monument to the Constitution of Cádiz (the Spanish Constitution of 1812) in St. Augustine, Florida.[63]

Nor has international law escaped the field. Contributors to a recent work discuss material items (many of them 'ready-mades' if we press the analogy) and their importance in international law.[64] Despite the work's focus on objects rather than artworks, authors employ similar approaches in contributions related to works such as the Axum Stele, paintings of international law textbooks, and stained glass windows at the Peace Palace, The Hague.[65]

---

58   Ibid., 7.
59   Ibid., 8.
60   José Ramón Narváez H., *Cultura jurídica: ideas e imágenes* (México: Editorial Porrúa, 2010) 93–133.
61   Hensel, Bock, Dircksen and Thamer, *Constitutional Cultures*.
62   Viven Green Fryd, 'Representing the Constitution in the US Capitol Building: Justice, Freedom and Slavery' in *Constitutional Cultures*, 227–249; Martin Knauer, 'Embodiments of Ideal Order: Visualisations of Constitutions in Early Southern German Constitutionalism' in *Constitutional Cultures*, 251–271.
63   Matthew C. Mirow, 'Translating into Stone: The Monument to the Constitution of Cádiz in Saint Augustine, Florida', in *Translation in Times of Disruption: An Interdisciplinary Study in Transnational Context*, eds David Hook and Graciela Iglesias-Rogers (London: Palgrave Macmillan, 2017) 101–117.
64   *International Law's Objects*, eds Jessie Hohmann and Daniel Joyce (Oxford: Oxford University Press, 2019). Depsite its promising title for our purposes, a recent symposium, 'The Art of International Law,' at Case Western Reserve University School of Law addresses artworks, antiquities, and cultural property only as objects of international law. See, 'The Art of International Law' (2017) 49 Case Western Reserve Journal of International Law 1–372.
65   Jean d'Aspremont and Eric De Brabandere, 'Paintings of International Law' in *International Law's Objects*, eds Jessie Hohmann and Daniel Joyce (Oxford: Oxford University Press, 2018) 330–341; Daniel Litwin, 'Stained Glass Windows, the Great Hall of Justice of the Peace Palace' in *International Law's Objects*, 463–477; Lucas Lixinski, 'Axum Stele' in *International Law's Objects*, 130–140.

Scholars have studied a multitude of artistic expressions of law. Studies have placed photographs into their legal context and interpreted photographic archives recording genocide.[66] American legal education has recently explored the promises of the visual in the classroom.[67] The field has also expanded in geographical scope.[68] Alfred Brophy argues that American ante-bellum landscape paintings reveal a world of changing attitudes toward technology, notions of property, and property law itself.[69] Gregory Alexander has viewed property through the works of Félix González-Torres.[70] Ellesworth Kelly's abstract monochromes displayed in the Boston Courthouse, titled *The Boston Panels*, have been the subject of varied interpretations related to democracy and law.[71]

With expansion into so many promising regions, mediums, and periods and with so many methodological and theoretical approaches, the discipline of legal iconography is flourishing. Some even argue that modern law is on the cusp of a transition from writing to image and that technological changes impel the law towards the visual and a new form of interpretation. Noting this transition and despite some contrary evidence presented here, Boehme-Neßler encapsulates the older paradigm this way, 'So far the law is the one area of society which is fundamentally and very deeply skeptical about images and which is vehemently opposed to visualification.'[72] If Boehme-Neßler's predictions that

---

66 Maria Elander, 'Images of Victims: The ECCC and the Cambodian Genocide Museum' in *Law and the Visual*, 210–228; Jennifer L. Mnookin, 'The Image of Truth: Photographic Evidence and the Power of Analogy' (1998) 10 Yale Journal of Law & the Humanities 1–74; Sherally Munshi, '"You Will See my Family Became So American": Race, Citizenship, and the Visual Archive' in *Law and the Visual*, 161–188.

67 Michael Asimow and Ticien Marie Sassoubre, 'Introduction to the Symposium' (2018) 68 Journal of Legal Education 2–7 (Symposium on Visual Images and Popular Culture in Legal Education); Timothy J. Innes, 'Art and Legal History' (2013) 53 American Journal of Legal History 414–417.

68 Shane Chalmers, 'The Visual Force of Justice in the Making of Liberia' in *Law and the Visual*, 141–157; Rahela Khorakiwala, 'Depictions of Justice in the Colonial Courts of British India: The Judicial Iconography of the Bombay High Court' in *The Art of Law: Artistic Representations*, 433–449; Rahela Khorakiwala, 'Judicial Iconography in India' (2014) 1 Asian Journal of Legal Education 89–101.

69 Alfred L. Brophy, 'Property and Progress: Antebellum Landscape Art and Property Law' (2009) 40 McGeorge Law Review 603–659.

70 Gregory S. Alexander, 'Objects of Art; Objects of Property' (2017) 26 Cornell Journal of Law & Public Policy 461–468.

71 Brian Soucek, 'Not Representing Justice: Ellsworth Kelly's Abstraction in the Boston Courthouse' (2012) 24 Yale Journal of Law & the Humanities 287–304.

72 Volker Boehme-Neßler, *Pictorial Law: Modern Law and the Power of Pictures* (Heidelberg: Springer, 2011) ix.

modern law will become 'pictoral law' are true, then legal iconography will become an essential tool for lawyers, judges, and all who practice or are subject to the law.

2   Xavier Cortada's *May It Please the Court*

Despite this burgeoning interest in legal iconography, little academic work has explored law and art in the United States. Inspired by the established discipline of legal iconography in Europe and more recent theoretical treatments of law and image, this volume moves in a different direction by focusing on contemporary art, scholarly analysis, Florida, and the United States Constitution. These chapters explore law and art on the ground. Their authors are law professors who teach and write about constitutional law; they thus eschew high cultural theory for the praxis of examining images with expert eyes and thoughtful minds versed in the legal issues presented by each painting. These chapters and authors revel in the novelty of the process. And while some critics may proffer cries of 'dilettantism,' they would miss the effort employed, the sound results, and that the root of dilettante is 'to delight.'[73] Similar to Manderson's collection of essays, these chapters take on particular laws (as judicial decisions) in Cortada's artistic manifestation of them.

Building on established methodologies in legal iconography constructed over the past three decades, this book seeks to disrupt established perspectives on constitutional law by asking highly respected scholars to see their fields through Cortada's vivid images. This produces fresh and expansive explorations of essential themes in American law and life. Nonetheless, several features tie Cortada's series to the long sweep of legal depictions and the study of these depictions within the history of western law. These include an attention to the idea of justice and a critique of injustice, the effects of law on the individual's life, and the relationship between good administration of law and good governance. Cortada's works reflect some perennial themes in law: fair trial (in this case through the Anglo-American adversary process and jury), property ownership, good government, marriage, and the spectacle of execution. It reflects new themes as well: freedom of the press, religious freedom, sovereignty of indigenous tribes, and the right to counsel.

---

73   George Chambers Calvert, *A Defense of the Dilettante* (Indianapolis: The Studio Press, 1919) sixth unnumbered page.

These chapters reveal the way Cortada's depictions critique law. They evoke aesthetic and emotional responses to racism; the power of the state to intrude, to incarcerate, and to kill; the vagaries of judicial resolution of elections; the boredoms and biases of juries; and legal reconceptualizations of native peoples, the environment, and the family. Their critique exhorts the viewer to do better, to judge better, to rule better, and to place the individual and human dignity at the core of law's functions. Each painting is a concrete study in the failure or success of achieving justice and mercy.

From another perspective, this work differs significantly from the body of extant legal iconography as to time, legal system, and place. By examining a series of contemporary paintings, this work falls outside standard approaches to legal iconography that have developed over the past thirty years. Constitutional decisions of the Supreme Court of the United States not only offer current examples of the proper interpretation and application of constitutional law but also become part of the nation's legal history. Each new decision retells and reinterprets language that has guided some of the country's most important legal and social questions for more than 225 years, each a step in a continuously evolving standard or rule. All of Cortada's cases properly belong within the legal history of the United States.

From the perspective of comparative law, Cortada's paintings reflect the common law, and particularly the Unitedstatesian view of law. These are individual cases with individual facts about individual people. The common law's fetishism of the case and the facts pours onto Cortada's canvases. These paintings graphically portray the common law's and the 'legal realist infatuation with facts.'[74] These paintings are not idealized representations of justice, mercy, or judgment. Cortada paints facts in legal context – a dog sniffs a house, sand spews onto a beach, presidential candidates are showered with the hanging chads of ballots, meat is severed in ceremonial offering, parents hold their child, a jury deliberates, a newspaper speaks, an isolated prisoner petitions the Court, and sparks shoot from the head of the executed convict. Nothing better depicts the common law, its approach to specific cases, and its love of facts; the specificity, individuality, and personal quality of these cases spring from the canvas in an onslaught of powerful color. Each color selected by the artist not only conveys a present, aesthetic choice, but also deep historical meaning through various colors' ties to religion, authority,

---

74   Stephen N. Subrin, 'How Equity Conquered the Common Law: The Federal Rules of Civil Procedure in Historical Perspective' (1987) 135 University of Pennsylvania Law Review 968.

and law. Black, red, white, blue, purple, gold (in fabrics, clothing, and elsewhere) have signaled meaning in western art for centuries, including meaning in law.[75]

This work is also distinguished by place. These are cases arising from one state of the United States that wound up before the Supreme Court of the United States as indicia of particularly important constitutional principles. As Howard Wasserman argues in his contribution, there is something unusual about Florida and its ability to produce so many unexpected scenarios that implicate federally protected constitutional rights. Florida in the United States is highly unusual, even unique.

This is what has drawn me as a legal historian to the study of Florida's law and legal development. Florida has spent most of its history as a Spanish province. St. Augustine was founded in 1565 and was the capital of Spanish Florida until 1763, when the province became the British province of East Florida that lasted for 20 years until it was transferred back to Spain. During the British period, however, East Florida remained loyal to the crown and in fact became saturated with loyalists refugees during the American Revolution. Its second Spanish period, from 1783 to 1821, ended when it was ceded to the United States as a territory, becoming a state in 1845. It seceded from the United States just about fifteen years later to join the Confederacy, but Key West remained a Union stronghold in the South for much of the war.

Florida experienced centuries of slave society under Spain, Britain, and the United States. It passed through Reconstruction, then saw more racial murders and lynchings per capita than its southern neighbors during Jim Crow. It saw waves of land speculation in booms and busts. It saw hurricanes. It experienced massive growth with the end of World War II and residential air conditioning. It was home to the space program, Disney World, and various influxes of rich and poor exiles and refugees from the Caribbean and central and south America – Cubans, Colombians, Nicaraguans, Salvadorians, Haitians, and Venezuelans. Official documents for public consumption in Miami are in English, Spanish, and Haitian Creole. Perhaps only a land with this rich diversity of experiences, sorrows, joys, and peoples could yield the cases of Cortada's *May It Please the Court*.

---

75   Jean-Paul Andrieux, 'Les couleurs du droit (I/II): Notes de lectures' (2018) 96 Revue historique de droit français et étranger 305–334; Jean-Paul Andrieux, 'Les couleurs du droit (II/II): Notes de lectures' (2018) 96 Revue historique de droit français et étranger 447–478.

Recommended Reading

Alciat, André. *Emblemata: Les Emblèmes: Fac-similé de l'édition lyonnaise Macé Bonhomme de 1551.* Paris: Les Belles Lettres, 2016.

Alexander, Gregory S. 'Objects of Art; Objects of Property.' *Cornell Journal of Law and Public Policy* 26 (2017): 461–468.

Andrieux, Jean-Paul. 'Les couleurs du droit (I/II): Notes de lectures.' *Revue historique de droit français et étranger* 96 (2018): 305–334.

Andrieux, Jean-Paul. 'Les couleurs du droit (II/II): Notes de lectures.' *Revue historique de droit français et étranger* 96 (2018): 447–478.

Antaki, Mark, Angela Condello, Stefan Huygebaert, and Sarah Marusek. *Sensing the Nation's Law: Historical Inquries into the Aesthetics of Democratic Legitimacy.* London: Springer, 2018.

Asimow, Michael and Ticien Marie Sassoubre. 'Introduction to the Symposium.' *Journal of Legal Education* 68 (2018): 2–7 (Symposium on Visual Images and Popular Culture in Legal Education).

Becker-Moelands, M.A. 'An Introduction to the Iconographical Study of Legal History: The Netherlands.' In *Legal History in the Making: Proceedings of the Ninth British Legal History Conference Glasgow 1989*, edited by W.M. Gordon and T.D. Fergus, 88–94. London: The Hambledon Press, 1991.

Behrmann, Carolin. 'Law, Visual Studies, and Image History.' In *The Oxford Handbook of Law And Humanities*, edited by Simon Stern, Maksymilian Del Mar, and Bernadette Meyler, 39–64. New York: Oxford University Press, 2020.

Boehme-Neßler, Volker. *Pictorial Law: Modern Law and the Power of Pictures.* Heidelberg: Springer, 2011.

Brophy, Alfred L. 'Property and Progress: Antebellum Landscape Art and Property Law.' *McGeorge Law Review* 40 (2009): 603–659.

Capers, Bennett. 'On Andy Warhol's Electric Chair.' *California Law Review* 94 (2006): 243–260.

Capers, Bennett. 'On Justicia, Race, Gender, and Blindness.' *Michigan Journal of Race and Law* 12 (2006): 203–233.

Curtis, Dennis E. & Judith Resnik. 'Images of Justice.' *Yale Law Journal* 96 (1987): 1727–1772.

Dauchy, Serge, Georges Martyn, Anthony Musson, Heikki Pihlajamäki, and Alain Wijffels eds., *The Formation and Transmission of Western Legal Culture: 150 Books that Made the Law in the Age of Printing*, Cham: Springer, pp. 99–102.

Douzinas, Costas and Lynda Nead, eds. *Law and the Image: The Authority of Art and the Aesthetics of Law.* Chicago: University of Chicago Press, 1999.

Edgerton, Samuel Y. Jr., *Pictures and Punishment: Art and Criminal Prosecution during the Florentine Renaissance.* Ithaca: Cornell University Press, 1985.

Estética y république (siglos xviii-xix). 9 November 2018. Mexico City. https://www.casa-develazquez.org/es/investigacion/novedad/estetica-y-republica-siglos-xviii-xix/.

Jäger, Felix. "Framing the Law: Joos de Damhouder and the Legal Iconography of the Grotesque." In *The Art of Law: Artistic Representations and Iconography of Law and Justice in Context, from the Middle Ages to the First World War*, edited by Stefan Huygebaert, Georges Martyn, Vanessa Paumen, Eric Bousmar, and Xavier Rousseaux, 223–244. Cham: Springer, 2018.

Goodrich, Peter. *Legal Emblems and the Art of Law:* Obiter depicta *as the Vision of Governance.* Cambridge: Cambridge University Press, 2014.

Goodrich, Peter, and Valérie Hayaerts, eds. *Genealogies of Legal Vision.* London: Routledge, 2015.

Hayaert, Valérie. 'Emblems.' In *The Oxford Handbook of Law And Humanities*, edited by Simon Stern, Maksymilian Del Mar, and Bernadette Meyler, 757–778. New York: Oxford University Press, 2020.

Hensel, Silke, U. Bock, K. Dircksen and H.U. Thamer, eds., *Constitutional Cultures: On the Concept and Representation of Constitutions in the Atlantic World.* Newcastle upon Tyne: Cambridge Scholars Publishing, 2012.

Hohmann, Jessie and Daniel Joyce, eds., *International Law's Objects*, Oxford: Oxford University Press, 2019.

Holladay, Joan A. *Genealogy and the Politics of Representation in the High and Late Middle Ages.* Cambridge: Cambridge: Cambridge University Press, 2019.

Huygebaert, Stefan, Georges Martyn, Vanessa Paumen, Eric Bousmar, and Xavier Rousseaux, eds. *The Art of Law: Artistic Representations of Law and Justice in Context, from the Middle Ages to the First World War.* Cham: Springer, 2018.

Huygebaert, Stefan, Georges Martyn, Vanessa Paumen, and Tine Van Poucke. *The Art of Law: Three Centuries of Justice Depicted.* Tielt: Lannoo, 2016.

Innes, Timothy J. 'Art and Legal History.' *American Journal of Legal History* 53 (2013): 414–417.

Khorakiwala, Rahela. 'Judicial Iconography in India.' *Asian Journal of Legal Education* 1 (2014): 89–101.

Manchester, A.H. 'An Introduction to Iconographical Studies of Legal History: England and Wales.' In *Legal History in the Making: Proceedings of the Ninth British Legal History Conference: Glasgow 1989*, edited by W.M. Gordon and T.D. Fergus, 85–88. London: The Hambledon Press, 1991.

Manderson, Desmond, ed. *Law and the Visual: Representations, Technologies, and Critique.* Toronto: University of Toronto Press, 2018.

Manderson, Desmond and Cristina S. Martinez. 'Justice and Art, Face to Face.' *Yale Journal of Law & the Humanities* 28 (2016): 241–263.

Martínez Martínez, Faustino. *Imágenes de la Justicia*. Ariccia: Aracne, 2020.

Meyers, Nancy Illman. 'Painting the Law.' *Cardozo Arts and Entertainment Law Journal* 14 (1996): 397–406.

Mezey, Naomi Jewel. 'Teaching Images.' *Journal of Legal Education* 68 (2018): 74–81.

Mirow, Matthew C., 'Translating into Stone: The Monument to the Constitution of Cádiz in Saint Augustine, Florida.' In *Translation in Times of Disruption: An Interdisciplinary Study in Transnational Context*, edited by David Hook and Graciela Iglesias-Rogers, 101–117. London: Palgrave Macmillan, 2017.

Mnookin, Jennifer L. 'The Image of Truth: Photographic Evidence and the Power of Analogy.' *Yale Journal of Law & the Humanities* 10 (1998): 1–74.

Narváez, H., José Ramón. *Cultura jurídica: ideas e imágenes*. México: Editorial Porrúa, 2010.

Perry, Barbara A. 'The Israeli and United States Supreme Courts: A Comparative Reflection on their Symbols, Images, and Function.' *The Review of Politics* 63 (2001): 317–339.

Resnik, Judith and Dennis Curtis. *Representing Justice: Invention, Controversy, and Rights in City-States and Democratic Courtrooms*. New Haven: Yale University Press, 2011.

Scharf, Michael P. and Katie Steiner. 'Foreward: The Art of International Law.' *Case Western Reserve Journal of International Law* 49 (2017): 1–4.

Scheurmann, Ingrid, ed., *Frieden durch Recht: Das Reichskammergericht von 1495 bis 1806*. Mainz: Verlag Philipp von Zabern, 1995.

Sherwin, Richard K. *Visualizing Law in the Age of the Digital Baroque: Arabesques and Entanglements*. London: Routledge, 2011.

Solórzano Pereira, Juan. *Emblemata centum, regio politica in centuriam unam redacta*. Madrid: Garcia Morras, 1653; reprint Madrid: Tuero, 1987.

Soucek, Brian. 'Not Representing Justice: Ellsworth Kelly's Abstraction in the Boston Courthouse.' *Yale Journal of Law & the Humanities* 24 (2012): 287–304.

Weisberg, Ruth. 'The Art of Memory and the Allegorical Personification of Justice.' *Yale Journal of Law & the Humanities* 24 (2012): 259–270.

Widener, Michael & Mark S. Weiner, *Law's Picture Books: The Yale Law Library Collection*. Clark, NJ: Talbot Publishing, 2017.

Woodlock, Douglas P. 'Communities and the Courthouses Tey Deserve. And Vice Versa.' *Yale Journal of Law & the Humanities* 24 (2012): 271–285.

Young, Alison. *Judging the Image: Art, Value, Law*. Abingdon: Routledge, 2005.

Young, Alison. *Street Art, Public City: Law, Crime and the Urban Imagination*. London: Routledge, 2011.

CHAPTER 3

Xavier Cortada

Socially Engaged Activist Artist

Renée D. Ater

> In using arts and culture to build community, we often forget that the greatest resource isn't necessarily the program we design, or the object we create, or the idea we generate. It is the people themselves. We somehow forget that art is theirs; that for a very long time now people have intuitively used it to better connect one with another.
> XAVIER CORTADA

∴

The above epigraph marks Xavier Cortada as a socially engaged activist artist who is committed to deploying art as a community-building tool. For Cortada, art has the profound ability to bring public awareness to pressing social, environmental, and political issues. His activist art-making includes painted and collaged murals, easel painting, mosaics, site-specific installations, performance, textiles and banners, and interventions in the environment. In this introductory essay to *Painting Constitutional Law*, I consider the diverse range of Cortada's work, including murals such as *Bridging the Gap*; *Stepping into the American Dream*; and *Protecting America's Children: A National Message Mural*. I give sustained attention to each of the ten easel paintings that make up the *May It Please the Court* series, which are the subject of this volume. Lastly, I consider Cortada's science-art projects, including the environmental community-sourced *Reclamation Project* and the science-art installations *The Markers (South Pole)* and *Ancestral Journeys*. In this work, Cortada asserts the power of art to build community and make social connection.

Born in 1964 to a Cuban–American family in Albany, New York, Cortada moved to Miami with his family when he was three years old. He studied psychology as an undergraduate in the mid-1980s at the University of Miami, then earned a master's degree in public administration and a juris doctor degree from the University of Miami in 1991. During this period, he was involved in a range of activities in Miami, including working as an orderly at Jackson Memorial Hospital, conducting cardiology research at the Veterans Affairs Medical Center, serving on the University's Board of Trustees and the Council of International Students and Organizations, and running for the Florida House of Representatives. After passing the Bar, Cortada served as a Research Assistant Professor and Director of the Juvenile Violence and Delinquency Prevention Programs. Since 2000, he has been engaged full-time as an artist while serving as a Professor of Practice in the Department of Art and Art History at the University of Miami.[1]

Although Cortada's path to becoming an artist appears circuitous, he was immersed in art as a child. His father and uncle were artists, influenced by Cuban modernism and such early twentieth-century *vanguardia* artists as Eduardo Abela, Carlos Enríquez, Antonio Gattorno, Wifredo Lam, Victor Manuel, Amelia Peláez, and Fidelio Ponce.[2] Cortada's visual language borrows from Cuban modernism, including the tropical palette and strong black lines of Amelia Peláez and the syncretic Surrealist aesthetic of Wifredo Lam. He also references diverse modern artists, including the geometric forms of Pablo Picasso, the elongated faces and figures in the portraits of Amedeo Modigliani, the slashing gestures of Willem de Kooning, and the deeply emotive canvases depicting traumatized humanity of Francis Bacon. Besides these well-known modern painters, a range of popular sources inform Cortada's art, including 'the visual barrage of advertising, the iconography of *estampas religiosas*, Saturday morning cartoons, the stained-glass windows of Gesu Catholic Church in Miami, and importantly his travels through Africa and Latin America.'[3] Cortada paints in a bold expressionist style with bright colors, fractured form, and the human figure in exaggeration.

---

1 Meredith Camel, 'X Factor: From the North Pole to the South Pole and Everywhere in Between, the Art of UM Alumnus Xavier Cortada Bridges Conflict, Inspires Action, and Teaches the World about Science that Matters', University of Miami Alumni Association, February 15, 2018, accessed February 7, 2019, https://news.miami.edu/stories/2018/02/x-factor.html, and Xavier Cortada, 'Biography', http://cortada.com/about/.
2 Juan A. Martínez, *Cuban Art and National Identity: The Vanguardia Painters, 1920s-1940s* (Gainesville: University Press of Florida, 1994); Segundo J. Fernandez, et al., *Cuban Art in the 20th Century: Cultural Identity and the International Avante Garde* (Tallahassee: FSU Museum of Fine Arts, 2016); and 'Cuban Art in Miami: A Quick History Lesson from Ramon Cernuda', Cuban Art News, September 20, 2016, accessed February 14, 2019, https://cubanartnews.org/2016/09/20/cuban-art-in-miami-a-quick-history-lesson-from-ramon-cernuda/5574/.
3 'Cubaba', Generation Ñ Magazine, Miami, Florida, May 1998, https://cortada.com/press/1998/cubaba.

1   Mural Painting as Consciousness-Raising

Cortada's painting style is best seen in a series of commissioned murals he completed in the late 1990s and early 2000s. In 1995, he completed his first commission: a mural for the historic mining town of Leadville, Colorado. Lake County High School installed the mural, entitled *Hand to Hand*, inside the school to honor the diverse history of the area. Cortada intended the mural to help a 'conflicted community of new and established immigrants to bridge their divide.'[4] Done in a figurative style that would become his signature, the artist used the human figure in exaggerated proportions, bold geometric designs, and vibrant colors to convey the power of mural painting to act as a source for community engagement and as a consciousness-raising tool. Following this mural, Cortada engaged in a global effort to use art to heal communities around issues of violence and drugs, with mural projects in Madrid, Spain; Johannesburg, South Africa; Freetown, Sierra Leone; Port Louis, Mauritius; and Dar es Saalam, Tanzania.[5]

Through the years, Cortada has focused on pressing social issues and involved a range of community participants in his mural projects. Three collaborative murals exemplify his practice.

His 1998 movable mural, *Bridging the Gap*, addresses AIDS and its effects on the global community. Cortada created it onsite for the Twelfth World AIDS Conference in Geneva, Switzerland. At 19 ½ feet long, the mural includes images of men and women whose arms are outstretched. The canvas is painted in a kaleidoscope of deep reds, magentas, yellows, oranges, and blues, evoking the broken planes of Cubism and the color aesthetic of Fauvism (an early twentieth-century art movement that used high-keyed colors and bold, expressionistic brushwork) and Synchromism (an early modern movement that developed a color theory based on analogies between color and music). The participant-driven mural also includes small pieces of paper collaged onto the surface. Cortada invited attendees at the conference to draw images or write thoughts about AIDS on these paper remnants 'to capture the diverse stories of people with AIDS.'[6] He then embedded hand-written comments onto the surface of the painting, weaving the small pieces of paper around the figures.

Cortada created *Stepping into the American Dream* in 2002 for the White House Conference on Minority Homeownership under President George

---

4   Camel, 'X Factor'; and Xavier Cortada, 'Biography', http://cortada.com/about/.
5   See Cortada's website for press information on these murals, https://cortada.com/press/1994/.
6   'Bridging the Gap: About', Xavier Cortada, https://cortada.com/1998/BridgingTheGap/About.

W. Bush. Similar to *Bridging the Gap*, the large mural contains painting and collaged pieces of paper with messages from conference participants, new minority homeowners, President Bush, and Secretary of Housing and Urban Development Mel Martinez. Measuring 8 × 8 feet, the large-scale canvas includes three vignettes. In the far background in front of a house with a yellow front, Cortada shows a brown couple shaking hands with a man—the realtor. From the house flows a banner with signed mortgage documents. In the lower left hand, a woman with grey curly hair hands a man a writing implement so that he can sign the document before him. A piggy bank represents his savings and down payment for the home. Looming in the right-hand side of the painting, a smiling family of four enters their new home; the father grasps the door while the young son holds the key. Representing the 'Blueprint for the American Dream Partnership', a program to increase the number of minority homeowners, the mural illustrates 'the various avenues through which individuals and families can achieve homeownership—homebuyer education, adequate supply of affordable homes, down payment assistance, and mortgage financing.'[7]

In 2005, Cortada completed *Protecting America's Children: A National Message Mural*. Commissioned by the Child Welfare League of America (CWLA), Cortada unveiled the mural at the IDEA Public Charter School in Washington, D.C. According to Shay Bilchick, then-president of CWLA, 'This mural will serve as a powerful and visible reminder of how the IDEA students overcame their struggles and their fears from first-hand experience of violence in their community and, through artistic expression and civic engagement, created a masterpiece for their fellow and future students to enjoy for years to come.'[8] An exuberant contrast of red background and blue/green forms, the mural includes representations of six children rendered in a stained glass effect: five figures are rendered in blue and outlined in black, while a sixth figure is painted in red and outlined in white, symbolizing a child lost to violence.

Like his other murals, Cortada included drawings and messages from IDEA students and concerned citizens about the issues of child abuse and neglect, violence prevention, and non-violent resolution of problems. In the case of *Protecting America's Children*, individuals submitted their responses online and Cortada added their messages to the canvas rather than an onsite interaction.

---

7 'Martinez Unveils Home Ownership Mural by Miami Artist', HUD Archives: News Release, HUD No. 02-146, December 3, 2002, accessed February 15, 2019, https://archives.hud.gov/news/2002/pr02-146.cfm.
8 'Cuban American Artist, Xavier Cortada, Unveils Murals Honoring Children's Memorial Flag', Child Welfare League of America Press Release, April 14, 2005, Xavier Cortada, https://cortada.com/press/2005/cwla-pressrelease.

Messages include the words of the famous such as Martin Luther King Jr., 'Our lives begin to end the day we become silent about the things that matter,' to the wishes of ordinary citizens, 'The most powerful emotion we have is love and compassion. Share it freely with the children of the world and the world will be a better place for their children. Protect the children of the world.'[9] Long used as a pedagogical art form, mural painting here is exploited to its fullest potential to prompt community building around difficult issues.[10] Cortada's murals represent a sustained attention to human connection. The process of individuals coming together in consciousness-raising activities is as important as the final paintings.

2   Law, Advocacy, and Painting

The paintings that comprise *May It Please the Court* align with Cortada's large-scale mural projects in their social messaging and in their artistic form. Painted for the rotunda of the Supreme Court of Florida in 2004, the series originally included seven easel paintings of landmark cases that originated in the State of Florida and made their way to the Supreme Court of the United States. Measuring 48 × 36 inches and using oil and acrylic paints, the seven images include *Gideon v. Wainwright*; *Palmore v. Sidoti*; *The Miami Herald Publishing Company v. Tornillo*; *Williams v. Florida*; *Church of the Lukumi Babalu Aye, Inc. v. City of Hialeah*; *Seminole Tribe of Florida v. Florida*; and *Proffit v. Florida*. He finished the series in 2017 with three additional paintings, depicting *Bush v. Gore*; *Stop the Beach Renourishment, Inc. v. Florida Department of Environmental Protection*; and *Florida v. Jardines*. Informed by his training as a lawyer, Cortada is concerned with the power of art to tell difficult stories about freedom: 'I care passionately about the law. Going to law school informed my career as an artist, which is why I paint these things instead of landscapes and flowers. I use art as a tool of advocacy.'[11] Through his use of strong visual language in *May It Please the Court*, Cortada presents a range of cases that reveal individuals engaging and challenging the law as activist citizens and communities.

---

9   'CWLA Messages', Xavier Cortada, https://cortada.com/2005/CWLA.
10 Renée Ater, 'The Search for a Usable Past: American Mural Painting, 1880–1940' in *Rising Up: Hale Woodruff's Murals at Talladega College*, ed. Stephanie Mayer Heydt (Atlanta: High Museum of Art, 2012), 107–123.
11 Jan Pudlow, 'Artist's Brush Brings Court Cases to Canvas', The Florida Bar News, March 15, 2004, accessed January 4, 2019, https://www.floridabar.org/the-florida-bar-news/artists-brush-brings-court-cases-to-canvas/.

2.1 *Gideon v. Wainwright*

May It Please the Court begins with *Gideon v. Wainwright*. Cortada based the image on a quotation from Robert Kennedy that stressed the groundbreaking nature of Clarence Earl Gideon's effort to be heard and to receive a fair trial with the right to counsel. The oil painting shows a diminutive Gideon seated with bare feet dangling between the oversized steel bars of his cell. Dressed in an orange jumpsuit, Gideon holds a pen in his hand as he writes on a large undulating piece of paper that dominates the foreground of the composition. Cortada suggests that this scroll is a roll of toilet paper. Between the layers of red and pink paint on the right side of the composition, a white toilet bowl jarringly pops out. Below the toilet bowl, a triangle of white 'toilet paper' touches one of the bars. Directly above Gideon, another prisoner lays on his cot, inactive and completely resigned to his fate. Cortada paints Gideon in action, writing his truth, despite his circumstances. As the viewer, we are meant to reflect upon the power of one individual to make change.[12]

Blues, yellows, oranges, and reds dominate the canvas. Cortada also drew a hard-edged black line around his forms to delineate them and fracture the surface. Although of different subject matter, the artist connects the ten paintings of the series through the use of saturated color and bold line. Here, Cortada's approach to color and line aligns with the rich palette and dark lines seen in the work of Cuban modernists Amelia Peláez and Wifredo Lam.

2.2 *Palmore v. Sidoti*

At the center of *Palmore v. Sidoti*, Cortada painted a bi-racial couple with a white child between them. Cortada uses abstract compositional elements to suggest unity and division. The couple is connected through a series of embraces: the woman holds the child around the waist, the man reaches his arm around the woman while he holds the child's hand in his much larger hand, and the child holds onto the woman's thumb. Touch underscores that the three figures are an entity, a family unit. Cortada's exploitation of color hints at the racial divide at the center of the case. With blond hair, blue eyes, and pink skin, the woman, Linda Sidoti, is dressed in a swirl of green. Her partner, Clarence Palmore, Jr., is shown wearing a purple tank top and blue shorts. Cortada painted Palmore with bare feet, juxtaposing them to Sidoti's high heeled shoes. Palmore's dark brown skin is highlighted with daubs and streaks of orange, red, and green. His skin stands in stark contrast to Sidoti's pink skin and the pink skin of the blond-haired, blue-eyed child. The family is enveloped in a plane of

---

12   Xavier Cortada, Interview with Renée Ater, February 4, 2019.

sunny yellow that rises from the bottom of the canvas. On the left side of the painting, however, bands of blue and pink fractured rectangles and triangles intrude into Sidoti's body. Cortada's use of expressive brushwork, sweeping flows of color, and black line disrupt the unity of the family.

This metaphor of intrusion is fully realized in the staring blue eyes set in waves of pink, magenta, and orange acrylic that dominate the upper third and left side of the image. Not only is their gaze directed towards the couple, but the blue eyes stare out at the viewer, implicating them in entrenched attitudes about race, interracial sex, and who gets to constitute family. As Cortada describes: 'Eyes, can't believe what they are seeing … Eyes, bewildered that she could marry someone of another race. Eyes, horrified that she's taken her daughter—one of their own—to live with him.'[13] Through his use of the blue eye, Cortada makes a visual reference to Surrealism's fantastical eye but he does so in order to convey the destructive power of the white discriminatory gaze.[14]

2.3 *Miami Herald Publishing Company v. Tornillo*

Miami Herald Publishing Company v. Tornillo is one of the most visually successful of the paintings. Cortada exploited his knowledge of Cuban modernism to create a dynamic and powerful image. He accomplished this through color, abstraction, and the human body. Set against a saturated crimson red background, the painting is an abstracted image of a newspaper, held by two disembodied white hands. Eight large fingers grip the edges of the newspaper, pressing it into accordion folds of cool blues and greens and warm yellows. Cortada uses the bold black outline to achieve a kaleidoscopic effect, similar to Amelia Peláez's brightly colored, quasi-abstract paintings such as *Peces (Fishes)* (Museum of Modern Art) and *Marpacífico (Hibiscus)* (Art Museum of the Americas). Trapezoids and rectangles dominate, suggesting doorways and portals. Populated with at least seven mouths with red lips and large white teeth, the mouths are open in full expression of free speech, except for one mouth with pursed lips, surely a reference to Pat Tornillo. This image reminds us that

---

13 Xavier Cortada, Text Panel for *'Palmore v. Sidoti*, May It Please the Court: A Solo Exhibit by Xavier Cortada', March 1–July 15, 2004, Florida Supreme Court, Tallahassee, Florida; chapter 8.
14 Alexandre Werneck, 'The Apparitions of the Surrealist Eye' Studio International, December 17, 2007, https://www.studiointernational.com/index.php/the-apparitions-of-a-surrealist-eye-dal-iacute---amp--film and Christina Cacouris, 'The False Mirrors: Disembodied Eyes as Disengaged Subjects' Medium, July 30, 2016, https://medium.com/@christinacacouris/the-false-mirrors-disembodied-eyes-as-disengaged-subjects-91fa07228152.

the freedom of press clause of the First Amendment is essential for successful public debate in a democratic society.

2.4 *Williams v. Florida*

In *Williams v. Florida*, a group of six stand in a juror room with institutional green walls and a doorway with a drawn shade behind them. A bright white bulb under a metal shade illuminates the scene. According to Cortada, this white light represents the union of all the colors and symbolizes truth.[15] Engaged in discussion, the jurors stand on two sides of a long rectangular table. The front of the table is covered in a color wheel of papers and juts into the picture plane. In the center of the table sits a brass-colored scale in equal balance. In this image, Cortada foregrounds the importance of juries to the U.S. judicial system. He writes: 'Nowhere can citizens have a more direct, immediate and substantial role in their government. Jurors are the arbiters of facts. They determine truth.'[16] The painting captures six diverse citizens actively engaged in the jury process: referencing their notes, evaluating the evidence, and determining a fair verdict.[17]

Cortada self-consciously engaged the color wheel to represent the Supreme Court's decision about the composition of juries. He used primary (red, yellow, blue) and complementary (green, purple, orange) hues to create the skin tones, hair, and clothing of the individuals. Three women represent the primary colors: a red woman wearing a green shirt on the left side of the composition; a yellow woman with purple shirt at the center of the table; and a blue woman with orange dress with her hand to her chest. By painting women in primary hues, Cortada advocates for the importance of women's voices in the jury process. He applied complementary, sometimes called secondary, colors to the three men. An orange man in a blue suit holds a piece of paper in his hand; a solemn-looking purple man in yellow shirt points upward with two fingers; and a green man with dark green short hair wears a red turtleneck. 'I see truth as light. I see light as color. I wanted to represent the jurors in six different colors', writes Cortada, 'each bringing their own perspectives and experiences into the jury room.'[18] For Cortada, the jury system and a diverse group of jurors is essential to a democratic system and to the successful administration of the law.

---

15 Xavier Cortada, Interview with Renée Ater, February 4, 2019.
16 Xavier Cortada, Text Panel for '*Williams v. Florida*, May It Please the Court: A Solo Exhibit by Xavier Cortada', March 1–July 15, 2004, Florida Supreme Court, Tallahassee, Florida; chapter 5.
17 Xavier Cortada, Interview with Renée Ater, February 4, 2019.
18 Cortada, Text Panel for *Williams v. Florida*; chapter 5.

2.5   Church of the Lukumi Babalu Aye, Inc. v. City of Hialeah

At the center of *Church of the Lukumi Babalu Aye, Inc. v. City of Hialeah* hangs a slab of pink butchered goat divided into four cuts, set against a white background made of swirls of yellow, blue, red, and white pigment. The leg of the goat hangs from a swath of dark grey in the shape of a hook attached to a dark grey bar that stretches across the top of the canvas. The meat is 'dressed' in a purple cape with white edging and gold designs, and on either side of the cape, two pale yellow crutches emerge. Cortada has anthropomorphized the meat to suggest the body of the Santería *orisha*, Babalú-Ayé, a syncretized form of Saint Lazarus in the Afro-Caribbean religion. Traditionally, Babalú-Ayé is shown hobbling on crutches accompanied by two dogs, who Cortada includes in the bottom left and right corners of the painting. Cortada's image is strangely opaque—it could be read as a butcher shop scene or, if one is familiar with Santería, as a reference of the role of sacrifice within its religious practices. He writes: 'The Hialeah ordinance would have had no problem with the activity depicted in the painting, unless you imbued it with meaning. ... If that goat was being carved up for Babalú instead of "Bob" or "Lou" or either of the dogs, the City would have made it illegal. The Court killed the ordinance and gave life to the free exercise of religion.'[19]

2.6   Seminole Tribe of Florida v. Florida

Similar to *Church of the Lukumi Babalu Aye*, *Seminole Tribe of Florida v. Florida* lacks the human body and is a bold painting dominated by green, blue, red, and yellow. Cortada combined a men's Seminole patchwork jacket with the American flag. The green jacket has three rows each of the map of Florida, the state flag of Florida, and the initials 'FL'. The stripes and stars of the American flag undulate in the background and can been seen through two vertical 'tears' in the jacket, also evoking the number '11.' A case about the Eleventh Amendment, Cortada suggests the ripped jacket is a slot machine benefiting the State of Florida, not the Seminole Tribe.

2.7   Proffitt v. Florida

The most viscerally powerful painting in the series is *Proffitt v. Florida*, a shocking image of a prisoner being executed by electric chair. Convicted of first-degree murder, Proffitt challenged both the constitutionality of his death sentence as 'cruel and unusual' and the arbitrary nature of Florida's capital-sentencing procedure.

---

19   Xavier Cortada, Text Panel for *Church of the Lukumi Babalu Aye, Inc. v. City of Hialeah*, May It Please the Court: A Solo Exhibit by Xavier Cortada, March 1–July 15, 2004, Florida Supreme Court, Tallahassee, Florida; chapter 9.

Dressed in an orange prison jump suit, the condemned Proffitt is shown strapped at his arms to a wooden chair with his left leg shackled to an electric cord that extends out of the picture plane on the lower right. Against a black background, the chair rests in a blue pool. The exaggerated proportions of the man's body outlined in black line—smaller head to enormous feet—as well as the man's screaming mouth suggests his agony. Radiating from the prisoner's head to the right are sharp shards of color, symbolic of the surge of electricity used to kill him.

Cortada again turned to color to create a dynamic composition: the primary color blue and its complement orange dominate the palette against a black void. Two blue panels with Roman numerals frame the man; on the left, Cortada painted the numbers I to VII; on the left, I to VIII. These numbers represent the formula used to determine the mitigating and aggravating factors in sentencing someone to death. Cortada has imagined the formula as $7M + 8A = 0 \, (CU)$, where M = mitigating, A = aggravating, and CU = cruel and unusual. 'Although the idea was to put some objectivity into the decision making, at some point it's almost absurd to think that we can objectify a decision that is so laden with emotion,' states Cortada. 'In my opinion, adding the formula de-emotionalizes the death penalty so that it can be carried out.'[20] In an unflinching and vigorous style, the artist represents the tension between the 'impartial' numbers and the ramifications of the violence of the death penalty.

Cortada based his composition on Francis Bacon's infamous *Study after Velázquez's Portrait of Pope Innocent X* (1953), itself a copy of a Diego Velázquez painting of Pope Innocent X from 1650. By overtly referencing Bacon, Cortada links himself to a long history of artists' responding to and dialoging with each other's work. Bacon's *Study after Velázquez's Portrait of Pope Innocent X* depicts the seated pontiff clinching the arms of his chair, which is bound to the picture plane with gold-colored cords. Dressed in purple and white, Pope Innocent X's 'screaming mouth, isolated from other facial features and divorced from any narrative context, suggests existential agony.'[21] Using saturated color and the human form, Cortada conveys the same horrifying agony as Bacon's study—a question of the existential right of humans to lawfully kill one another. 'Naturally, it is a fantastic painting, it is loud and brash. But then again, there is nothing more fantastic than the death penalty, whether by lethal injection or

---

20 Xavier Cortada, Text Panel for *Proffitt v. Florida*, May It Please the Court: A Solo Exhibit by Xavier Cortada, March 1–July 15, 2004, Florida Supreme Court, Tallahassee, Florida; chapter 7.

21 'The Truth Behind Francis Bacon's Screaming Popes', Phaidon, February 8, 2013, https://www.phaidon.com/agenda/art/articles/2013/february/08/the-truth-behind-francis-bacons-screaming-popes/.

some other process.'²² *Proffitt v. Florida* challenges viewers to think about the death penalty and the inescapable horror of such state sanctioned violence.

2.8 Bush v. Gore

At the center of *Bush v. Gore*, one of three paintings added to the series in 2017, is an hourglass painted in blue with short strokes of yellow. On the top and bottom of the hourglass, Cortada included ballot boxes: one blue box contains GORE in white letters, while the red box is inscribed with BUSH in black. The Gore box is on top of the hourglass and the Bush box is painted upside down on the bottom of the hourglass; this allows the painting to be displayed in either orientation, with Bush at the top of the hourglass and Gore at the bottom. Ballots with punched-out chads stick out of each ballot box. On the either side of the hourglass, stand two men dressed in judicial robes, holding ballots. Cortada states that he wanted to capture the idea of time running out during the recount of the ballots for the contested presidential race in 2000. He also proposes that the hourglass with ballots swirling inside, 'serves as an instrument to measure the passage of time as American democracy continues to (d)evolve. The hourglass is the perfect metaphor for the chaos to come. A nation that grows more and more polarized, a democracy that becomes more fragile with the passage of time.'²³ The composition is divided diagonally from the bottom left corner to the upper right into blue and red zones, symbolic of the Democratic and Republican parties. Painted over the blue and red zones are yellow ballots, hanging chads, butterfly ballots, and ballots that will never be counted. For Cortada, *Bush v. Gore* revealed the partisan nature of the Supreme Court and its intervention to hand the election to Bush.

2.9 Stop the Beach Renourishment, Inc. v. Florida Department of Environmental Protection

The most abstract composition in the series, *Stop the Beach Renourishment, Inc. v. Florida Department of Environmental Protection*, is dominated by four bands of color: dark blue, blue-green, yellow, and red-burgundy. This striation suggests that the boundary between ocean and beach is always in flux. Painted with pigment and sand, Cortada notes 'the media I used mattered: I used sand I personally collected at the water's edge to depict the original seabed in the paintings backdrop. Then, using multi-purpose sand I purchased

---

22   Cortada, Text Panel for *Proffitt v. Florida*; chapter 7.
23   Xavier Cortada, Text Panel for *Bush v. Gore*, May It Please the Court: A Solo Exhibit by Xavier Cortada, March 1–July 15, 2004, Florida Supreme Court, Tallahassee, Florida; chapter 11.

in a 60-pound bag at Home Depot, I created globs splattering dredged sand from the deep to depict the brutal process of artificially restoring shorelines. As that happens, water drips back in ... Or is it flowing up?'[24] His use of sand also brings to mind the work of French modernist Jean Dubuffet, who incorporated into his radically innovative paintings such materials as sand, gravel, straw, and mud. In this abstracted image of ocean and beach, Cortada painted a dark blue pipe at the bottom of the composition that spews out tan, sandy pigment towards the shoreline. The incorporation of sand in the pigment adds three-dimensional volume to the surface. It also suggests the core problem at the heart of the case: the issue of private property, public land, and the dredging of sand from the Gulf of Mexico to replenish beaches impacted by erosion and storm damage. As Cortada writes, 'It is an endless dance, seen sharply at the water's edge, even if for a moment, as the waterline recedes with the tide. It is most dramatic as it erases shorelines. The dance creates an ever-changing landscape—one that wasn't made for us, but one we want to control so that it best works for us.'[25] Of all the paintings in *May It Please the Court*, this is most tied to Cortada's science and environmental activist community projects and performance art, which he began in 2006.

2.10   *Florida v. Jardines*

The last painting depicts *Florida v. Jardines*. A swirling, undulating composition, the image is comprised of a tilted room with a dog's large grey-brown snout bursting through a bright orange doorway, which is nearly off its hinges. Cortada created the tilted room with three catawampus walls and an askew gold light fixture. The whole composition seems to dance. The three walls are painted in an early modern Pointillist style using small dots of red, yellow, and blue juxtaposed next to each other to suggest vibrations and pulsations. Cortada plays with sensorial sensation of smell through the curlicue shapes in green and yellow emanating from the dog's nose. These twisting serpentine forms dominate the entire composition and suggest the olfactory power of trained drug-detection dogs. Rather than remaining on the porch to sniff out drugs, the artist depicts the dog's nose invading the interior of the home, an unlawful search in violation of the Fourth Amendment.

• • •

---

24   Xavier Cortada, Text Panel for *Stop the Beach Renourishment, Inc. v. Florida Department of Environmental Protection*, May It Please the Court: A Solo Exhibit by Xavier Cortada, March 1–July 15, 2004, Florida Supreme Court, Tallahassee, Florida; chapter 12.
25   Ibid.

Gideon v. Wainright and *Proffitt v. Florida* bracket the original seven paintings in the series, connected through color and subject matter. Both paint the cases of two prisoners who insisted on being heard, but with different outcomes. Breaking through the prison bars, Gideon used the power of the pen for self-advocacy; he challenged his conviction and sentence on the grounds that his constitutional rights were violated. The Supreme Court agreed that the Sixth Amendment's guarantee of counsel is a fundamental right. For Proffitt, the outcome of his advocacy was death. The Supreme Court ruled that the death penalty was not 'cruel and unusual punishment' and that Florida's procedures were not capricious. Despite the Court's ruling, Cortada reminds viewers that jurors must consider in their decision-making the reality of putting someone to death. Taken as a whole, *May It Please the Court* signifies the power of individuals to challenge and participate in the judicial system and to use the law to create a more just society.

3 Art, Science, and Building Community

Besides an activist painting practice, Cortada is dedicated to an art praxis that confronts the environment and participates in current science concerns. His *Reclamation Project* (2006–2012) is an ecological art intervention and community-engagement project. The purpose of the project was to plant mangrove propagules in the Miami-Dade County area. Fascinated with mangroves since his childhood and disturbed by the destruction of mangrove forests near his Florida Keys retreat, Cortada initially planned to create an art project based on the replanting of his retreat area with mature mangroves.[26] But in 1996, the State of Florida passed the Florida State Mangrove Trimming and Preservation Act that strictly regulated the care and preservation of mangrove wetlands in the state. Cortada discovered that he would need to plant mangrove propagules, the germinated seed pod that looks like a skinny green and brown cigar, at designated mitigation sites (specific public lands designated for replanting in order to prevent further damage to the ecosystem).[27]

---

26   Mary Jo Aagerstoun, 'Cortada's Eco-Art' Xavier Cortada, accessed October 22, 2020, https://cortada.com/press/2007/eco-art-essay.
27   'Mangrove Species Profiles' Florida Museum of Natural History, accessed February 15, 2019, https://www.floridamuseum.ufl.edu/southflorida/habitats/mangroves/species/ and 'Mangrove Wetlands' Miami-Dade County Environmental Resources Management, accessed February 14, 2019, http://www.miamidade.gov/environment/wetlands-mangroves.asp.

With the assistance of Gary Milano, Habitat Restoration Program Director for the Miami-Dade County Department of Environmental Resources Management, Cortada developed a community art project to grow individual propagules. Working with volunteers and the Miami Science Museum (now the Phillip and Patricia Frost Museum of Science), Cortada designed his first art installation related to the project in 2006. It featured mangrove propagules placed in water-filled plastic cups displayed in storefront windows along Lincoln Road in Miami Beach. Weeks later, volunteers who had assisted in collecting the propagules planted the mature seedpods along Biscayne Bay in a ritual-laden ceremony. As volunteers planted the propagules, they repeated the phrase: 'I hereby reclaim this land for nature.'[28] Cortada has described the project as slow activism: 'I don't care that a mangrove was planted; I care that you planted a mangrove. I go through all these crazy processes to create a sense of community, to create a strategy to make you more curious. Most of what I do is slow activism, creating a cadre of citizens who are more science literate and more loving and supportive to one another as we face the greatest challenge of our time.'[29] The *Reclamation Project* sums up Cortada's commitments to the creative act, community engagement, and the environment.

A year after starting the *Reclamation Project*, Cortada traveled to McMurdo Station, the U.S. Research Center on Ross Island in Antarctica, on a National Science Foundation Antarctic Artists and Writers fellowship. Cortada used the three-kilometer thick, moving glacial ice sheet to mark time and significant historical events. Named *The Markers (South Pole)* (2007), Cortada embedded fifty-one flags on the ice sheet. The flags were spaced 10 meters apart and marked the spot where the shifting geographic South Pole stood from 1956 to 2006. The artist used colored flags to also mark the coordinates of specific locations tied to important historical events: for example, 1963 is geo-located to Washington, DC—38.8893° N, 77.0502° W—and represents the March on Washington for Jobs and Freedom.

Cortada also planted an ice replica of a mangrove seedling on the moving ice sheet, where it began a 1,400 km journey from McMurdo Station to the Weddell Sea. This symbolic journey will take approximately 150,000 years. *The Markers (South Pole)* 'invites viewers to reflect on our role on this planet. Juxtaposing geological time frames (the 150,000-year journey) with human time frames (the markers), Cortada reaffirms the notion that we are merely

---

28   Mary Jo Aagerstoun has written an in-depth analysis of Reclamation Project, describing its aesthetic value, activist impulse, and science focus. Mary Jo Aagerstoun, 'Xavier Cortada's Reclamation Project,' exhibition brochure, 2017.
29   Camel, 'X Factor'.

custodians who should live in harmony with nature during the brief time we are here.'³⁰ The project also reminds us of the interconnectedness of our world, the mangrove serving as link between the South Pole and Biscayne Bay. During his time at McMurdo Station, Cortada also created a series of mixed media Ice Paintings using ice and sediment samples from the nearby Ross Sea. Playing with the ideas of beauty and horror, Cortada states: 'With the ice paintings, I wanted to melt the very ice that threatened to drown my city [Miami]. The work, beautiful and serene, would be a precursor of horrors to come. ... I melted the ice on paper to create works, adding painting and sediment. The works were made in Antarctica, about Antarctica, using Antarctica as the medium.'³¹ In such images as *Astrid* (2007), the blue pigment and areas of white suggest aerial maps and satellite images of Antarctica, as well glacial disintegration caused by climate change: 'Viewed in terms of materiality instead of the metaphor of representation, *Astrid* functions as a token or specimen of a place undergoing irrevocable change wrought by human actions elsewhere.'³²

From his Antarctica art installation and paintings, Cortada began to create an 'evolving body of work that used genetic data to explore how nature influenced human migration and history.'³³ Similar to *Reclamation Project*, Cortada relied on community participants to make the art and imbue it with local meaning. In *Ancestral Journeys* (2010), exhibited at Deering Estate in Palmetto Bay, Florida, Cortada collected DNA samples of people living in Miami to trace ancestral journeys and to explore ideas of deep ancestry and interconnectedness across the Western Hemisphere. At what is known as the 'Cutler Fossil Site', archaeologists have discovered human and animal remains dating to 10,000 years ago, including a Paleo Indian shelter from the end of the Pleistocene Era and burial mound of the native Tequesta people. This ancient history, along with Dr. Spencer Well's work with the National Geographic's Genographic Project, inspired the artist.

Cortada created *Ancestral Works*, a series of twenty digital paintings; *The Ancestral Dinner Party*; *Ancestral Journeys: Paternal Lineage*; and *Ancestral Journeys: Maternal Lineage* were site-specific installations and participatory events at Deering Estate. Working with local Miamians, Cortada traced the ancestral

---

30 'Xavier Cortada: Using a Moving Ice Sheet to Mark Time', Association of Polar Early Career Scientists, accessed February 14, 2019, https://www.apecs.is/outreach/international-polar-week/past-polar-weeks/polar-week-march-2017/polar-art/1703-xavier-cortada-using-a-moving-ice-sheet-to-mark-time.html.
31 Xavier Cortada, email message to Alan C. Braddock and Renée Ater, June 3, 2014.
32 Alan C. Braddock and Renée Ater, 'Art in the Anthropocene' (2014) 28(3) American Art 3.
33 'Artist's Statement: Ancestral Journeys', Xavier Cortada, https://cortada.com/statement.

journeys of men and women through their DNA. Twelve men submitted DNA to discover their respective paternal ancestral journeys; their countries of origins include Costa Rica, El Salvador, Haiti, Spain, and Venezuela. For the maternal lineage installation, nine male and female participants were tested for genetic markers in their Mitochondrial DNA (maternal lineage) to discover their respective maternal ancestral journeys, from Columbia, Ecuador, Mexico, and Uruguay. Cortada created digital maps representing individuals and their DNA markers as well as an icon for each person. Each map includes a red line demarking the migratory path of their ancestors. On the grounds of the estate, Cortada placed white flags depicting these global journeys in response to climate change. 'Visitors were encouraged to reenter the forest [at Deering Estate] and to retrace their ancestors' steps as they populated the planet in response to a changing environment.'[34] *Ancestral Journeys* focused on genetic data to reveal human's interconnectedness and relationship to the natural world. By selecting citizens of Miami as the subject of the project, Cortada created a diverse portrait of the Miami community: 'In their blood they capture evidence of the routes their deep ancestors took in response to climatic changes from their original journey out of Africa 60,000 years ago.'[35]

Works such as *Reclamation Project*, *The Markers* (*South Pole*), and *Ancestral Journeys* reveal an artist committed to science and to participatory art projects. Through his eco-art practice, Cortada reveals the ways in which local communities and recent science can be connected to raise consciousness about pressing environmental concerns.

4 Conclusion

May It Please the Court is part of a larger artistic practice based in process, community, activism, consciousness raising, and advocacy. From his early mural paintings to the easel paintings of *May It Please the Court* to his environmental participatory projects, Cortada works across media to edge individuals and communities into action. In the past decade, his work has included a site-specific installation of five huge banners for CMS at CERN (2011), the largest particle physics laboratory in the world; *Flower Force* (2012), a participatory eco-art project to encourage communities in Pennsylvania to plant native wildflowers; *Five Action Steps to Stop Sea Level Rise* (2015), a performance/video

---

34 'Ancestral Journeys: Xavier Cortada' exhibition brochure, 2010, Xavier Cortada, https://cortada.com/2010/AncestralJourneys/About.

35 'Ancestral Works', Xavier Cortada, https://cortada.com/2010/AncestralWorks.

piece funded through the Robert Rauschenberg Foundation; and the *Diatom Fountain* (2017), a public art project located in Little Havana in Miami, a mosaic of a diatom based on samples from scientists at FIU's Florida Coastal Everglades LTER (Long Term Ecological Research) project to study the ecology of the Everglades and sea-level rise. Xavier Cortada exploits a range of materials and processes to insist that art is a tool for social and political engagement.

Recommended Reading

Aagerstoun, Mary Jo. 'Cortada's Eco-Art.' Xavier Cortada, accessed October 22, 2020, https://cortada.com/press/2007/eco-art-essay.

Braddock, Alan C. and Renée Ater. "Art in the Anthropocene." *American Art* 28(3) (Fall 2014): 2–8.

"Cubaba." *Generation Ñ Magazine* (Miami, Florida), May 1998, Xavier Cortada, https://cortada.com/press/1998/cubaba.

Pudlow, Jan. 'Artist's Brush Brings Court Cases to Canvas.' *The Florida Bar News*, March 15, 2004, accessed January 4, 2019, https://www.floridabar.org/the-florida-barnews/artists-brush-brings-court-cases-to-canvas/.

'X-Factor: From the North Pole to the South Pole and Everywhere in Between, the Art of UM Alumnus Xavier Cortada Bridges Conflict, Inspires Action, and Teaches the World about Science that Matters.' University of Miami Alumni Association, February 15, 2018, accessed February 7, 2019, https://news.miami.edu/alumni/stories/2018/02/x-factor.html.

Gideon v. Wainwright, 372 U.S. 335 (1963)

Xavier Cortada

∴

> If an obscure Florida convict named Clarence Earl Gideon had not sat down in his prison cell with a pencil and paper to write a letter to the Supreme Court, and if the court had not taken the trouble to look for merit in that one crude petition, among all the bundles of mail it must receive every day, the vast machinery of American Law would have gone on functioning undisturbed. But Gideon did write that letter, the court did look into his case; and he was retried with the help of competent defense counsel, found not guilty and released from prison after two years of punishment for a crime he did not commit—and the whole course of legal history has been changed.
>
> ROBERT F. KENNEDY, 1963

In researching *Gideon v. Wainwright,* 372 U.S 335 (1963), I found that Bobby Kennedy quote and instantly came up with my composition about the landmark case on 'the right to an attorney.' Instead of focusing on what Gideon was unable to do in the courtroom without an attorney ('lawyers in criminal courts are necessities, not luxuries'), I focused on what he did accomplish after he was sentenced.

Gideon could have literally done what his cell mate is doing in my painting, just sitting back and rotting away in jail. He could have used that paper as toilet paper. Instead, what Gideon decided to do is act. Because Gideon decided to write from his cell, others were guaranteed a right to counsel before being sent to theirs.

Even in the most isolated, remote place, he said, 'I am going to challenge.' For someone who is marginalized to that level: no money, no nothing, no power; a roamer, a drifter now sitting in jail. And you can single-handedly change the course of history.

I think it speaks volumes for what we as individuals in a society can do.

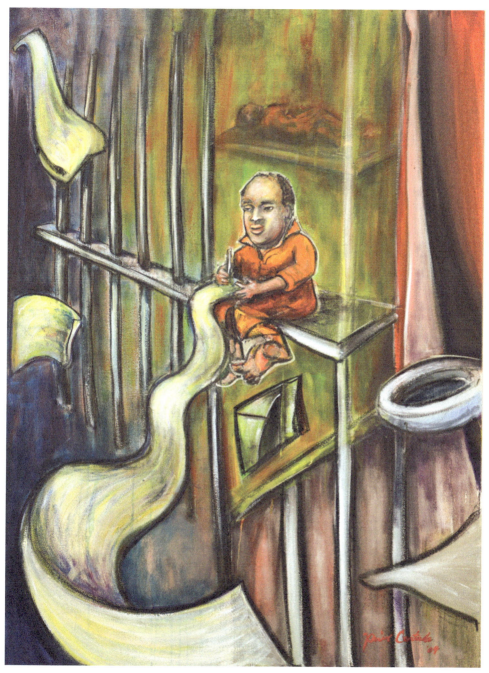

FIGURE 4.1   Xavier Cortada, *Gideon v. Wainwright*, 372 U.S. 335 (1963), 48" × 36", oil on canvas, 2004.
PHOTO: ZENAIDA PIRRI, MIAMI, FLORIDA

CHAPTER 4

Gideon v. Wainwright

The Surprising Power of a Prisoner Petition

Paul Marcus and Mary Sue Backus

'You have a right to an attorney.' That phrase is deeply embedded in the American criminal justice lexicon. Most Americans can recite that foundational principle without hesitation, having been schooled in its importance through countless television crime dramas. Very few, however, would picture the genesis of that right as artist Xavier Cortada depicts it—a lone prisoner handwriting a petition to the Supreme Court of the United States. Cortada captures the fascinating story of long odds and perseverance in his portrait of Clarence Earl Gideon and his role in establishing a poor criminal defendant's right to an attorney.

1   The Road to *Gideon v. Wainwright*

Do you suppose most people in the United States understand that the right to a defense lawyer in criminal cases was not guaranteed until the mid-1960s? Of course not. After all, we have known for a long time about those great attorneys who represent us at trial. Advocates such as Jackie Chiles (*Seinfeld*), Atticus Finch (*To Kill a Mockingbird*), Billy Flynn (*Chicago*), Vincent Gambini (*My Cousin Vinny*), Saul Goodman (*Breaking Bad*), Lionel Hutz (*The Simpsons*), *Ally McBeal*, and *Perry Mason* were there to protect our rights against government over-reach. True enough, at least in television and in the movies. In the actual criminal justice system, though, the reality is not as uplifting.

Our story begins in 1791, with the states' ratification of the Sixth Amendment to the United States Constitution as part of the Bill of Rights. It provides, in material part: 'In all criminal prosecutions, the accused shall enjoy the right … to have the Assistance of Counsel for his defense.' There can be little doubt that our framers did not intend to insure that even poor people would be provided counsel. No, the Supreme Court insisted, this involved 'the right to the aid of counsel when desired and provided by the party asserting the right.'[1]

---

1   *Powell v. Alabama*, 287 U.S. 45, 68 (1932).

The guarantee to a lawyer for all came closer to reality when the Justices held in *Johnson v. Zerbst* in 1938 that the right applied to the destitute defendant in federal cases.[2] Closer, but not close enough, for the vast majority of criminal cases are handled in state courts for violations of state criminal law. Still, the language in *Johnson* was so strong that many believed it would also be applied in state cases. 'The purpose of the constitutional guaranty of a right to counsel is to protect an accused from conviction resulting from his own ignorance of his legal and constitutional rights. ... Compliance with this constitutional mandate is an essential jurisdictional prerequisite to a federal court's authority to deprive an accused of his life or liberty.'[3] That broader application was not to be, at least not for another quarter century.

Four years later, the Court held that the Due Process Clauses of the Fifth and Fourteenth Amendments, not the Sixth Amendment, would only require a lawyer for a poor person accused of a crime if exceptional circumstances showed that basic fairness dictated the need for an attorney.[4] It was not enough that the penniless defendant had no legal education or that—if convicted—he could be imprisoned for many years. The Justices softened this view in 1962, stating that an exceptional circumstance was present if it could be shown that 'an imaginative lawyer' might have considered legal claims beyond the ability of a layperson.[5] That rather odd holding lasted but a year, when the Court took on the basic question of whether its earlier decision establishing the exceptional circumstances principle should be overruled.

2   *Gideon v. Wainwright*

When Clarence Earl Gideon stood before a Florida state court judge in 1961, arguing strenuously that he was entitled to be represented by counsel in his trial for breaking into the Bay Harbor Pool Hall in Panama City, he did not understand the nuances of the Supreme Court's Sixth Amendment doctrine. Gideon asked the court to appoint a lawyer to represent him because he could not afford to hire his own. The trial judge denied his request because, at that moment, the Sixth Amendment, as understood by the Court and by Florida law, did not guarantee an indigent defendant such as Gideon a lawyer in state court.

What Gideon knew, and what the Supreme Court would later acknowledge as an 'obvious truth,' was that he could not get a fair trial without a lawyer to defend him. Gideon was an uneducated man who struggled to make a living.

---

2 *Johnson v. Zerbst*, 304 U.S. 458 (1938).
3 Ibid., 467.
4 *Betts v. Brady*, 316 U.S. 455 (1942).
5 *Chewning v. Cunningham*, 368 U.S. 443, 447 (1962).

From the time he was a teenager, he was in and out of prison on assorted robbery and larceny charges, some more serious than others. When arrested for breaking and entering the pool hall, he was a career petty criminal, having amassed multiple arrests and a number of felony convictions over his 51 years.

Even the knowledge he gained from his encounters with the criminal justice system was not enough to help Gideon when he was forced to represent himself at trial. He did the best he could—calling witnesses, making arguments, and cross examining the state's witnesses. Unsurprisingly, despite his efforts, the jury convicted him and he was sentenced to the maximum of five years in prison. Gideon could have given up and served his time as he had done on a number of other occasions, but he did not. He petitioned the Supreme Court of Florida to overturn his conviction and sentence on the ground that his constitutional right was violated by the trial judge's refusal to appoint counsel. When that petition was denied, Gideon wrote to the Supreme Court of the United States.

It is remarkable that Clarence Gideon's handwritten letter to the Supreme Court, in pencil no less, produced this legal revolution. As United States Attorney General Eric Holder wrote:

> Nearly half a century ago, the Supreme Court's decision in *Gideon v. Wainwright* marked a watershed moment—and a critical step forward—in our nation's enduring pursuit of equal justice for all. This landmark case provided that criminal defendants have a constitutional right to counsel, even if they cannot afford an attorney, and—as my predecessor, Attorney General Robert Kennedy, stated a few months after the 1963 ruling—'[changed] the whole course of American legal history.'[6]

Two years after receiving his letter, the Court unanimously agreed with Gideon and held that 'any person haled into court, who is too poor to hire a lawyer, cannot be assured a fair trial unless counsel is provided for him.'[7] The Court found that the average citizen lacks the necessary legal skills to mount an effective

---

[6] Eric H. Holder, Jr. and Dick Thornburgh. 'Reflections on *Gideon*' (2012) NACDL, *available at* https://www.nacdl.org/Champion.aspx?id=24999. The Supreme Court has established a complex body of law for when a rule of criminal procedure applies retroactively, to convictions that became final prior to the rule being announced. One exception is for "watershed rules of criminal procedure' implicating the fundamental fairness and accuracy of the criminal proceeding.' *Saffle v. Parks*, 494 U.S. 484, 495 (1990) (citing *Teague v. Lane*, 489 U.S. 288, 311 (1989) (plurality opinion)). The Court has cited *Gideon* as the paradigm, if not sole example, for that exception. *Saffle*, 494 U.S. at 495.

[7] *Gideon*, 372 U.S. at 344.

defense. States must provide legal counsel to anyone charged with a felony who cannot afford a lawyer. As Gideon stubbornly insisted to the Florida state court judge, the Supreme Court found that the Sixth Amendment's guarantee of counsel is a fundamental right, essential to a fair trial. And he was proven right, at least in his case. On remand, Gideon was retried, represented by his chosen lawyer, and acquitted.

Gideon did not answer every question about the right to counsel for poor people. The Court gave no guidance as to when the Sixth Amendment right to counsel attaches; what level of counsel is guaranteed; how to provide indigent defense services; or how to fund those services. But its ringing language endorsing effective representation for poor criminal defendants is celebrated as a guarantee that every criminal defendant, no matter his education or her economic resources, stands equal before the law. That constitutional guarantee is a cornerstone of equality and fairness in the judicial process: a criminal defendant's right to counsel 'may not be deemed fundamental and essential to fair trials in some countries, but it is in ours.'[8]

3   The Retreat from *Gideon*

The Court's opinion was both powerful and inspirational. And with no dissent, hopes were high that later decisions would broaden the *Gideon* holding. In particular, many argued that the right to counsel for even the desperately poor should apply to all criminal prosecutions, not only felonies, and should attach as soon as the defendant was arrested, questioned, and identified, not only at trial. A majority of Justices held different notions, such that the hope for strengthening of the Sixth Amendment was dashed over the intervening years.

Soon after *Gideon*, the Justices left little doubt that while the Constitution spoke of counsel 'in all criminal prosecutions' the actual application of the right to counsel for indigent defendants would be to some criminal prosecutions. In a series of decisions, the right was restricted to cases in which the defendant was actually ordered imprisoned. That is, a judge at sentencing could not order any term of imprisonment unless she had offered to the indigent defendant the assistance of counsel. The Sixth Amendment is not violated absent imprisonment. But defendants are not guaranteed counsel to protect against the often-severe non-imprisonment collateral consequences of conviction. These include disadvantages in employment opportunities, licensing, student

---

8   Ibid.

loans, government housing, and even deportation. It includes the use of one conviction, obtained without counsel, to enhance a sentence for a later conviction where counsel was appointed. But the Court has held that a suspended sentence that may 'end up in the actual deprivation of a person's liberty' may not be imposed unless the defendant was accorded 'the guiding hand of counsel' in the prosecution for the crime charged.[9] Thus a probation violation may not result in imprisonment if the underlying conviction was uncounseled.

The Court also limited the right to counsel to trial. Unfortunately, the vast majority of criminal convictions in the United States do not result from trials. Rather, the norm is a negotiated plea. Pre-trial proceedings thus are important, as they may determine the ultimate bargain as to charged offenses or sentence. Once again, the Court painted with a narrow brush, concluding that the right to counsel did not begin with the arrest of the suspect, but only with an adversarial judicial proceeding. Thus, a lineup could be held without a defense lawyer present, so long as that lineup occurred before a formal charging event such as a preliminary hearing or the issuance of an indictment.

The Court also required counsel only when the defendant herself was confronted in some sort of proceeding related to the determination of guilt. This may not seem like much of a limitation, but it is of major practical significance. For instance, the notoriously unreliable photo display used to identify a suspect may proceed, even after commencement of adversarial judicial proceedings, without defense counsel present. No lawyer for the defendant is present to note the witness's reaction to photos, to view the body language of the investigating officer, or to consider the time given for viewing each photo. Such involvement by defense counsel could be invaluable in shaping trial strategy and in determining whether to accept a plea offer. But the poor defendant's lawyer cannot be required to participate simply because it is a photo display rather than an in-person identification.

The core of the right to counsel is that assistance of counsel be effective. But the Court's decisions have made clear that it will not review with great care claims that counsel was provided but ineffective. In the leading decision, issued more than three decades ago, the Justices imposed on the defendant the full burden 'to show that counsel's representation fell below an objective standard of reasonableness.'[10] And much deference is given to the lawyer in the work done. Even if that hurdle can be cleared, the defendant prevails only if she 'show[s] that there is a reasonable probability that, but for

---

9   *Alabama v. Shelton*, 535 U.S. 654 (2002).
10 *Strickland v. Washington*, 466 U.S. 668, 688 (1984).

counsel's unprofessional errors, the result of that proceeding would have been different.'[11]

One federal judge revealed the true height of these hurdles, stating 'the Constitution does not guarantee that a defendant will have a perfect lawyer.' It does not guarantee that he will have a good lawyer. It does not even guarantee that he will *not* have a 'really bad one.'[12] As the Supreme Court recently reminded us, a violation of the Sixth Amendment right to effective representation is not 'complete' until the defendant is prejudiced and the rules 'must be applied with scrupulous care.'[13]

The Court's failure to guarantee aggressively the Sixth Amendment right of poor criminal defendants is disappointing, but it is the failure of the states to provide effective public defense that most undermined *Gideon*'s promise. *Gideon* makes clear that the fundamental right to counsel is a foundation of an adversary system of justice, which is based on the idea that the truth will emerge where skilled advocates on each side have a full opportunity to present their side of their story in a dispute. Sadly, in criminal proceedings across the country, this model of adversarial fairness is near fantasy, leaving many defendants without an effective advocate.

Gideon left it to the states to determine how to provide adequate representation to criminal defendants who cannot afford a lawyer. The result is a patchwork of public-defense systems in state courts—from fully state-funded public defender programs to appointed counsel paid by the hour and contract attorneys who handle all cases in a jurisdiction. Whether by design or by lack of political will, states have largely failed to construct independent, competent public-defender systems to deliver on *Gideon*'s promise of adversarial fairness. Given that poor criminal defendants are not a particularly popular or sympathetic constituency and the Supreme Court's less than vigorous standards for declaring representation inadequate, there is little incentive for states to create, staff, and fund effective defense systems.

The failure of states to provide adequate representation for poor criminal defendants is well documented. Each major anniversary of *Gideon* inspires panels, conferences, and news articles bemoaning the sad state of its unrealized promise. Over the five decades since the decision, multiple reports and

---

11   Ibid., 694.
12   *Fields v. White*, (E.D. Ky. 2016), 2016 WL 3574396, *22 (E.D. Ky. 2016); *see Storey v. Vasbinder*, 657 F.3d 372, 374 (6th Cir. 2011) ('[T]he Supreme Court has gone out of its way to make clear that, in order to obtain a new trial on ineffective-assistance grounds, the petitioner must do more than show that he had a bad lawyer—even a really bad one.').
13   *Weaver v. Massachusetts*, 137 S. Ct. 1899, 1910–12 (2017).

studies attempting to diagnose the problem have identified the drastic underfunding as the root cause of the intractable problems plaguing indigent-defense systems. Scarce resources for public defense mean crushing caseloads for attorneys and little time or money for investigations, pretrial motions, or experts. Although there are a few exceptions where indigent-defense systems are adequately structured and funded, across the country the basic rights guaranteed under *Gideon* have yet to be fully realized. Overall, the state of indigent defense continues to be referred to as 'in crisis.'[14] And that was before Justice Thomas questioned the constitutional basis for *Gideon* and the existence of any right to state-provided counsel for indigent defendants.[15]

Had Clarence Gideon been tried, convicted, and imprisoned in Florida today, he may have found himself writing a petition to the Supreme Court alleging that his appointed public defender lacked the time or resources to investigate his case and prepare for trial. His lawyer's time and attention would have been occupied by the hundreds, sometimes thousands, of other defendants she was assigned to represent. His publicly funded defense counsel may have only had enough time to encourage him to accept a plea bargain. Gideon may have sat in jail for months without any contact from his overwhelmed attorney. In short, Gideon might have discovered that much remains to be done to ensure that other poor criminal defendants receive the right he stubbornly insisted he was entitled to in his 1963 letter to the Supreme Court.

Nevertheless, we must not forget the monumental importance of *Gideon*. Prior to that ruling, most criminal defendants never were represented by lawyers. Most criminal defendants today are assigned attorneys because of *Gideon*, even if grave concerns remain as to the practical state of the right to counsel.

4 *May It Please the Court*

Xavier Cortada's *Gideon v. Wainwright* painting depicts a stylized jail cell occupied by two inmates, each wearing the standard-issue prisoner orange jumpsuit. The prisoner in the forefront, who is obviously meant to be Clarence Earl Gideon, is perched on the edge of the cell, not entirely contained within its bars. There is a long red curtain to Gideon's right, not unlike a theater curtain, which is drawn back as if to reveal the drama of the cell and its occupants. Gideon writes on a long stream of paper that floats and spirals through the air. A toilet seat juts into the cell, suggesting that the paper Gideon is writing

---

14 Mary Sue Backus and Paul Marcus, 'The Right to Counsel in Criminal Cases: Still a National Crisis?' (2018) 86 George Washington Law Review 1564.
15 *Garza v. Idaho*, 139 S. Ct. 738, 756 (2019) (Thomas, J. dissenting).

on may be toilet paper. The prisoner in the back of the painting is blurred and turned away and appears to be sleeping on a bunk bed.

At first glance, Cortada's painting cannot be described as uplifting or optimistic. The prison setting is depressing, the colors muted and dark. The toilet hulking in the corner gives the scene a grimy air and the central figure is not particularly attractive. One would be forgiven for turning away from the dark and unappealing images. But a closer look reveals that the artist has captured some of the most compelling elements of Clarence Gideon's story and his remarkable contribution to the bundle of procedural protections for criminal defendants. Gideon's handwritten petition to the Supreme Court was the longest of long shots. It was an act of desperation born of his circumstances and an act of faith in the United States Constitution. Cortada's rendering captures the unlikelihood of the success of that jailhouse plea. But the painting also captures Gideon's single-minded persistence despite the towering odds against him.

By all accounts, Clarence Gideon was not a particularly heroic figure. He was uneducated, likely an alcoholic. Although not violent, he was a career criminal who made a living primarily through petty crime and spent a considerable portion of his adult years in jail. He was married and divorced multiple times, lost custody of his children to the state, and, as a result of tuberculosis, was in chronically poor health and had to have portions of his lungs removed. Life, and his own choices, had certainly kicked Clarence Gideon around. In a letter to his appointed lawyer, Gideon referred to the 'utter folly and hopelessness [of] parts of my life.'[16]

Having landed in prison again, Gideon might have been resigned to his fate and given up, like the unidentified prisoner in the background curled up in his bunk, out of focus and with his back to the world. Even from his desolate prison cell, however, Gideon refused to surrender to his circumstances. His perseverance, which shines through the darkness of the painting, saved him. It is what led to the iconic principle enshrined in the decision bearing his name—even poor criminal defendants are entitled to lawyers, Gideon's accomplishment is remarkable, as the artist notes, 'for someone who is marginalized to that level: no money, no nothing, no power; a roamer, a drifter now sitting in jail.'

When Gideon stood up before the Florida trial judge and stubbornly proclaimed that 'the United States Supreme Court says I am entitled to be represented by Counsel,' he was, of course, wrong. The Supreme Court had said no such thing to that point. But this lack of understanding of Supreme Court precedent did not dampen Gideon's conviction that the Constitution guaranteed

---

16   Anthony Lewis, *Gideon's Trumpet* (New York: Vintage, 1964), 68.

this basic level of fairness to those who were unable to finance their own defense. He was convinced that he was entitled to a lawyer, and his single-minded determination fueled his efforts to seek his own justice. Gideon believed he had been treated unfairly. His petition to the Supreme Court declared that the Florida court had violated his due process rights by not providing him a lawyer when he could not afford one and was 'incapable adequately of making his own defense.'[17]

One aspect of Cortada's painting is puzzling: his portrayal of Gideon himself. At the time of the break-in, Gideon was just shy of six feet tall and under 150 pounds. Photos of him show a gaunt, Caucasian male with receding, graying hair and glasses, not unlike Henry Fonda's look in the 1980 television movie version of *Gideon's Trumpet*.[18] Cortada's Gideon looks nothing like that. The Clarence Gideon in the painting seems short and rather stocky and of indeterminant ethnic background. Perhaps the artist sought to have his Gideon represent a wider array of those most marginalized by our criminal justice system, including people of color. Perhaps he represents the small individuals fighting the weight of the giant prosecutorial machine. Or, perhaps, Gideon's physical appearance and ethnicity are simply not central to his story and his achievement.

Cortada's label for the painting indicates that he was inspired by a quote from Robert Kennedy:

> If an obscure Florida convict named Clarence Earl Gideon had not sat down in his prison cell with a pencil and paper to write a letter to the Supreme Court, and if the court had not taken the trouble to look for merit in that one crude petition, among all the bundles of mail it must receive every day, the vast machinery of American Law would have gone on functioning undisturbed. But Gideon did write that letter, the court did look into his case; and he was retried with the help of competent defense counsel, found not guilty and released from prison after two years of punishment for a crime he did not commit—and the whole course of legal history has been changed.[19]

---

17   Petition for a Writ of Certiorari from Clarence Gideon to the Supreme Court of the United States at 3 (1961), *available at* https://www.docsteach.org/documents/document/gideon-petition-writ-certiorari.

18   *Gideon's Trumpet* (CBS Television Broadcast, Apr. 30, 1980).

19   Robert F. Kennedy, Attorney General of the United States, Address, the New England Conference on the Defense of Indigent Persons Accused of Crime, November 1, 1963, https://www.justice.gov/sites/default/files/ag/legacy/2011/01/20/11-01-1963Pro.pdf.

Cortada's painting is true to that vision of Gideon's contribution to a critical component of the criminal-justice system—that poor criminal defendants are entitled to an attorney. Without Gideon's tenacity and stubborn insistence on fairness in the face of his depressing and demoralizing circumstances, would there have come a day when a different right to counsel case would have made its way to the Supreme Court and established that principle? Probably. But Clarence Earl Gideon will forever remain an icon in our legal history. This individual represents the right to counsel principle he helped establish and fortifies the hope that our justice system is capable of righting wrongs even when it seems like the longest of long shots.

Recommended Reading

Backus, Mary Sue and Marcus, Paul. 'The Right to Counsel in Criminal Cases: Still A National Crisis?' *George Washington Law Review* 86 (2018): 1564.

Caplan, Lincoln. 'The Right to Counsel: Badly Battered at 50.' *New York Times,* March 9, 2013, *available at,* https://www.nytimes.com/2013/03/10/opinion/sunday/the-right-to-counsel-badly-battered-at-50.html.

Cohen, Andrew. 'How Americans Lost the Right to Counsel, 50 Years After *Gideon.*' *The Atlantic,* March 13, 2013.

Davies, Andrew and Clark, Alyssa. 'Gideon in the Desert: An Empirical Study of Providing Counsel to Criminal Defendants in Rural Places.' *Maine Law Review* 71 (2019): 245.

Drinan, Cara H. 'Getting Real About Gideon: The Next Fifty Years of Enforcing the Right to Counsel.' *Washington and Lee Law Review* 70 (2013): 1309.

Israel, Jerold H. '*Gideon v. Wainwright*—From a 1963 Perspective.' *Iowa Law Review* 99 (2014): 2035.

Jacob, Bruce. 'Memories of and Reflections about *Gideon v. Wainwright.*' *Stetson Law Review* 33 (2003): 201.

Krash, Abe. 'Right to a Lawyer: The Implications of *Gideon v. Wainwright.*' *Notre Dame Law Review* 39 (1964): 150.

Lewis, Anthony. *Gideon's Trumpet.* New York: Vintage, 1964.

National Right to Counsel Committee, *Justice Denied: America's Continuing Neglect of our Constitutional Right to Counsel.* Open Society Foundations, available at https://www.opensocietyfoundations.org/publications/justice-denied-americas-continuing-neglect-our-constitutional-right-counsel

Williams v. Florida, 399 U.S. 78 (1970)

Xavier Cortada

In art there's this color wheel. It starts with three primary colors: red, yellow, blue. Then, between them, you see the secondary colors; those that are formed by the blending of primary colors: Orange (when one mixes yellow and red). Green (when one mixes blue and yellow). Purple (when one blends red and blue). Each one is as strong a color. Some become complementary to each other. Side by side, green and red, stand out more. The same with other colors on the opposite side of the color wheel: yellow and purple, blue and orange.

In physics, there's a light spectrum. We see it when prisms break up light into its component colors, much like a rainbow. One needs to have all the colors come together to make true light. As a lawyer, I understand the importance of juries to our judicial system and to our democracy. Nowhere can citizens have a more direct, immediate, and substantial role in their government. Jurors are the arbiters of facts. They determine truth.

The question becomes, how many jurors does it take to find the truth. To see the light? Common law had that number at 12. *Williams v. Florida*, 399 U.S. 78 (1970), challenged that number's reduction to six in criminal cases. The Supreme Court ruled that six jurors was a diverse enough pool of citizens to search for the truth.

I see truth as light. I see light as color. I wanted to represent the jurors in six different colors, each bringing their own perspectives and experiences into the jury room. The impact of each other's deliberations can be seen on the (complementary) colors of their clothes. They'll go back and forth, over and over, listening and speaking, until they find the truth.

Only when all six come together, do we really begin to see the light. The Spectrum of Truth.

FIGURE 5.1 Xavier Cortada, *Williams v. Florida*, 399 U.S. 78 (1970), oil on canvas, 2004.
PHOTO: ZENAIDA PIRRI, MIAMI, FLORIDA

CHAPTER 5

Williams v. Florida

What's in a Number? Jury Function and Jury Numbers

Jenny E. Carroll

In *Williams v. Florida*, the Supreme Court considered how many jurors are required in a criminal trial under the protection of the Sixth Amendment.[1] It was not a new question. The Court had previously maintained that the Constitution required a twelve-person jury.[2] In *Williams*, however, the Court abandoned this well-established position and held that, while nearly five centuries of history (and mythology) set the ideal number at twelve, a twelve-person jury was 'not an indispensable component' of the Sixth Amendment's promise of an impartial jury.[3] As a result, Florida's decision to supply Johnny Williams with a six-person jury in his robbery prosecution neither deprived him of his Sixth Amendment right nor undermined the function of the jury.

Eight years later in *Ballew v. Georgia*, reflecting on *Williams*, the Court stated that, while there is no magical number for an impartial jury, any number must be sufficient to promote the jury's function.[4] A five-person jury was constitutionally invalid because it failed to achieve a sufficient quorum necessary for meaningful representation or debate. In *Ballew* lies the challenge and the true legacy of *Williams*. *Williams* was as much about a number as about the fundamental question of the jury's function. Were jurors mere passive observers to the unfolding drama of a trial, endorsing the position of one formal actor or another in their verdict? Or did jurors serve some other role, one steeped in notions of direct democracy and true self-governance, engaged community-based

---

1 *Williams*, 399 U.S. 78 (1970).
2 The Court first set the requisite number of jurors at twelve in *Thompson v. Utah*, 170 U.S. 343 (1898). It referenced that number in subsequent cases. *See Patton v. United States*, 281 U.S. 276, 288 (1930); *Rassmussen v. United States*, 197 U.S. 516, 519 (1905); *Maxwell v. Dow*, 176 U.S. 581, 586 (1900).
3 In *Duncan v. Louisiana*, 391 U.S. 145, 151–154 (1968), the Court laid out the admittedly dubious history of the twelve-person jury requirement. Juror numbers varied historically and justifications for the twelve-person jury were offered only after the number was established, as opposed to prior to the establishment of the number—suggesting that such explanations were not the motivators for the settlement.
4 *Ballew v. Georgia*, 435 U.S. 223 (1978).

debate about the real-world application of law? For the Court, the jury was more than the sum of its parts; the number of jurors mattered only as it facilitated the jury's democratic function. Six jurors were adequate for Williams's trial because six jurors could get the job of the jury 'done,' even if five jurors could not.

In his painting on *Williams*, Xavier Cortada captures this conversion of number to function. He depicts Williams's six jurors alone in the jury room, left to sort through the case that they watched unfold in the trial. As they struggle to sort through evidence and law, they engage in direct democracy—laying law against fact to reach a verdict.

This Chapter explores the role of Johnny Williams's six-person jury as imagined by Cortada. In this exploration, I consider the jurors' interaction and their diversity of perspectives, as opposed to their number, as—to borrow the *Williams* Court's phrase—an indispensable component of the Sixth Amendment's jury.

1   **Numbers and Jury Function**

Cortada's jurors are, like all jurors, exceptional in their ordinariness. His painting depicts three women and three men. Each juror is a different color and each juror's face bears a different expression. The light of a single bulb shines upon their deliberations. The jurors appear to represent a wide array of demographics: different ages, different socioeconomic classes, different genders, different races. Their lives may hold still more diversity. They may be married or not. They may have children or grandchildren or not. They may vote Republican or Democrat or not at all. They may be white-collar or blue-collar workers or they may not work outside their homes. They may struggle for solvency or live comfortably. Their variance is endless.

Each person was likely a stranger to the others when she walked into the courthouse to report for jury duty. The tie that binds them to the room Cortada depicts is not some special interest or talent, but that they live their ordinary lives in the community in which Johnny Williams allegedly committed robbery. The jurors likely do not know the victim or the defendant (or they should not have survived the voir dire process for selecting the jury). They may not live in close proximity to any of the witnesses, attorneys, or the judge. They are strangers to each other and to the case. Yet in the courtroom and later in the jury room, they represent not only themselves, but some aspirational notion of community—one capable of regulating itself through the criminal law while recognizing the fallacies of a case to prevent an unjust conviction.

In this process, the jurors search for something more complicated than truth. They search for some multi-dimensional concept of justice that encompasses the crime that may have been committed, the quantum of proof required for conviction, and the evidence presented at trial. The sum of those component parts—allegation, proof, evidence—is filtered through each juror's notions of credibility, righteousness, and justice. Only then can the verdict be debated and, if consensus can be reached, returned.

In the grey space of the jury room, Cortada's jurors represent the myriad of perspectives and beliefs that drive the calculus of the verdict. They are everyday citizens who shine in primary colors in simultaneous contrast and union with one another. Together they tell a whole story of doubt and credibility and the choice between conviction or acquittal. As they deliberate, they fulfill their calling to summon into the grey, dimly lit room of the jury the community or communities they represent. To the *Williams* Court, their numbers mattered not because they were magical or extraordinary, but because they promoted the hard debate that must occur when citizens decide the fate of another in their midst. The 'essential feature of a jury obviously lies in the interposition between the accused and his accuser of the commonsense judgment of a group of laymen, and in the community participation and shared responsibility that results from that group's determination of guilt or innocence.'[5]

The number of jurors promotes the jury's function. To understand this requires consideration of the function itself. Despite the diminishing number of criminal jury trials in the United States, jurors still play a critical role in shaping criminal law. To the Founders, the jury was a citizen sentry, checking the power of the overzealous prosecutor or police or the biased judge. To the Court, the jury is a 'safeguard against the corrupt or overzealous prosecutor and against the compliant, biased, or eccentric judge,'[6] a 'bulwark of liberty,'[7] and 'circuit breaker in the State's machinery of justice.'[8] These citizens, installed by the luck of the venire process as the judges of fact, offered the court and the parties their lived experiences and sense of the world outside the doors of the jury room.

At the Founding of the United States, this idealized jury role was both important and admittedly curtailed. As the new nation struggled with competing identities and competing visions of democracy, questions about the ability of a centralized source of law—whether federal or state—inevitably emerged.

---

5 *Williams*, 399 U.S. at 100.
6 *Duncan v. Louisiana*, 391 U.S. 145, 156 (1968).
7 *Apprendi v. New Jersey*, 530 U.S. 466, 477 (2000).
8 *Blakely v. Washington*, 542 U.S. 296, 306 (2004).

Would federal legislators understand the complexity and nuance of each state? Would state or even local legislators be able to account for diverse perspectives in the community? Would any written or constructed law be able to anticipate the facts to which it would one day be applied? The answer to each of these questions was inevitably no. States had and have divergent visions that no federal government could hope to accommodate at all times and vice versa. Citizens often disagree about what is, was, or ought to be law. To complicate further the debate, static law, while valuable for its knowability and permanence, cannot be applied both justly and in a rote fashion. Law requires molding and interpretation in a myriad of discretionary moments—moments guided by citizens who live under that law.

These questions are not confined to the construction of law. Once the legislative body constructs the law, police and prosecutors make choices about how and against whom to enforce it. Judges confronted with ambiguity in law interpret its meaning to produce a just result. Each of these discretionary moments creates the opportunity to hone law's accuracy and, in so doing, to allay the fears that law would not and could not account for the experiences of the governed. And yet, each discretionary moment belonged to formal actors—the legislator, the sheriff, the prosecutor, and the judge were more than ordinary citizens. They moved within a specific realm with specific obligations. That they may have been elected by ordinary citizens did not render them ordinary themselves.

So the Founders installed an informal actor to check formal power–the ordinary people to whom the law applied and in whose midst the alleged crime had occurred. Formal actors presented the case to citizen jurors. But those citizen jurors retreated to Cortada's room to deliberate not only the fate of the defendant but the meaning of the law that would be applied to him. As notions of jury, government, and law have changed as the nation has grown in population and political maturity, a constant has remained: Whatever limitations may be placed on citizen jurors, at the end of the case, in a closed jury room, the law returns to the citizens for whom it was created and applied.

2 Cortada's Jury

In Cortada's grey room, the jurors gather without specialized knowledge or the resources that might provide specialized knowledge, hoping to animate the law with their lived experiences. The drab room in which they struggle is impersonal, silent to the work that must be done there. There is no art on the walls, nothing personal or human. The door to the room shows light through its glass pane, suggesting a brighter corridor beyond, but the jury room is lit by a single light that seems to contribute more to the room's industrial impersonality than to its illumination.

The table around which the jurors gather is equally drab and non-descript. It serves its necessary function, offering a space for something more significant to occur. In this drab space, the jurors shine with unnatural color. Their glow exceeds the gaunt lighting and décor of the room. They study papers that mirror the drabness of the room. Perhaps these are documents produced by the formal actors in the case: jury instructions or transcripts or exhibits—necessary and serving a critical function, but also distant and oddly bound by the formality of the law and court process.

In contrast, the scales of justice on the table shine as an ideal. Beyond these scales, colored pages appear to fall off the edge of the painting. These pages, tied by color to each juror, represent each one's input on the case. They diverge, overlap, curl in upon one another, as their authors seek to reconcile their visions of the world and the case with that of their fellow citizens in the jury room.

In the background, the jurors debate the meaning of the case as they know it, not as some distant matter or one reduced to the pages some of them hold, but as an animating force in their lives and the lives of the defendant, Johnny Williams, and his alleged victim. Cortada depicts the jurors' struggle to reach consensus. Whatever overlap or commonality exists in their votes, none precisely mirrors the others. The jurors in the background strike different poses that evince different levels of engagement as they move towards a verdict. A man in a suit studies a white page with a smile on his face, having found some comfort or consistency in this external and formal presentation of law or fact. Beside and behind him slightly, another man appears more distant, self-absorbed and dissatisfied with the debate. He is more casually dressed and appears focused on his own hand. Like his suited brethren, he struggles not only to contextualize the law and facts he must consider but also to reach consensus.

On the right side of the painting, two jurors actively debate the case. They face one another, each with hands clutched to the chest. One holds a white sheet of paper. The other holds the edge of the table. They anchor their arguments of law, fact, and guilt in the formal environs of the jury room, yet their debate is infused with notions of who they are. They speak to and with one another while clutching themselves, moving law beyond its mired formal existence into their own bodies and the body of the community they represent. The struggle to do so is apparent on their faces. Both hold their convictions as firmly as they seek to engage and convince the other.

A fifth juror points skyward as she gestures toward the scales on the table. In doing this, she makes a point about the case or draws some parallel toward a higher function of law and the debate—to reach not merely a conclusion, but a just conclusion. She is assertive in her posture, yet seated and deferential as the debate rages behind her. Does she invoke God or divine justice and compromise in her argument? Does she testify to the reality of the case or the law as she knows it? Is she engaged or unable to engage as she struggles to reconcile her own perspective and vote, which appears to shift and cascade off the top of the pile of votes, with the underlying perspectives in the room and the community?

Finally, one juror sits alone, eyes cast skyward as she points to papers and the table. Her lips are closed. She appears the most disengaged of all jurors. As she clings to these formal aspects of the room (the paper and table), does she ground herself there? Or does she reject these constructs as she realizes how foreign they are to her lived experiences or to the story she heard in Williams' case? Like her fellow seated juror, does she gaze skyward invoking some greater concept than she finds in the jury room? Or is she lost in thought and the realization that a verdict must emerge from the chaos or a deadlock must be declared?

Each juror shows aspects of engagement and distance. Each measures and tests the law's existence against his or her expectations and ideals. Alone in the room, each would not obtain a shared identity. He or she might reach a conclusion more quickly, but the conclusion would be poorer for the absence of his or her fellow jurors. By coming together, these six, separated in many ways from the Founding of the nation, realize the Founders' vision by engaging in active debate of the law in their midst. They are drawn from the community in which the trial occurs, but they function as independent entities, examining and debating the meaning of evidence and law until they arrive at a decision—a verdict reflecting an agreement of individual decisions or a deadlock reflecting a decision not to agree.

This is why their numbers matter. Without sufficient numbers, perspective is limited. Without sufficient numbers, debate is illusory or an act of singular contemplation. With too many jurors, debate may be stifled, as majorities smother dissent and drive toward an inevitable conclusion. As the Court stated,

> the performance of [the jury's] role is not a function of the particular number of the body that makes up the jury. To be sure, the number should probably be large enough to promote group deliberation, free from outside attempts at intimidation, and to provide a fair possibility for obtaining a representative cross-section of the community.[9]

---

9   *Williams,* 399 U.S. at 100.

3   Juror Consensus and Decisions

Despite their undoubted value, assembly and debate alone are not enough to achieve the grander function of the jury as a community check on the power of formal law and governance. To serve this checking role, the jury must represent the community from which it is drawn and must engage in decision-making that reflects that representation. This is no small feat, especially when contemplating assemblies of six to twelve citizens. Notions of representation and inclusion are complex. On the most basic level, the jury must be diverse. But superficial diversity will not elevate jury decisions to the larger imagined function, nor will it render a body magically representative. Communities are not one-dimensional ecosystems. And within any group, perspectives emerge, linger, and merge as holders sift and prioritize their places in the community. For a verdict to have some meaning, the jury who produced it must reflect that varied and complex community on multiple levels.

A jury composed entirely of white males may lack the critical perspectives of those who live under the law but do not check the same demographic boxes on their census forms. This is not to say the presence of a minority-identified juror will guarantee diversity of perspective. Nor is it to say that there is a singular minority perspective that can be offered by any member of a minority group or that the presence of a single minority juror will guarantee robust debate and consideration of other perspectives. It is to say that inclusion in the decision-making room matters. As criminal law enforcement falls disproportionately on minority populations, excluding members of those populations from the 'citizen-based' check on law carries a special irony that undermines the function of the jury: those most likely to have direct contact with law lack access to one of the fundamental mechanisms to check law. Further, if the jury is composed entirely of the very citizens most likely to hold formal positions— white, educated men—it appears as little more than an extension of formal lawmaking structures.

Ironically, the Founders contemplated juries composed of the same citizens who could serve in government—white, landed, literate men. As notions of inclusion, democracy, and politics have progressed in the wake of civil rights movements (including #metoo and Black Lives Matter), the importance of inclusion within the criminal justice system has become increasingly evident. The visual presence of female jurors or jurors of color signals an acknowledgement that such individuals are stakeholders in the law.

For the community gazing on the jury, a jury that reflects the population of the community legitimizes the verdict, even if a community member doing the gazing finds himself at odds with the verdict. Diversity of perspective certainly matters, but so does visual diversity. In cases preceding and following *Williams*, the Court acknowledged that reducing the number of jurors present in the jury room did not diminish the importance of diversity among those jurors. Read in conjunction with cases that prohibited excluding women from venire panels[10] and prohibiting peremptory strikes to exclude Black[11] and women[12] jurors, *Williams* reduces the total number of participants without compromising the critical role of diversity.

Beyond this, jurors carry an array of perspectives. Women or members of minority or marginalized groups in a community may carry a divergent sense of what the law ought to be or do or may interpret facts in a different way than a fellow juror who did not share their experiences. A gun tucked into a purse could signal premeditation to cause harm to a victim or it could signal fear of harm that may be visited upon the gun's owner. It may signal bravado or it may signal cultural norms. Such inferences drive verdicts crafting the same set of facts into a guilty verdict for premeditated murder or an acquittal based on a successful claim of self-defense or a justified shooting. As criminal law is increasingly called upon to settle larger social issues, the diversity of the deciders—the jurors—matters more than ever. From police shootings to allegations of rape to vigilante claims of self-defense, verdicts rendered by non-inclusive juries spark distrust and protests within communities that see the jury as one more forum of exclusion and one more lost opportunity for meaningful self-governance.

Juror diversity matters on multiple levels. Within the jury room, jurors, in each of their lived experiences, offer perspectives that drive a verdict not only to a just result but a result that achieves the broader contemplated function of checking government power. Outside the jury room, visual diversity on the jury panel promotes a sense of inclusion to the community viewing the trial or anticipating the verdict. Six or twelve assembled to deliberate become the voice of the whole in the confines of that room, with a power to curb abuse of power or to sanction a controversial act.

Cortada represents this diversity in the characteristics of his jurors. Not only are they physically different colors, but their physical appearance signals other aspects of diversity. Their clothing ranges from a suit and tie to a t-shirt and casual pants. While clothing is a deceptive indicator of wealth—one can only assume that Mark Zuckerberg would show up for jury duty in his ubiquitous hoodie, t-shirt, and jeans—it signals at least two significant possibilities in this

---

10 *Taylor v. Louisiana*, 419 U.S. 522 (1975).
11 *Batson v. Kentucky*, 476 U.S. 79 (1986).
12 *J.E.B. v. Alabama*, 511 U.S. 127 (1994).

painting. The most obvious is that the man in the suit is a member of an upper socioeconomic class and carries the accompanying education and privilege, while the man in the jeans and t-shirt is a member of a lower socioeconomic class and carries the lack of opportunity and perhaps lower education level. An alternative explanation, one that still hints at diversity, is that the man wears the suit to signal respect for the court process or to show dignity for his perspective or his interpretation of the facts and the law. He dresses up to serve on a jury, either because he likens it to attending a church or because he seeks to push the system to recognize his dignity, akin to civil rights activists who dressed in 'Sunday go to meeting' clothes when they registered to vote or marched through the streets (even as they knew they would face arrest). In contrast, the man in the t-shirt may reflect, in a Zuckerberg-esque way, that he has no need to dress up to present his perspective—his view is entitled and dominant and he needs no suit to signal either respect or his own dignity.

Regardless of one's interpretation of the clothing choices, the array of clothing and appearances reflects divergences in the jurors' identities, signaling a degree of diversity that may exceed the superficial indicators used to identify them. The suit suggests more than a trip to Saville Row or Men's Wearhouse. The t-shirt, the dress, the earrings remind the viewer that the American community is a complicated, multi-layered entity.

Other juror characteristics reinforce this assessment. Gender diversity is clearly present—half the jurors appear to be women. So is age—three jurors appear noticeably older than the others. Differences in body language also reflect diversity—some jurors gesture to themselves as they debate their position, others point outward.

The most compelling aspect of Cortada's painting is that everyone to whom I show it sees something different in the jurors. A juror whom I viewed as Black, others believed was white or Latina. A juror whom I viewed as Latino, others viewed as white. A juror whom I viewed as white, several friends insisted was Asian. The list could go on and is important to the issue of diversity—not because there is a singular right answer to the identity of Cortada's jurors, but because it underscores the importance of visual diversity on a decision-making body such as a jury.

Regardless of how friends and colleagues interpreted each juror's identity, each person who viewed this jury found diversity in it. Everyone saw at least one Black juror, at least one Latinx juror, at least two female jurors, at least one wealthy juror, at least one poor juror, and at least one elderly juror. Some saw four female jurors, some saw an Asian juror. Some carried physical traits into imagined belief systems—the suit became an indicator of a conservative businessman, one juror's t-shirt became a 'Make America Great Again' red shirt.

In seeing diversity, each saw a jury that represented the community, albeit at times imprecisely or generally. In this visual perception of difference lay confidence that this jury was capable of performing the larger function of the jury.

In this imagined and actual diversity, the verdict resonates with the larger community that the jury represents. This is not to say that every verdict produced by a diverse jury will seem 'just' to outside observers. Rather, it is to say that a diverse jury is more likely to represent accurately the larger population and more likely to consider an array of citizens' lived experiences, thereby achieving some larger goal. But this level of diversity must be sufficient to signal more than mere token representation; it must be sufficient to produce a debate that is inclusive of many perspectives.

True diversity on a jury of six is no small feat. Indeed, the Supreme Court has indicated that diversity on individual jury panels is a constitutional luxury, not a constitutional necessity. Instead, the Court demands the absence of impermissible racial or gender bias during selection and the representation of a fair cross section of the community in the larger venire panel from which jurors are selected.[13] Such a long view of juror diversity, while promoting efficient administration of the jury process, is not without problems. With respect to juror challenges, such an approach relies on an ideal that makes it difficult to prove or to remedy bias. A recent study demonstrates that, whether due to conscious or implicit bias, prosecutors are far more likely to use peremptory strikes to remove minority jurors and defense counsel is far more likely to strike white male jurors.[14] Despite the study's conclusion, proving that any particular peremptory challenge was based on the impermissible trait of race is another matter. The question is whether it should matter that the strike was based on race if the result is the removal of a minority voice from the jury. Even if race was not the conscious basis of the strike, non-race-based grounds for strikes may produce a doubly damaging blow to the function of the jury.

First, strikes that appear to be non-race based often evoke characteristics disproportionately experienced by minority identities. Many voir dire questions, while not based on race or gender per se, disproportionality affect minority and women jurors—asking if they know anyone who has been arrested or incarcerated or whether they have completed secondary education or whether they have a wage versus a salaried job or whether they have care responsibilities for small children or elderly parents. Questions such as these and the answers that trigger peremptory strikes target the people who already

---

13   *Duren v. Missouri*, 439 U.S. 357 (1979).
14   Ronald F. Wright, Kami Chavis and Gregory Scott Parks, 'The Jury Sunshine Project: Jury Selection Data as a Political Issue' (2018) 2018 Illinois Law Review 1407.

are among the fewest in the jury pool based on characteristics they possess because of their minority status.

Second, the use of such characteristics to support a peremptory strike signal that their perspectives have no place in the jury room. If a Latino potential juror is struck when he expresses distrust of the police based on his lived experience of repeated encounters that appear to him to be without justification, the remaining jurors learn that distrust of the police is not appropriate for juror consideration. To voice distrust of the police in the jury room is therefore to raise a perspective that is unwelcome and impermissible. This, in turn, endorses the counter perspective—police are trustworthy—as one welcome in the jury room.

These realities lay bare the disconnect between the ideology and reality of jury selection. The ideal of selection in furtherance of impartiality is noble and constitutionally necessary. The practice of selection paints a different portrait. The Latino juror who has suffered repeated encounters with the police may both know others who have suffered similar fates and may also genuinely and (as stop-and-frisk litigation revealed)[15] accurately believe that he has suffered these encounters as a result of his race. This may alter his perception of the reliability of any officer's testimony. If legal standards such as reasonable suspicion and probable cause are malleable on the street when a police officer sees a brown man walking or talking on a street corner with friends, he may believe that similar distortions will arise in the construction of a case against a defendant of color. From the juror's perspective, prosecutors, like police, may overlay a suspect's action with their own assumptions of their meaning based on his race. The case may be suspect before the first piece of evidence is presented. Another juror who has not personally experienced this type of police encounter may believe, either through lived experience or secondary exposure such as media coverage, that inequities exist in law enforcement and police treatment of minority populations. Statistically, she would be correct—police presence and activity in poor and minority communities are different than in suburban, wealthy, and predominately white communities.

The concern is that this reality—based on lived experience or otherwise—may color the potential juror's view of the officer's testimony. And that reality may be used to support striking either juror as based on something other than an impermissible trait—distrust of police or prosecutor. But this removes from that jury a lived experience and silences the stirrings of empathy or sympathy for that experience among remaining jurors. The perspective that police or

---

15   *Floyd v. City of New York*, 959 F. Supp. 2d 540, 573–74 (2013).

prosecutors may target the poor or people of color is removed as partial. The perspective that police or prosecutors are a fictionally benign presence in that community, or at least a presence that should be accorded juror trust, lingers. This false construction of juror reality through the selection process creates a dissonance from the moment of empanelment. Can a member of the struck juror's community find him or herself in the empaneled jury when the reality he or she lives has been struck as too impermissibly partial to warrant a seat in the jury box?

The selection process also may color the decision-making process. As the Court stated in *Williams*, the jury, whether of six or twelve, should meld individual perspectives to produce a single, unified verdict. In Cortada's painting, each juror's paper bears color, while the official papers of the court or proceeding are white. Deliberation transforms the white paper from drab and impersonal to reflect all the jurors' perspectives in the verdict form. Seen as a reflection of all color rather than an absence of it, the white verdict form literally and figuratively reflects the myriad of perspectives each juror signals in his or her color. No one color or perspective dominates; all, in theory, are equally reflected.

For this to occur, however, jurors must be free to engage in meaningful and constructive debate. That debate depends on their varied lived experiences and those of the varied communities in which they live. If minority representation on a jury is limited or if particular perspectives are removed in jury selection, the possibility and reality of such a debate is likewise limited.

Cortada's jury initially appears engaged in meaningful and thoughtful debate. Closer inspection, however, suggests another possibility—jurors locked in their own reflective worlds, unable or unwilling to engage one another. Even the two jurors who appear to speak most directly to one another, hands to respective chests, appear hopelessly locked in the wisdom of their respective positions. They make no direct eye contact. They do not appear to speak to one another. They gesture to themselves, as if to say they alone carry justice and truth inside of them. All of which raises the question whether this is a true debate. Will their verdict be the product of consensus? Or will it not exist at all, as each remains committed to her own world view, unable or unwilling to account for the different experiences in the room?

4   The Future of *Williams*

The Supreme Court in *Williams v. Florida* imagined that six citizens might achieve what twelve often fail to do—create a jury in which a community's perspective is laid beside formal actors' creation, application, and interpretation of the law to produce a just result. That this ideal fails every day does not lessen its lofty aims or undermine the need for the function it imagined. Nor does it stop the Court from evoking that vision year after year in criminal jury cases.

The solution is an expansion of *Williams*'s own ideal, applied not to numerosity but to perspective. Rather than enlarge the size of the jury, enlarge the breadth of its vicinage to include the community with the greatest stake in the verdict—that of the victim and of the defendant.

Xavier Cortada imagines Johnny Williams's jury as a diverse and lively group. They bring color and light to a process that might otherwise be impersonal and sterile. As they struggle and stumble toward a verdict, despite their small number, they achieve a direct democratic function, holding the law accountable to the people it would govern. In answering the question of how many jurors are constitutionally required, *Williams* considered something far more fundamental than the number of bodies sitting in a courtroom. It weighed the function of the jury within a republican system and concluded that at the moment in which the law touched Johnny Williams directly, his fellow citizens, not a formal actor, should weigh his case's merit and render judgment.

Recommended Readings

Carroll, Jenny E. 'The Jury's Second Coming.' *Georgetown Law Journal* 100 (2012): 657–707.

Ferguson, Andrew Guthrie. *Why Jury Duty Matters: A Citizen's Guide to Constitutional Action*. New York: NYU Press, 2012.

Larsen, Joan L. 'Ancient Juries and Modern Judges: Originalism's Uneasy Relationship with the Jury.' *Ohio State Law Journal* 71 (2010): 959–1002.

Miller, Robert H. 'Six of One is Not a Dozen of the Other: A Re-Examination of *Williams v. Florida* and the Size of State Criminal Juries.' *University of Pennsylvania Law Review* 146 (1998): 621–686.

Smith, Alisa and Michael J. Saks. 'The Case for Overturning *Williams v. Florida* and the Six-Person Jury: History, Law and Empirical Evidence.' *Florida Law Review* 60 (2008): 441–470.

Miami Herald Publishing Company v. Tornillo, 418 U.S. 241 (1974)

Xavier Cortada

∴

In 2000, I accompanied my Dad on a trip to Cuba to see family members. I was able to bring my grandfather photos of his siblings—he hadn't seen them since he fled the Communist island in the 1960s. My grandfather's life ended the year after my trip, as did the life of a sister and brothers I had visited. Unlike them, he lived in an open society and died a free man.

I remember wanting to stay with family during my trip but being denied. I could only stay in state-sponsored housing. The appeal was lost at some Interior Ministry office in the provincial capital of Camaguey.

We had taken a long ride in a crappy car to get there, and I needed to defecate. I remember interrupting my meeting with the Cuban official, asking to use his bathroom. He obliged, but told me they had no toilet paper, and offered me a few sheets of *Granma* newspaper. The official newspaper of a regime that has never met a First Amendment right it liked.

The stuff of the First Amendment is poison to totalitarian regimes. Free exchange of ideas and a free press belittle state propaganda. Even the smallest concession to independent journalists can tinker with the apparatus of state control. That is why the only information Cubans on the island can receive comes from state-run radio, state-run television, and state-run newspapers. Anything that state does not control is illegal.

In *Miami Herald Publishing Company v. Tornillo*, 418 U.S. 241 (1974), the Court threw out a 1913 state statute that forced newspapers to give equal Opinion page space to any political candidate who it had criticized. This concession thwarted the paper's free expression: Having the State tell someone what to print is the same as telling them what not to print.

Because the statute tinkered with the apparatus of a free press, it was relegated to toilet paper status.

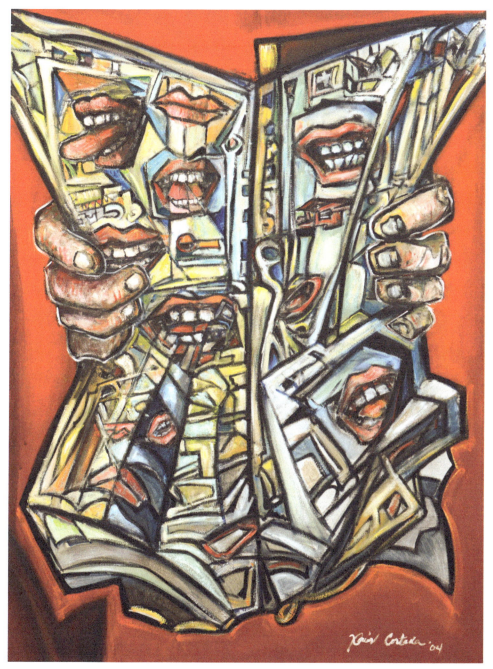

FIGURE 6.1 Xavier Cortada, *Miami Herald Publishing Company v. Tornillo*, 418 U.S. 241 (1974), 48" × 36", oil on canvas, 2004.
PHOTO: ZENAIDA PIRRI, MIAMI, FLORIDA

CHAPTER 6

Miami Herald Publishing Company v. Tornillo
Freedom of Speech for Whom?

Leslie C. Kendrick

Xavier Cortada's painting for *Miami Herald Publishing Company v. Tornillo* depicts a pair of hands clutching a crumpled newspaper. The reader is otherwise invisible to us, hidden behind the newspaper that occupies the canvas. The newspaper pages are in full, dazzling color and they are covered with mouths—bright red lips, wagging tongues, caught midsentence, talking all at once. The effect is that of a colorful cacophony, many voices speaking all at once. Whose mouths are these? Are they speaking as one or in many different voices? Is the unseen reader absorbed in this chorus or is he in the middle of crumpling up the newspaper and squelching it?

This visual depiction of *Miami Herald v. Tornillo* gets to the heart of the case. Whose voices are represented in the media? Who decides that question? Should the media represent a diversity of voices and viewpoints? Or is media access controlled by media ownership? *Tornillo* asked the Supreme Court to decide these questions as a matter of First Amendment law. In doing so, the Court confronted two different visions of the First Amendment: one that mandated media access for multiple voices and one that protected the media from interference, including access by third parties. Rarely has the Supreme Court faced such a stark choice between First Amendment paradigms. And rarely has it stated its view of the First Amendment as clearly as it did in *Tornillo*, adopting the latter paradigm and rejecting the former.

How the issue came to the Court and what the Court said about it are stories of constitutional and media history. They are also Florida stories, involving two larger-than-life parties—Pat Tornillo and the *Miami Herald*. Without them, this particular issue may never have reached the Supreme Court, at least not in this particularly stark way.

1 The Case Begins

James Beasley was a young lawyer in Miami when his boss came into his office, put a stack of papers down on his desk, and said, 'I've got a Supreme Court case for you.' Beasley soon found himself on a team representing the *Miami Herald*.

Jerome Barron had recently become dean of Syracuse University Law School when Tobias Simon, a Miami labor lawyer, asked if he would be willing to work on a case representing a Miami union leader. Barron initially passed, saying that his new duties prevented him from taking on any cases. 'You have to take this one,' Simon said, and traveled to Syracuse to persuade Barron.

The case they were brought became *Miami Herald v. Tornillo*.[1] On one side was the *Miami Herald*, the leading newspaper of South Florida, 'big, dominant, and aggressive.'[2] On the other was Pat Tornillo (pronounced Tor-NIH-lo), 'one of Florida's larger-than-life figures,' a South Florida power broker and leader of the Miami-Dade County teachers' union.[3] As Barron described his client in oral argument before the Supreme Court, 'He is a very controversial fellow, and he intends to remain being a very controversial fellow.'[4]

On September 20, 1972, the *Miami Herald* ran an editorial on Tornillo's candidacy for the state legislature:

> The State's Laws And Pat Tornillo
>
> Look who's upholding the law!
>
> Pat Tornillo, boss of the Classroom Teachers Association and candidate for the State Legislature in the Oct. 3 runoff election, has denounced his opponent as lacking "the knowledge to be a legislator, as evidenced by his failure to file a list of contributions to and expenditures of his campaign as required by law."
>
> Czar Tornillo calls "violation of this law inexcusable."
>
> This is the same Pat Tornillo who led the CTA strike from February 19 to March 11, 1968, against the school children and taxpayers of Dade County. Call it whatever you will, it was an illegal act against the public interest and clearly prohibited by the statutes.

---

1 418 U.S. 241 (1974). The author would like to thank Jim Beasley and Jerome Barron for generously agreeing to be interviewed for this piece. The author would also like to thank Kent Olson of the University of Virginia Law Library for invaluable research assistance.
2 Randall P. Bezanson, *How Free Can the Press Be?* (Champaign: University of Illinois Press, 2003), 59.
3 'The Rise and Fall of Pat Tornillo', The Ledger, Aug. 30, 2003.
4 *Miami Herald v. Tornillo*, Oral Argument Transcript 18 (Apr. 17, 1974) at https://www.supremecourt.gov/pdfs/transcripts/1973/73-797_04-17-1974.pdf

> We cannot say it would be illegal but certainly it would be inexcusable of the voters if they sent Pat Tornillo to Tallahassee to occupy the seat for District 103 in the House of Representatives.[5]

On September 27, Tornillo wrote the *Herald* with a response:

> Five years ago, the teachers participated in a state-wide walkout to protest deteriorating educational conditions.
> Financing was inadequate then and we now face a financial crisis.
> The Herald told us that what we did was illegal and that we should use legal processes instead. We are doing just that through legal and political action.
>
> My candidacy is an integral part of this process. During the past four years:
>
> - CTA brought suit to give Dade County its share of state money to relieve local taxpayers.
> - CTA won a suit which gave public employees the right to collectively bargain.
> - CTA won a suit which allowed the School Board to raise $7.8 million to air-condition schools and is helping to keep this money.
>
> Unfortunately, the *Herald* dwells on past history and ignores CTA's totally legal efforts of the past four years.
> We are proud of our record.[6]

The *Herald* did not run Tornillo's response. Instead, on September 29, 1972, it ran a second editorial:

> From the people who brought you this—the teacher strike of '68—come now instructions on how to vote for responsible government, i.e., against Crutcher Harrison and Ethel Beckham, for Pat Tornillo. The tracts and blurbs and bumper stickers pile up daily in teachers' school mailboxes amidst continuing pouts that the School Board should be delivering all this at your expense. The screeds say the strike is not an issue. We say maybe it wouldn't be were it not a part of a continuation of disregard of any and all laws the CTA might find aggravating. Whether in defiance of

---

5 *Miami Herald Pub. Co. v. Tornillo*, 418 U.S. 241, 243 n.1 (1974).
6 Bezanson, *How Free*, 60.

zoning laws at CTA Towers, contracts and laws during the strike, or more recently state prohibitions against soliciting campaign funds amongst teachers, CTA says fie and try and sue us—what's good for CTA is good for CTA and that is natural law. Tornillo's law, maybe. For years now he has been kicking the public shin to call attention to his shakedown statesmanship. He and whichever acerbic proxy is in alleged office have always felt their private ventures so chock-full of public weal that we should leap at the chance to nab the tab, be it half the Glorious Leader's salary or the dues checkoff or anything else except perhaps mileage on the staff hydrofoil. Give him public office, says Pat, and he will no doubt live by the Golden Rule. Our translation reads that as more gold and more rule.[7]

Tornillo again wrote the paper with a substantive response, along with a request that 'under Florida Statute 104.38, the *Herald* print the following record of affirmative and legal action.'[8] The *Herald* did not oblige.

Florida Statute 104.38 was a 'right-of-reply' statute, providing that any newspaper criticizing a political candidate's personal character or official record had to provide space on demand for any reply that the candidate wished to make, free of charge. The reply had to be as conspicuous and in the same font as the original criticism, so long as it did not take up more space than the original criticism. Violations constituted a first-degree misdemeanor.[9]

Tornillo sued the *Herald* under the right-of-reply statute in state court, and the *Herald* argued that the statute violated the First Amendment.[10] The *Herald* engaged well-known Miami lawyer Dan Paul and his firm, Paul & Thomson, to represent the newspaper. Paul brought on Beasley, a recent Harvard graduate and young Paul & Thomson associate, who immersed himself in the case and the drafting of briefs.

Tornillo was represented by Miami labor lawyers Tobias Simon and Elizabeth duFresne, who reached out to Barron at Syracuse. In 1967, Barron had published *Access to the Press: A New First Amendment Right*[11] in the *Harvard Law Review*, arguing that the First Amendment required the mass media to represent a diverse range of speakers, including unpopular speakers. A First

---

7   *Miami Herald*, 418 U.S. at 243 n.1.
8   Bezanson, *How Free*, 61.
9   *Miami Herald*, 418 U.S. at, 244. Although the statute provided for criminal penalties, the Supreme Court of Florida held that civil remedies, including damages, also were available. Ibid., 246.
10 Ibid., 244.
11 Jerome A. Barron, 'Access to the Press: A New First Amendment Right' (1967) 80 Harvard Law Review 1641.

Amendment that merely protected media owners' ability to speak became 'a rationale for suppressing competing ideas.'[12] Existing conceptions of the First Amendment as a negative right against interference served only to reinforce existing property distributions and the status quo in the marketplace of ideas.

Barron's article had received a great deal of attention. 'I mean, for a law review article,' Barron says now, 'I was astonished at the reaction to it.'[13] Simon had read the article and contacted Barron because Tornillo's claims implicated Barron's: Tornillo wanted access to respond to the newspaper's criticisms, and the newspaper asserted a First Amendment right to keep him out.

2 The Right of Reply

Florida enacted the right-of-reply statute in 1913 as part of the Trammel Corrupt Practices Act.[14] According to the Florida Supreme Court, it complemented a 1909 law that attempted to eradicate corruption in primary elections. In the Court's words, the right-of-reply statute

> was enacted not to punish, coerce or censor the press but rather as a part of a centuries old legislative task of maintaining conditions conducive to free and fair elections. The Legislature in 1913 decided that owners of the printing press had already achieved such political clout that when they engaged in character assailings, the victim's electoral chances were unduly and improperly diminished. To assure fairness in campaigns, the assailed candidate had to be provided an equivalent opportunity to respond; otherwise not only the candidate would be hurt but also the people would be deprived of both sides of the controversy.[15]

Barron characterizes the law as 'very unusual in the United States.'[16] Beasley agrees it essentially was a dead letter when Tornillo invoked it, obscure and unused.

Yet Beasley believes it was not Tornillo who made it newly relevant, but the turbulent nature of South Florida politics at the time. 'If it had not been Pat

---

12   Ibid., 1642.
13   Telephone Interview with Jerome A. Barron, Harold H. Greene Professor of Law Emeritus, George Washington University Law School, Jan. 21, 2019, [hereinafter 'Barron interview'].
14   *Ex parte Hawthorne*, 156 So. 619, 621 (1934).
15   *Tornillo v. Miami Herald Pub. Co.*, 287 So. 2d 78, 81 (Fla. 1973).
16   Barron Interview.

Tornillo at that time, it could have been someone else a couple years before or after', Beasley says, 'because the atmosphere was so heated.'[17] Political and legal culture increased the chances that Tornillo's claim would gain traction. Barron's article and its reception indicated some level of concern that the media had become too consolidated, with detrimental effects for disadvantaged speakers.

In 1968, the Supreme Court decided *Red Lion Broadcasting v. FCC*,[18] upholding the Fairness Doctrine for broadcast television and radio against a First Amendment challenge. Under the Fairness Doctrine, recipients of broadcast licenses were obligated to cover public issues and to give fair coverage to all sides. As part of this obligation, if a broadcast licensee criticized a public figure or endorsed one political candidate over another, it had to offer a timely opportunity for response by the criticized figure or the endorsee's opponent.[19] This was a right of reply for broadcasting, similar to the right mandated for newspapers by the 1913 Florida statute.

Red Lion relied in part on broadcast licensees' receiving a privilege from the government, on which the government could impose certain conditions, consistent with the public's interest in receiving diverse information and perspectives.[20] This rationale could not carry into the newspaper context, because the government does not grant newspaper licenses in the same way it issues licenses to portions of the broadcast spectrum.

But the *Red Lion* Court also relied on broader arguments about the meaning of the First Amendment. The broadcast regime must 'function consistently with the ends and purposes of the First Amendment', and 'it is the right of the viewers and listeners, not the right of the broadcasters, which is paramount.'[21] In the words of the Court, 'It is the purpose of the First Amendment to preserve an uninhibited marketplace of ideas in which truth will ultimately prevail, rather than to countenance monopolization of that market, whether it be by the Government itself or a private licensee.'[22] Applied to media such as private newspapers, this vision of free speech would mean that the First Amendment protects viewers and listeners and does not countenance speaker monopolies. Tornillo's lawyers relied and elaborated

---

17   Telephone Interview with James W. Beasley, Jr., Partner, Beasley & Galardi, P.A., Oct. 10, 2018, [hereinafter 'Beasley Interview'].
18   395 U.S. 367 (1969).
19   Ibid., 372–73.
20   Ibid., 389.
21   Ibid., 390.
22   Ibid.

upon *Red Lion*'s vision of the First Amendment in their briefing before the Supreme Court of Florida.

Beasley now describes the *Herald*'s response as 'freedom of the press means freedom of the press'.[23] *Herald* lawyers distinguished *Red Lion* as a case about government grant of privileges, while their own case struck at the heart of the First Amendment Press Clause's protection of the press from governmental interference.

The Supreme Court of Florida sided with Tornillo and upheld the right-of-reply statute as constitutional.[24] '[T]his statute enhances rather than abridges freedom of speech and press protected by the First Amendment',[25] because the 'right of the public to know all sides of a controversy and from such information to be able to make an enlightened choice is being jeopardized by the growing concentration of the ownership of the mass media into fewer and fewer hands, resulting ultimately in a form of private censorship.'[26] The court quoted extensively from *Red Lion* and from *Associated Press v. United States* (1945), which rejected the Associated Press's claim of First Amendment immunity from antitrust laws.[27] The court rebuked the *Herald*:

> What some segments of the press seem to lose sight of is that the First Amendment guarantee is 'not for the benefit of the press so much as for the benefit of us all.' Speech concerning public affairs is more than self expression. It is the essence of self government.[28]
>
> The 'fundamental purpose of the First Amendment [is] to inform the people.'[29]

The supreme court remanded to the trial court for further proceedings. Tornillo had sought injunctive relief and damages, and the state supreme court held that the statute would support either type of relief, were liability established at trial.[30] But the *Herald* appealed the First Amendment holding to the Supreme Court of the United States, and the case proceeded there.

---

23   Beasley Interview.
24   *Tornillo v. Miami Herald Pub. Co.*, 287 So. 2d 78, 80 (Fla. 1973).
25   Ibid.
26   Ibid., 82–83.
27   Ibid., 83 (citing *Associated Press v. United States*, 326 U.S. 1, 18 (1945)).
28   *Tornillo*, 287 So. 2d at 81.
29   Ibid., 85.
30   Ibid., 90 (rejecting petition for rehearing).

3   The Court Decides

The Supreme Court heard argument on the afternoon of April 17, 1974. Dan Paul argued for the *Herald* and Barron for Tornillo. Paul mostly faced questions on whether the Court had jurisdiction to hear the constitutional claim, a question the Court summarily answered in the affirmative in its opinion.[31]

Paul also articulated the paper's First Amendment vision: 'Compelling a newspaper to print is the same as telling it what not to print. It is censorship forbidden by the First Amendment. ... If there is any area where the role of the press under the First Amendment must remain unfettered, it is criticism of political candidates of the very kind expressed in this case.'[32] Paul raised a hypothetical: 'Will the 12 black newspapers, serving the black community in Florida have to give equal time to George Wallace to reply as a candidate, despite the views of the particular editor of that newspaper in the community which it serves?'[33] He argued that '[f]reedom of the press, not fairness, is what the First Amendment is concerned with. Fairness has been left to the editors.'[34]

Barron argued that the statute was justified as an exercise of state police power. Because the statute 'adds to expression rather than detracts from expression, that what it does really is instead of offending the First Amendment, it implements it.'[35] Pressed by Justice Blackmun with the proposition that '[f]or better or for worse, we have opted for a free press not for free debate', Barron responded, 'Well, Mr. Justice Blackmun, I hope that is not so. I hope we have, we can work out an accommodation between the two.'[36] Barron posited:

> We live here in the 20th century when economics and technology have given us a world perhaps we did not want. And what our task is is to try to make an adjustment so that freedom of speech and press as we understand it and as we believe in it can endure. That's our problem.[37]

On June 25, 1974, the Court unanimously held that the Florida statute violated the First Amendment. In an opinion authored by Chief Justice Burger,

---

31   *Miami Herald v. Tornillo*, Oral Argument Transcript 9–10, Apr. 17, 1974, https://www.supremecourt.gov/pdfs/transcripts/1973/73-797_04-17-1974.pdf
    Miami Herald Pub. Co. v. Tornillo, 418 U.S. 241, 246 (1974).
32   *Miami Herald v. Tornillo*, Oral Argument Transcript 13–14, Apr. 17, 1974.
33   Ibid., 17.
34   Ibid., 14.
35   Ibid., 32.
36   Ibid., 29.
37   Ibid., 26.

the Court observed that for many years it had 'expressed sensitivity as to whether a restriction or requirement constituted the compulsion exerted by government on a newspaper to print that which it would not otherwise print.'[38] It viewed the Florida law as such a compulsion. In fact, the statute functioned as a speech restriction, by exacting a penalty on a newspaper for taking positions on political candidates.[39] The law put the paper to the choice of ceding column inches or remaining silent to avoid having to provide the print space.[40] The Court also posited that this penalty had a chilling effect on criticism of political candidates, thereby impoverishing public debate.[41]

Conspicuously absent from the Court's analysis was *Red Lion*. The opinion did not refer to it. It discussed the problem of increasingly concentrated media ownership, stating that 'the result of these vast changes has been to place in a few hands the power to inform the American people and shape public opinion.'[42] The Court further recognized that the 'obvious solution'—creation of additional newspapers—was unrealistic given the barriers to entry.[43] Nevertheless, any solution involving 'governmental coercion' of access ran afoul of the First Amendment. Despite the absence of any discussion of *Red Lion*, Barron says now that the Chief Justice Burger's opinion does a fairly good job of laying out the arguments in favor of a constitutional right of access, if only to reject them. 'Basically, I think his position was that the Constitution guaranteed a free press but not a fair one.'[44]

4   Liberty, Equality, and First Amendment Law

Xavier Cortada's rendering of *Miami Herald v. Tornillo* raises the same questions as the case itself. Whose mouths speak from this newspaper? Do they represent a diversity of voices and viewpoints? Or are they effectively one voice, controlled by the entity that owns the pages? Whose voices does the public hear and who decides that question? The Court's answer: he who owns the pages chooses the voices.

---

38   *Miami Herald*, 418 U.S. at 256.
39   Ibid., 256–57.
40   Ibid.
41   Ibid., 257.
42   Ibid., 250.
43   Ibid., 252.
44   Barron Interview.

Miami Herald v. Tornillo represented a clash between two conceptions of the First Amendment, one liberty-based, the other equality-based. One emphasized the history of press freedom and the specter of censorship, the other economic and informational equality. One focused on the media as speakers, the other on the public as listeners and on other speakers seeking access to the media's powerful platforms. The Court's decision about that clash is important on its own terms; it chose press freedom over press fairness, foreclosing a fairness doctrine for print media akin to the one for broadcast media upheld in *Red Lion*.

But *Miami Herald* is important for its further implications. Other businesses have invoked *Miami Herald* with increasing frequency to gain similar immunity from governmental regulation.

Google and other search engines have successfully argued that they should be immune to claims that their search algorithms violate antitrust or fair-competition laws by advantaging certain businesses or disadvantaging others.[45] Internet service providers argue that net neutrality laws similarly violate their First Amendment rights.[46] These laws prohibit internet service providers, such as cable internet giants Verizon and AT&T, from picking the content their subscribers can access—by blocking certain content from their services or 'throttling' (slowing down) some content in favor of other content. These search engines and service providers claim that their decisions about what businesses or content to privilege, what to slow down, and what to block are editorial decisions like those of a newspaper's editorial page, immune from governmental regulation under *Miami Herald*. Although the federal government has at this point abolished net-neutrality regulations, prior to that the D.C. Circuit rejected a First Amendment challenge to them patterned on *Tornillo*.[47]

These examples could be only the beginning. In an information economy, more businesses and industries can characterize their activities as 'speech'. Any entity that collects and uses data—from health-care providers to Facebook—could argue that its decisions about how to use information are 'editorial' in nature. It is hard to imagine that the Justices had anything of the sort in mind in 1974. But does *Miami Herald* compel this? Can those who own information claim immunity from regulation?

---

45 *S. Louis Martin v. Google Inc.*, No. CGC-14-539972 (Cal. Sup. Ct. Nov. 13, 2014); *Langdon v. Google Inc.*, 474 F. Supp. 2d 622 (D. Del. 2007); *Search King Inc. v. Google Tech Inc.*, 2003 WL 21464568 (W.D. Okla. 2003).

46 *U.S. Telecom Ass'n v. FCC*, 825 F.3d 674 (D.C. Cir. 2015); *Verizon v. F.C.C.*, 740 F.3d 623 (D.C. Cir. 2014).

47 *U.S. Telecom Ass'n v. FCC*, 825 F.3d 674, 740–44 (D.C. Cir. 2015).

There are three possible answers.

One is that *Miami Herald* was rightly decided and dictates this outcome. The Court considered the clash between a freedom- or liberty-based First Amendment and a fairness- or equality-based First Amendment and chose the latter over the former.

Another view is that *Miami Herald* was wrongly decided and its extension into these new areas highlights what was wrong about it. Barron believes it is predictable that new litigants in communications and data industries would seek immunity from regulation under *Red Lion*. 'It's the same argument, they do indeed use it, and so far they've been successful.'[48]

The third option is that whether *Miami Herald* can be justified on its own terms, it can be distinguished from new technologies and businesses. *Miami Herald* required the Court to reconcile two parts of its case law on freedom of the press. The First Amendment protects against abridgement of 'the freedom of speech, or of the press'. The Speech Clause and the Press Clause convey rights that can confer immunity from otherwise valid regulation; an otherwise legitimate law that violates the First Amendment immunizes rights-holders from the law's operation. The Court's First Amendment jurisprudence is an effort to describe the scope and strength of the claims that First Amendment rightsholders can assert—to determine how far First Amendment rights go and how strongly they push back against regulation.[49]

Cases involving the press have carved an important distinction. On one hand, the Court has been very skeptical when the media industry has invoked the Press Clause to claim immunity from general economic regulation. In the early to mid-twentieth century, the Court rejected the Associated Press's claims that the Press Clause immunized it from both wage-and-hour regulations[50] and antitrust laws.[51] Freedom of the press did not give the media special exceptions from economic regulation; the press as an industry had to follow the same rules as other businesses.

On the other hand, the Court has been suspicious of laws that affect what newspapers can and cannot print. This 'sensitivity'[52] grew over the twentieth century, as the Court limited various longstanding doctrines when they

---

48   Barron Interview.
49   Leslie Kendrick, 'Free Speech as a Special Right' (2017) 45 Philosophy and Public Affairs 87; Frederick Schauer, 'Must Speech Be Special?' (1983) 78 Northwestern University Law Review 1284.
50   *Associated Press v. National Labor Relations Board*, 301 U.S. 103 (1937).
51   *Associated Press v. United States*, 326 U.S. 1 (1945).
52   *Miami Herald Pub. Co. v. Tornillo*, 418 U.S. 241, 256 (1974).

interfered with what could be said in a newspaper—group libel,[53] defamation,[54] judges' criminal contempt powers,[55] executive national security authority.[56] Many of these cases contributed to and reflected a broader enmity toward any form of content discrimination in any sphere, not just the press. The Court articulated this wholesale suspicion of content discrimination clearly in the 1970s and it remains a mainstay of current First Amendment doctrine,[57] but it begins with a special solicitude for the press.

Miami Herald required the Court to decide in which bucket the Florida right-of-reply statute belonged. The statute required newspapers to publish certain content, implicating the Court's 'sensitivity' about governmental interference. But its justification was economic: a small number of newspapers controlled print media access and content for the public and a right-of-reply statute offset these inequalities in a modest way. In property terms, the right of reply functions as an easement—a right-of-way that an opposing voice has on the newspaper's property. It mitigates the fact that a small number of owners control valuable property providing essential information to the public. The statute could have been framed as either content regulation or economic regulation.

The Court had considered similarly bimodal regulations in the past. In *Grosjean v. American Press Co.*,[58] it declared invalid a Louisiana law imposing a two percent tax on all in-state newspapers with a circulation greater than 20,000 copies per week, justifying it as a 'license tax' imposed for the 'privilege' of selling advertising in high-circulation newspapers.[59] On its face and in its stated justification, the tax on was an economic regulation unrelated to the content of newspapers. In Louisiana, however, the tax was lambasted as an instrument to repress newspapers critical of Senator Huey Long.[60] The Court avoided discussing motives or the political climate surrounding the tax's passage, instead emphasizing the history of press suppression through taxation, including the colonial Stamp Act. This backdrop made the form of the tax sufficiently 'suspicious' to strike it down.[61]

---

53 *Near v. Minnesota*, 283 U.S. 697 (1931).
54 *Gertz v. Robert Welch, Inc.*, 418 U.S. 323 (1974); *New York Times Co. v. Sullivan*, 376 U.S. 254 (1964).
55 *Craig v. Harney*, 331 U.S. 367 (1947); *Bridges v. California*, 314 U.S. 252 (1941).
56 *New York Times Co. v. United States*, 403 U.S. 713 (1971).
57 *Iancu v. Brunetti*, 139 S. Ct. 2294 (2019); *Matal v. Tam*, 137 S. Ct. 1744 (2017); *Reed v. Town of Gilbert*, 135 S. Ct. 2218 (2015).
58 297 U.S. 233 (1936).
59 Ibid., 44.
60 Gary Feinerman, 'Unconstitutional Conditions: The Crossroads of Substantive Rights and Equal Protection' (1991) 43 Stanford Law Review 1369, 1408 n.206.
61 *Grosjean*, 297 U.S. at 248–51.

The Florida right-of-reply statute bore no similar evidence of improper motive, no indication that it was intended to penalize or to repress political speech. Indeed, the Supreme Court of Florida had characterized it as an anticorruption statute designed to give the public adequate information about candidates for office. But as *Grosjean* showed, the Court might find a law suspect by invoking the long history of press censorship, without investigating the actual motives behind it.

The Supreme Court took that approach subsequent to *Miami Herald* in a case involving a Minnesota use tax on paper and ink consumed in the production of publications.[62] The Court found no evidence of an invidious motive. Minnesota argued that the tax was a reasonable substitute for a sales tax, which was difficult to impose on newspapers because they were inexpensive and often sold in vending machines. Minnesota also argued that the tax favored the press, because a use tax on raw materials was cheaper than the same tax rate applied to finished products. Nevertheless, the Court declared the tax invalid because it singled out the press[63]—in fact, particular press entities, thanks to a carve-out for small publications.[64] The Court again erected a prophylactic rule to protect press freedom from possible encroachments.

From this perspective, *Miami Herald v. Tornillo* is unexceptional. As a press case, it fits a long tradition of suspicion toward government actions singling out the press, particular members of the press, or the substantive content of print media. Granting that the right-of- reply statute had economic justifications, the Court balked because it remedied economic inequalities by prescribing content. Regardless of government purpose, the effects on content were too close for comfort.

One may agree or disagree with the substantive outcome in *Miami Herald*. But viewing it as a press case reveals its limitations. *Miami Herald*—like *Grosjean* and *Minnesota Star Tribune*—viewed the challenged regulations as implicating a long and ugly history of press censorship and suppression. This reason for 'sensitivity' does not carry to application of antitrust laws to search engines or net neutrality laws to internet service providers. To argue that these regulations deserve the same level of scrutiny requires both (1) that the business functions at issue plausibly can be described as involving 'editorial discretion' and (2) that the businesses involved have endured a history of suppression similar to the print media. Otherwise, 'editorial discretion' looks like ordinary

---

62   *Minneapolis Star Tribune Company v. Commissioner*, 460 U.S. 575 (1983).
63   Ibid., 592.
64   Ibid., 590–91.

business decision-making and the sensitivity accorded to the press morphs into a generalized suspicion of regulation.

That this transmogrification is happening more frequently is a testament to trends in the Supreme Court since *Miami Herald*.

One trend is the collapse of the Press Clause into the Speech Clause, as the Court ignores the former and decides press cases under the Speech Clause. This trend erases the press-specific nature of cases such as *Miami Herald* and implies that suspicions aroused by the history of press censorship in that case attach to any regulation of speech by any speaker. This trend informs doctrine defining content discrimination as the primary First Amendment evil, as well as the increasing reliance on *Miami Herald* by non-media economic actors.

Another trend is an unreflective understanding of what counts as speech for purposes of 'the freedom of speech'. Courts assume the First Amendment is implicated whenever an activity can be described as speech—whether search engines, internet service providers, or tattoo parlors. Yet many forms of actual speech—such as contracts, wills, estates, insider trading, anti-competitive agreements—fall outside the freedom of speech. Assuming that any activity with a speech component always implicates the First Amendment is a good way to destroy the boundary between speech protection and economic regulation. First Amendment jurisprudence is predicated on the idea that freedom of speech and freedom of the press are special—that their regulation raises more concerns than general regulation of business activities. To make protection of speech a gateway to immunity for business interests is to erase what makes speech worth singling out in the first place.

This is not to say that the First Amendment has no role in an information economy. It would implicate the First Amendment if, for example, government regulated the content of search engines by suppressing anti-government ideas. But when a business claims that a search engine's algorithm favors the search engine's products over those of its competitors, it is not obvious that the First Amendment should foreclose the suit any more than it should in the context of some other business practice. There may be no easy answers to how much scrutiny to give regulations of new media. But that is why the questions cannot be answered by automatic analogy to *Miami Herald*. Granting immunity because an entity can be described as vaguely analogous to a newspaper ignores the long history of press censorship and the hard work of distinguishing suspect from permissible regulations that informed *Miami Herald v. Tornillo* in the first place.

This scope of freedom of speech and press is one of the most pressing legal questions of our time. Whatever answers the courts provide, *Miami Herald* will play a large role. Time will tell if its principle stays within the four corners of the newspaper or expands to major swaths of our economy.

5   Postscript

Much has happened since the Court decided *Miami Herald* in 1974. No one in the 1970s could have imagined what the newspaper industry would look like today. Print circulation has collapsed, and the media has consolidated to an even greater degree. First Amendment doctrine is further from Tornillo's arguments today than it was is 1974. The federal government abolished the Fairness Doctrine for broadcast licensees in the 1980s; in the unlikely event that it were reinstated, the current Supreme Court almost certainly would view it as violating the First Amendment. Meanwhile, other industries continue to invoke *Miami Herald* as a source of immunity from regulation.

At the same time, the rise of the internet and social media has fundamentally altered the information landscape. The institutional press is no longer the near-exclusive gateway for receiving or disseminating information. It shares that role with a variety of platforms that facilitate and mediate information-sharing by individuals and other entities, including the media. Displacement of the press has meant displacement of the journalistic norms informing the 'editorial discretion' that the *Herald*'s lawyers defended as the source of fairness in communications. While the mainstream media adheres to journalistic norms regarding sourcing and fact checking, other speakers do not. The practices of modern information platforms are not transparent and their regulation is a subject of fierce debate.

But important similarities remain. Jerome Barron observes,

> If you look at the media today you could say that the internet is the answer to all we hoped to achieve in *Miami Herald v. Tornillo*. And to a certain extent that's true. People can go onto Twitter, Facebook, and innumerable websites and get their view across. But structurally the media landscape is very similar to what it was. They have the same kind of dominance to move around the news, to alter the news, to shape the news that the networks had when we were arguing *Tornillo*.[65]

Barron questions who freedom of the press is for: 'Is it the working journalists, or the corporation that owns it? These are the questions we had then, and we have the same questions now'.

Pat Tornillo died in 2007, having remained a controversial figure. He stepped down from the Miami-Dade teachers' union in 2003 in the face of federal

---

65   Barron Interview.

charges relating to extensive use of union funds for personal expenses.[66] He pleaded guilty to tax evasion and mail fraud and served 22 months in federal prison.[67]

The *Miami Herald* broke the story of the federal investigation into Tornillo's malfeasance.[68] On Tornillo's release from prison in 2005, he wrote an apology to the teachers and children of Miami-Dade County.[69] The *Herald* published his apology.

Recommended Reading

Abrams, Floyd. *Speaking Freely: Trials of the First Amendment.* New York: Penguin Books, 2006.

Barron, Jerome A. 'Access to the Press: A New First Amendment Right.' *Harvard Law Review* 80 (1967): 1641–1678.

Bezanson, Randall P. *How Free Can the Press Be?* Champaign: University of Illinois Press, 2007.

Schauer, Frederick. 'Must Speech Be Special?' *Northwestern University Law Review* 78 (1983): 1284–1306.

---

66 'Rise and Fall'.
67 Ibid.; Vaishali Honawar, 'Disgraced Union Leader Pat Tornillo Dies', Education Week, June 27, 2007.
68 Joe Mozingo and Manny Garcia, 'Union paid private bills for Tornillo', Miami Herald, May 11, 2003, https://www.miamiherald.com/latest-news/article1928929.html; 'Rise and Fall'; Stephen Greenhouse, 'F.B.I. Is Investigating Teachers' Union Leader in Miami Area', New York Times, June 1, 2003, https://www.nytimes.com/2003/06/01/us/fbi-is-investigating-teachers-union-leader-in-miami-area.html.
69 Honawar, 'Disgraced'.

Proffitt v. Florida, 428 U.S. 242 (1976)

Xavier Cortada

∴

Francis Bacon painted an image of a pope gripping the arms of his chair. I don't really recall when I first saw this beautiful piece, but I found it disturbing. Perhaps it's because the sitting pontiff looked as if he was being electrocuted. Except I wondered, who, if anyone, really belongs in an electric chair? Who should receive the ultimate punishment? Who should decide, and what should the circumstances be?

It is a controversial issue that our Country and our courts have struggled with for years, at one point barring all executions as cruel and unusual. Then, in 1972, the U.S. Supreme Court took up five cases to change its mind. One of those Death Penalty cases was *Proffitt v Florida*. The court provided relief to states like Florida who wanted to allow judges to make the determination. With a formula that addressed mitigating and aggravating factors judges could calculate whether they would be sentencing someone to death. I envision the Capital Punishment formula as an algebraic expression that would read something like:

$7M+8A=0(CU)$
M = mitigating
A = aggravating
CU = cruel and unusual

Although the idea was to put some objectivity into the decision-making, at some point it's almost absurd to think that we can objectify a decision that is so laden with emotion. In my opinion, adding the formula de-emotionalizes the death penalty so that it can be carried out.

Bacon's painting was in the back of my mind as I painted this piece. In it, I portray a Death Row inmate whose time is up. He sits in a vacuum, waiting for one of us to pull the switch. It's harder to do that when you see the individual face to face, regardless of the formulas. Naturally, it is a fantastic painting, it is loud and brash. But then again, there is nothing more fantastic than the death penalty, whether by lethal injections or some other process. I created this painting to make us all more aware about capital punishment, because in the end, it's all of us who have a firm grip on to that switch.

FIGURE 7.1 Xavier Cortada, *Proffitt v. Florida*, 428 U.S. 242 (1976), 48" × 36", acrylic on canvas, 2004.
PHOTO: ZENAIDA PIRRI, MIAMI, FLORIDA

CHAPTER 7

Proffitt v. Florida
Distorting Death

Corinna Barrett Lain

Xavier Cortada's depiction of *Proffitt v. Florida*[1]—one of a trio of Supreme Court decisions that revived the death penalty in 1976 after it had been declared invalid in 1972[2]—is a masterful work of art that shows a remarkable understanding of the decision and its failures. It is a fantastical piece, a piece that captures the horror of death by electrocution set against two columns of ominous looking Roman numerals. Cortada uses the visual to ask the cardinal questions of state-sanctioned death. 'Who, if anyone, really belongs in an electric chair?' he writes in a statement accompanying his piece. 'Who should decide, and what should the circumstances be?'

Cortada's painting leaves little doubt about who he thinks capital punishment punishes. The condemned inmate's skin is dark. The death penalty has a face, Cortada suggests in his painting, and it belongs to a racial minority.

As a factual proposition, the depiction is accurate.[3] Indeed, racial discrimination in the imposition of death was one of the prime reasons that the Justices invalidated the death penalty in 1972. *Furman v. Georgia*, the 1972 decision that struck down the death penalty as then applied, had no majority or plurality opinion; it consisted of five individual concurrences, and three of them discussed race. Justice Douglas wrote that the death penalty was 'pregnant with discrimination.'[4] Justice Brennan wrote that the burden of capital punishment fell upon 'the poor, and the members of minority groups.'[5] And Justice

---

1 428 U.S. 242 (1976). Thanks go to Howard Wasserman and M.C. Mirow for inviting me to participate in this worthy project; to Ron Bacigal, Erin Collins, John Douglass, Jessica Erickson, Jim Gibson, Michael Meltsner, Luke Norris, Scott Sundby, Allison Tait, and Kevin Woodson for their helpful suggestions along the way; and to MaryAnn Grover and Win Jordan for their excellent research assistance.
2 *Furman v. Georgia*, 408 U.S. 238 (1972).
3 United States General Accounting Office, Death Penalty Sentencing: Research Indicates Pattern of Racial Disparities 5 (1990) (documenting racial disparities in the imposition of the death penalty across a variety of studies).
4 *Furman*, 408 U.S. at 257 (Douglas, J., concurring).
5 Ibid., 366 (Brennan, J., concurring).

Stewart wrote that 'if any basis can be discerned for the selection of these few to be sentenced to die, it is the constitutionally impermissible basis of race.'[6] *Furman* is famous for prohibiting the arbitrary and capricious imposition of death, but lurking in the shadows was the ever-present specter of its imposition on the basis of race.

Proffitt was the answer to *Furman*—or, more accurately, it was part of the answer, because the full rebuttal consisted of three cases, the lead being *Gregg v. Georgia*.[7] In *Gregg*, the Supreme Court explained that the deficiencies in *Furman* could be remedied by giving the sentencer guidance in deciding whether to impose death; in *Proffitt*, the Court approved Florida's death penalty scheme as an example of how that could be done. Florida's scheme had a judge, rather than jury, make the life-or-death decision (a feature that has not survived constitutional scrutiny over time)[8] and required the judge to weigh eight aggravating factors against seven mitigating factors to determine whether death would be imposed. Hence the Roman numerals in Cortada's painting—seven in one column, eight in the other. When aggravators outnumber mitigators, the result is death.

Cortada resists this algebraic approach to death, which he contends 'de-emotionalizes the death penalty so that it can be carried out.' We numb ourselves with numbers. This distorts death penalty decision-making by obscuring what is fundamentally a moral decision, a value-laden judgment about the propriety of life or death.

Cortada's painting is an unequivocal success in depicting the death penalty as a quintessentially human enterprise—a human decision with human consequences, in contrast to the columns of Roman numerals that offer the pretense that it is something else. Florida's death penalty scheme removes the human element from the sentencing equation. Cortada's aim is to put it back.

The remainder of this essay expounds upon the insights of Cortada's painting, then turns to what Cortada identifies as the visual inspiration for his piece—a painting of a screaming pope by Francis Bacon. Bacon's pope was not a comment on the death penalty, but the themes he was exploring—pain, imprisonment, isolation, and obfuscation—turn out to be eerily apropos of the death penalty as well. Cortada's painting is in dialogue with these four themes, and each illuminates a point about the death penalty more broadly.

---

6 Ibid., 310 (Stewart, J., concurring).
7 428 U.S. 153 (1976). The third of the *Gregg* trio is *Jurek v. Texas*, 428 U.S. 262 (1976).
8 *Hurst v. Florida*, 136 S. Ct. 616 (2016) (invalidating Florida's capital sentencing scheme, under which an advisory jury makes a recommendation to the judge and the judge makes the findings necessary for imposing death).

1   What Guided Discretion Does to Death Penalty Decision-Making

Cortada's painting makes a statement about Florida's approach to death penalty decision-making, so a closer look at that approach is a fitting place to start. What does guided discretion do to death penalty decision-making? Before turning to what it does, the discussion first turns to what it does *not* do—guide death-sentencing discretion.

The idea behind guided discretion is first to narrow the death penalty's applicability so that it is available for only the most serious crimes and the most serious offenders. Guided-discretion statutes do this by enumerating aggravating circumstances, any one of which can render an accused criminal 'death-eligible.' These statutory aggravators delineate the difference between most first-degree murders and the special class of first-degree murders that are punishable by death. At least that is the way guided discretion is supposed to work; that is how it works in theory.

But that is not how it works in practice. Some aggravators are too vague to narrow the death penalty's applicability; they can be read to apply to most any first-degree murder. A famous example of this sort of aggravator is murder committed in an 'especially heinous, cruel or depraved manner.'[9] Another is murder that shows 'utter disregard for human life.'[10] Wait, *what?* Doesn't every intentional murder show utter disregard for human life?[11] As one judge observed, 'What first-degree murderer fails to show "callous disregard for human life"? I suppose this would be the "pitiful" slayer, who, prior to delivering the fatal blow, tells the victim, "Excuse me, pardon me, I know it's inconvenient, but I must now take your life." '[12] These sorts of aggravators cannot possibly serve their narrowing function because virtually every first-degree murder meets them.

Other statutory aggravators are more concrete, but the circumstances they name are exceedingly common so, again, most every first-degree murder is

---

9   *Walton v. Arizona*, 497 U.S. 639 (1990) (holding that 'especially heinous, cruel, or depraved' aggravating circumstance, as construed by state supreme court, furnished sufficient guidance to guide sentencer discretion).
10 *Arave v. Creech*, 507 U.S. 463 (1993) (holding that 'utter disregard for human life' aggravating circumstance, as construed by state supreme court, furnished sufficient guidance to guide sentencer discretion).
11 Granted, the mercy killer—the killer who murders because the victim is suffering from some incurable and painful disease—is an example of someone who murders without showing utter disregard for human life. But that is an exceedingly narrow exception, so narrow in fact that it hardly merits mention.
12 *State v. Charboneau*, 116 Idaho 129, 172 (1989) (Bistline, J., dissenting).

death-eligible. A prime example of this sort of aggravator is murder committed in the course of committing another felony. States vary in the felonies listed, but most include rape, robbery, burglary, abduction, and carjacking.[13] The problem with using felonies in this way is that murder rarely occurs in a vacuum. People do not usually just walk up to other people and kill them; people kill in the context of a break-in, or robbery, or rape, or abduction, or one of the other felonies on the list. Here again, rather than narrowing the class of death-eligible murders, these types of aggravators result in most murders being eligible for the penalty of death.

Yet even if statutory aggravators were not problematic in their own right, a larger systemic problem with guided-discretion statutes would undermine their ability to rein in the class of murders eligible for death: Aggravator creep. When the Supreme Court decided *Proffitt* in 1976, Florida's death penalty statute had eight aggravating circumstances, any one of which could render the defendant death-eligible (hence Cortada's column of eight Roman numerals on one side of the ledger). Today, Florida's statute has double that number of aggravators—sixteen—and some states, such as Alabama and California, have more than that.[14]

The result is nearly complete death eligibility for first-degree murder. In Arizona, for example, a study showed that the state's fourteen statutory aggravators rendered 856 of 866 first-degree murder cases—98 percent—death-eligible.[15] Relying on this data, condemned inmates in 2017 challenged Arizona's guided-discretion statute for failing to serve its constitutionally required narrowing function.[16] They lost in state court and the Supreme Court denied *certiorari*, albeit with a statement from four Justices noting the need for a more fully developed factual record.[17] Whether the Court will enforce the narrowing

---

13 For a state-by-state listing of aggravating circumstances, *see* https://deathpenaltyinfo.org/aggravating-factors-capital-punishment-state.
14 Ibid.
15 *State v. Hidalgo*, 241 Ariz. 543 (2017) (discussing data).
16 Ibid.
17 *Hidalgo v. Arizona*, 138 S. Ct. 1054 (2018) (denying certiorari on the question 'Whether Arizona's capital sentencing scheme, which includes so many aggravating circumstances that virtually every defendant convicted of first-degree murder is eligible for death, violates the Eighth Amendment.'). Justice Breyer, joined by Justices Ginsburg, Sotomayor, and Kagan wrote separately: 'In support of his Eighth Amendment challenge, the petitioner points to empirical evidence about Arizona's capital sentence system that suggests about 98% of first-degree murder defendants in Arizona were eligible for the death penalty. That evidence is unrebutted. ... Evidence of this kind warrants careful attention and evaluation. However, in this case, the opportunity to develop the record through an evidentiary hearing was denied. As a result, the record as it has come to us is limited and largely unexamined by experts and the courts below in the first instance. ... [T]he issue

function of guided-discretion statutes remains to be seen; what is clear is that they are not serving that function now.

None of this is shocking; we have known that guided-discretion statutes fail to guide sentencer discretion for nearly fifty years. Studies have shown that over ninety percent of those sentenced to death before *Furman* would have been death eligible after it.[18] Indeed, the year before *Furman*, the Supreme Court rejected a claim that guided discretion in death sentencing was constitutionally required, in part because the Court was convinced that those statutes could not perform their narrowing function.[19] Obviously, the Court changed its mind,[20] but what it said in 1971 merits mention here. 'It is apparent that such criteria do not purport to provide more than the most minimal control over the sentencing authority's exercise of discretion,' the Court stated in *McGautha v. California*, adding, 'To identify before the fact those characteristics of criminal homicides and their perpetrators which call for the death penalty, and to express these characteristics in language which can be fairly understood and applied by the sentencing authority, appear to be tasks which are beyond present human ability.'[21] All this the Court knew when it approved guided-discretion sentencing schemes five years later in *Proffitt* and *Gregg*.[22]

Over time, recognition that guided-discretion statutes do not work has only grown stronger. In 2009, the American Law Institute withdrew its guided-discretion statute from the Model Penal Code—the statute that had served as a model for the guided-discretion statutes approved in *Proffitt* and *Gregg*. According to the ALI, rescission was warranted 'in light of the current intractable institutional and structural obstacles to ensuring a minimally adequate

---

presented in this petition will be better suited for certiorari with such a record." Ibid., 1057 (Breyer, J., joined by Ginsburg, Sotomayor, and Kagan, JJ.).

18 David C. Baldus, George Woodworth and Charles A. Pulaski, Jr., *Equal Justice and the Death Penalty: A Legal and Empircal Analysis* (Lebanon: Northeastern University Press, 1990), 102.

19 *McGautha v. California*, 402 U.S. 183 (1971).

20 For those wondering about the backstory of a Supreme Court that first held that standards guiding death penalty decision-making were not constitutionally required, then invalidated the death penalty because there were no standards, then required the standards that it had said were not required and would not work, see Corinna Barrett Lain, '*Furman* Fundamentals' (2007) 82 Washington Law Review 1.

21 *McGautha*, 402 U.S. at 207–208 (1971).

22 In *Gregg*, the Supreme Court acknowledged *McGautha* only by vaguely referencing it in a footnote, stating, 'Some have suggested that standards to guide a capital jury's sentencing deliberations are impossible to formulate.' *Gregg*, 428 U.S. at 193. It was true, 'some' had— namely, four of the plurality Justices in *Gregg*.

system for administering capital punishment.'[23] As statements go, it was like Ford announcing that it could no longer stand behind the minimally adequate safety of cars.

Recognizing that guided-discretion statutes fail to do the very thing they were designed to do is one thing, but as Cortada astutely observes, guided-discretion statutes do something else—they do affirmative harm. Cortada describes this harm as 'de-emotionaliz[ing] the death penalty so that it can be carried out.' He is right about that, but how this happens is sufficiently complex to warrant some time unpacking it.

Sometimes guided-discretion statutes de-emotionalize the death penalty by suggesting to juries that a sentence of death is required when it is not. The work of the Capital Jury Project, a National Science Foundation-supported consortium of state research projects that study how capital jurors think,[24] has shown that a substantial portion of jurors who voted for death in a capital case erroneously believed that the law required it. In one study, close to five in ten jurors believed that the law required death if the murder was 'heinous, vile, or depraved,' and four in ten jurors believed that the law required death if they found a different statutory aggravator, future dangerousness.[25] Other studies have produced similar results,[26] suggesting that jurors often confuse a sentence of death that is authorized by law with one that is required by law.

Narrative responses from jurors interviewed through the CJP illustrate the point. Across a variety of capital trials conducted under a variety of guided-discretion statutes, jurors erroneously asserted that if they found an aggravating

---

23   Message from Lance Liebman, Director, American Law Institute, Oct 23, 2009, https://www.ali.org/media/filer_public/f0/17/f017bd1f-fd2f-46cb-8b11-838118005abd/2009-fall.pdf. Among the obstacles listed in a report supporting the decision was the failure of guided-discretion statutes to narrow eligibility for the sentence of death. Carol S. Steiker and Jordan M. Steiker, 'Part II: Report to the ALI Concerning Capital Punishment' (2010) 89 Texas Law Review 367, 377–380 (prepared at the request of ALI Director Lance Liebman).
24   For information about the Capital Jury Project, see https://www.albany.edu/scj/13189.php.
25   Ursula Bentele and William J. Bowers, 'How Jurors Decide on Death: Guilt is Overwhelming; Aggravation Requires Death; and Mitigation Is No Excuse' (2001) 66 Brooklyn Law Review 1011, 1041.
26   James Luginbuhl and Julie Howe, 'Discretion in Capital Sentencing Instructions: Guided or Misguided?' (1995) 70 Indiana Law Journal 1161, 1174 (finding that 63 percent of jurors interviewed in North Carolina thought the death penalty was required if the murder was 'heinous, vile, or depraved', and 43 percent thought it was required if they found future dangerousness); Theodore Eisenberg, Stephen P. Garvey, and Martin T. Wells, 'Jury Responsibility in Capital Sentencing: An Empirical Study' (1996) 44 Buffalo Law Review 339, 360 ('Nearly one-third of the jurors were under the mistaken impression that the law required a death sentence if they found heinousness or dangerousness, a result replicated in a multi-state study of the interview data.').

circumstance, they were required to vote for death.[27] When asked why they voted for death, for example, jurors responded with comments such as:

> J: In fact, we had to according to the judge's instructions give capital punishment. ...
>
> J: We went the first step, we all decided on the first step before we'd go to the second step. It's very structured. ...If you decide on this then it must be this. ...
>
> J: The instruction, what the law specified. From what I remember the law said if he's guilty of murder and the murder was committed with special circumstances that the death penalty was appropriate.[28]
>
> J: It seemed that the State of Florida called for the death penalty. There didn't seem to be any choice.[29]

To be clear, no state's death penalty scheme actually requires the imposition of death upon a finding of an aggravated circumstance.[30] Indeed, the Supreme Court declared mandatory death penalties invalid the same day that it upheld the guided-discretion statutes in *Proffitt* and *Gregg*.[31] The problem is not what the law says. The problem is that jurors believe it says something else.

Why don't capital jurors understand that the presence of a statutory aggravator merely makes the defendant death-eligible? The CJP's findings suggest that jurors treat statutory aggravators like elements of the offense in the guilt phase of a criminal trial. If they find the elements of the offense beyond a reasonable doubt, they are told they must convict—and so it is, jurors believe, with aggravators during the penalty phase of a capital trial.[32] Capital cases are exceedingly complex and capital jury instructions are notoriously difficult to understand; they are often dozens of pages long, written in legalese, and raise more questions than they answer.[33] Absent a clear sense of how guided-discretion

---

27   Bentele and Bowers, 'How Jurors Decide', 1032 ('Jurors in all the states in the study described this determinative role of aggravating factors.').

28   Ibid., 1032, 1035–36.

29   William S. Geimer and Jonathan Amsterdam, 'Why Jurors Vote Life or Death: Operative Factors in Ten Florida Death Penalty Cases' (1988) 15 American Journal of Criminal Law 1, 25.

30   Texas comes closest, but the Supreme Court in *Jurek v. Texas*, 428 U.S. 262 (1976), the third case in the *Gregg* trilogy, read the state's death penalty scheme to allow the consideration of mitigating circumstances. In accord, *Johnson v. Texas*, 509 U.S. 350 (1993).

31   *Woodson v. North Carolina*, 428 U.S. 280 (1976).

32   Bentele and Bowers, 'How Jurors Decide', 1057.

33   As one juror explained: "The instructions were confusing. Specifically, it was written in legal terminology. Very wordy. He gave us a forty-page booklet. He read a great deal to

schemes work, jurors fill in the blank with what they know: the rules for determining guilt in a criminal trial.

One reason, then, that guided-discretion statutes de-emotionalize death penalty decision-making is that jurors misunderstand them. Jurors believe they must vote for death; they think the law requires it. They are wrong about that. They are misreading the instructions. But they believe they have no choice, which allows them to detach themselves from the emotionally wrought decision of choosing life or death.

A more subtle version of this phenomenon is what Cortada surely has in mind in his depiction of *Proffitt*: jurors do not misunderstand the law in the sense that they confuse death eligibility with a death-sentence requirement, but they misunderstand the *role* that the law plays in death sentencing. They do not understand that guided-discretion statutes are intended to guide their discretion, as opposed to making the sentencing decision for them.

To understand the point requires pausing to consider the second purpose that guided-discretion schemes serve—guiding the sentencer's decision-making once a defendant is found to be death-eligible. States do this in different ways, but many (perhaps most) tell sentencers to weigh aggravating and mitigating circumstances to determine life or death.[34] This was the Florida scheme approved in *Proffitt*, and Cortada depicts this weighing exercise with the columns of Roman numerals—one representing aggravating circumstances, one representing mitigating circumstances—on both sides of the condemned inmate. The inmate is in the middle; his life hangs in the balance.

In this more subtle version of the point, jurors do as they are told, conscientiously weighing aggravating and mitigating circumstances to determine life or death, but they leave themselves out of it; the law serves as a calculator of sorts that tells them the 'right' answer. Research shows that a substantial minority of capital jurors—roughly one-fourth in one study[35]—believed that a death sentence was required under this algebraic framework when it was not, and a massive percentage—roughly eight out of ten capital jurors—exhibited the sort of emotional detachment from relying on the law that is the core of

---

us, and it took two hours, but it was confusing and not written where a lay person could understand it. We laughed, like what did you get out of this? Very little help to us. We were not allowed to ask questions. We were given the evidence and then we were told when you have [a] verdict you ring a bell and that is it." Joseph L. Hoffman, 'Where's the Buck?—Juror Misperception of Sentencing Responsibility in Death Penalty Cases' (1995) 70 Indiana Law Journal 1137, 1151.

34 For links to each state's guided discretion scheme, *see* https://deathpenaltyinfo.org/aggravating-factors-capital-punishment-state.
35 Luginbuhl and Howe, 'Discretion', 1173.

Cortada's critique.[36] Among capital jurors interviewed by the CJP, less than ten percent believed they were individually responsible for a death sentence, and less than ten percent believed that the jury as a whole was responsible.[37] Over thirty percent believed that the law was most responsible for a sentence of death.[38]

Here again, the responses of jurors interviewed through the CJP illustrate the point. Many jurors were explicit in relying on the law to relieve themselves of the awesome responsibility of deciding life or death, even when they appeared to understand their instructions correctly. Typical in this genre were comments such as:

> J: My justification of the whole thing is, it's not really my decision, it's the law's decision. They told me to just look at this in the penalty phase, mitigating, aggravating. I've done it.
>
> J: In my case, I found it would have been easier to vote for the death penalty than I thought it would. ... you're deciding on the law, really. You're not deciding death or no death. You're deciding what has happened and whether it meets the requirements of the law.
>
> J: You need guidelines. You know, that takes it off of how you feel. So that was the whole thing. It was very helpful to have the judge's instructions and the copy of the law that we were able to use that framework.[39]
>
> J: We are not sentencing him to death—we are just answering these questions. We talked about it. 'We are just answering these questions'—to get a clear mind so as not to feel guilty that I sentenced him to die. That's how the law has it—just answer these questions.[40]

---

36 William J. Bowers, 'The Capital Jury Project: Rationale, Design, and Preview of Early Findings' (1995) 70 Indiana Law Journal 1043, 1094; but see Eisenberg, Garvey, and Wells, 'Jury Responsibility', 366 (arguing that 'most jurors did employ some mechanical reasoning processes to arrive at a sentencing decision' but that the survey questions 'd[id] not probe *how* mechanistically that weighing process is being conducted' and thus it is possible that jurors retained a sense of responsibility for their verdict).

37 Ibid.

38 Ibid.

39 Craig Haney, Lorelei Sontag, and Sally Costanzo, 'Deciding to Take a Life: Capital Juries, Sentencing Instructions, and the Jurisprudence of Death' (1994) 50 Journal of Social Issues 149, 166; Ibid., 160 (noting 'there was a tendency from both [California and Oregon jury] samples to shift or abdicate responsibility for the ultimate decision—to "the law", to the judge, or to the legal instructions—rather than grapple personally with the life and death consequences of the verdicts they were called upon to render.').

40 Bowers, 'The Capital Jury', 1076.

The dynamic at work here is different from what is happening when jurors clearly misread their instructions, but the result is the same. Jurors believe they have no choice in deciding death; they believe that the law decides it, and this allows them to avoid the awesome responsibility of having to decide life or death for themselves.

Again, none of this is new. Thirty-five years ago, Robert Weisberg wrote that guided-discretion statutes allowed juries 'to reassure themselves that the sanctions they inflict follow inevitably from the demands of neutral, disinterested legal principles, rather than from their own choice and power.'[41] Craig Haney followed with empirical evidence to support the claim, concluding that guided-discretion statutes implicitly told jurors that the appropriate sentence in a capital case involved 'nothing more than simple accounting, an adding up of the pluses and minuses on the balance sheet of someone's life.'[42] Back in the day of unfettered discretion in capital sentencing—the same unfettered discretion that the Supreme Court invalidated in *Furman*—juries were told that the law would not save them from the momentous decision of life or death.[43] The law provided no guidance; jurors were told that 'whether you recommend or withhold mercy is a matter solely within your discretion, calling for the exercise of your very best and most profound judgment.'[44] Now jurors are told, as Weisberg puts it, 'that their apparently painful choice is no choice at all—that the law is making it for them.'[45] They need only know how to add.

Cortada sees all this clearly, commonsensically. And in his claim that guided discretion 'de-emotionalizes the death penalty so that it can be carried out', Cortada sees something else: the state's interest in rationalizing, even arithmetizing, death. Robert Cover famously observed that our discomfort with inflicting violence on others leads to mechanisms to reconcile the dissonance and relieve our anxiety, using the law's role in capital sentencing as a prime example.[46] The decision to take a life is so violent, so intense, so existentially monumental that perhaps it does not matter that guided-discretion statutes

---

41   Robert Weisberg, 'Deregulating Death' (1983) 1983 The Supreme Court Review 385.
42   Haney, Sontag, and Costanzo, 'Deciding to Take', 172.
43   Weisberg, 'Deregulating', 364.
44   Ibid., 363 (quoting pre-*Furman* jury instructions).
45   Ibid., 376.
46   Robert M. Cover, 'Violence and the Word' (1986) 95 Yale Law Journal 1601, 1622–28. For a riff on the theme, see Craig Haney, 'Violence and the Capital Jury: Mechanisms of Moral Disengagement and the Impulse to Condemn to Death' (1997) 49 Stanford Law Review 1447.

do not work. Perhaps their most important role is relieving jurors of their awesome responsibility. If that is the case, then jurors' conception of themselves as 'amoral calculators'[47] mechanically following legal instructions is not just a byproduct of guided-discretion statutes, but also their core contribution. It is what they do to keep death sentences flowing to maintain 'the machinery of death.'[48]

Cortada asks who should receive the ultimate punishment, but his point in asking is that the question cannot be answered by death-dealing arithmetic. It is a profoundly moral question that can only be answered by the soul-searching that comes with sitting in judgment over another person's life. Guided-discretion statutes distort this judgment process with legal formulas that obscure the excruciatingly difficult decision of life or death. As Haney observes, our formulaic approach to death 'removes the jurors' collective and individual sense of moral responsibility' and 'conveys to them a quality of legal compulsion that disengages their most critical ethical sensitivities.'[49] This is Cortada's point in his depiction of *Proffitt v. Florida*. Cortada forces us to see the face and not just the formula, to visually call out the distortion for what it is. And he does this exceedingly well.

2   Cortada's Inspiration in the Work of Francis Bacon

Cortada writes in his artist's statement that he was inspired by a painting by Francis Bacon of 'a pope gripping the arms of a chair.'[50] He found the image beautiful yet disturbing, perhaps because 'the sitting pontiff looked as if he was being electrocuted.'

The painting was not hard to find. Of Bacon's many works, *Study after Velázquez's Portrait of Pope Innocent X*[51] is distinctly reminiscent of a pope being electrocuted. The piece is considered to be one of Bacon's finest masterpieces and was created at the height of his artistic prowess.[52] It has

---

47   Stephen P. Garvey, 'The Emotional Economy of Capital Sentencing' (2000) 75 New York University Law Review 26, 39.
48   *Callins v. Collins*, 510 U.S. 1141, 1145 (1994) (Blackmun, J., dissenting from denial of certiorari) ('From this day forward, I no longer shall tinker with the machinery of death.').
49   Haney, 'Violence', 1485.
50   Artist's Statement.
51   Francis Bacon, *Study after Velázquez's Portrait of Pope Innocent X* (1953). https://www.francis-bacon.com/news/iconic-study-after-velazquezs-portrait-pope-innocent-x-1953-display.
52   David Sylvester, *Looking Back at Francis Bacon* (London: Thames and Hudson, 2000), 78.

DISTORTING DEATH

FIGURE 7.2 Francis Bacon, Study after Velázquez's Portrait of Pope Innocent X. 1953. Des Moines Art Center, Des Moines, Iowa.
PHOTO: RICH SANDERS, DES MOINES, IOWA

captured the attention of a number of prominent art scholars, one of whom described it as 'the finest pope Bacon produced.'[53] Bacon must not have liked popes much.

---

53 Ibid., 88.

Although it is hardly surprising that Cortada found inspiration in this painting for his depiction of *Proffitt*, Bacon's *Pope* is not a comment on the death penalty. It is an intentional distortion of Diego Velázquez's *Portrait of Innocent X*[54]—hence the name of Bacon's piece. At the time he painted it, Bacon was apparently coming to terms with the death of his father, who had brutally rejected him upon learning of his homosexuality, and with several deeply destructive sexual encounters reflecting his sado-masochistic approach to sex.[55] Bacon had been brought up in the church, but had lost his faith and was reportedly furious at religion and fervent in his disbelief.[56] One can see these disparate threads in Bacon's screaming *Pope*—the cage, which appears in other works by Bacon around this time and serves as a symbol of confinement; the thinly disguised veil covering a symbol of religious authority; and, most potently, the scream, a visual representation of abject pain. One cannot help but wonder if this is the sort of image that Patricia Williams had in mind when she wrote about 'spirit murder,' the inner destruction of the person in a world where institutional and other powerful constraints perpetuate harm to the self (there, in the context of racism).[57]

Although Bacon's painting may have been about existential pain as he worked through a number of his own tortured relationships, what Cortada saw instinctively—the image of a pope seemingly being electrocuted—captures more of the harsh realities of the death penalty than is apparent at first blush. This is not to say that Bacon's pope and Cortada's inmate are comparable; one had tremendous social status, the other none at all. But the larger themes that Bacon was exploring—pain, imprisonment, isolation, and obfuscation—are larger themes of the death penalty as well. The remainder of this essay explores

---

54   Bacon's interpretation of Velázquez's piece is arguably more interesting than Velázquez's piece itself, although Velázquez's portrait is considered 'by common consent one of the world's supreme masterpieces of portraiture.' https://www.wga.hu/frames-e.html?/html/v/velazque/07/0711vela.html. For a view of Velázquez's *Portrait of Innocent X*, and commentary about its magnificence, see Ibid. For a side-by-side comparison, see 'The Truth Behind Francis Bacon's "Screaming" Popes', at https://www.phaidon.com/agenda/art/articles/2013/february/08/the-truth-behind-francis-bacons-screaming-popes/.

55   A YouTube video from October 2012 features Sotheby's Oliver Barker and Bacon historian Michael Peppiatt discussing Bacon's work on Pope Innocent x. https://www.youtube.com/watch?v=isR4eDf8VBs&list=FLboJ_orflcWABYlmV-cyMzQ (Oct. 23, 2012). For a movie about Bacon's tumultuous, destructive relationships and their impact on his art, see Love Is the Devil: Study for a Portrait of Francis Bacon (BBC Films 1998), https://www.imdb.com/title/tt0119577/awards?ref_=tt_awd.

56   Ibid.

57   Patricia L. Williams, *The Alchemy of Race and Rights: The Diary of a Law Professor* (Cambridge: Harvard University Press, 1991), 73.

these four themes, drawing parallels between both artists' works and the death penalty more broadly.

First and foremost in the thematic comparison is pain—torturous, agonizing pain. Both paintings show gaping, open-mouthed screams of pain. Both show their subjects gripping the arms of the chairs in which they sit, a visceral response to the assault besieging them.

For a comment on the death penalty—particularly by an artist who lives in Florida—the theme of pain could hardly be more relevant. Florida's electric chair, dubbed 'Ol' Sparky,' is notorious for its frequent malfunctions and infliction of torturous pain. In 1997, Florida botched the electrocution of Pedro Medina, causing a foot-high flame to shoot from his head and his entire face-mask to catch on fire.[58] Two years later, it botched the electrocution of Allen Lee Davis, who bled profusely from his nose and made the sound of muffled screams before he died.[59] Gory pictures of Davis's body were posted on the Florida Supreme Court's website and received so many hits that the court's computer system crashed.[60] In the wake of these botches, Florida's attorney general coyly claimed, 'People who wish to commit murder, they'd better not do it in the state of Florida because we may have a problem with the electric chair.'[61]

Yet even when an execution is not botched, death by electrocution is a painful, tortuous death. An excerpt from Justice Brennan's description of the electrocution process is enough to provide the gist:

> The prisoner's eyeballs sometimes pop out and rest on the cheeks. The prisoner often defecates, urinates, and vomits blood and drool. The body turns bright red as its temperature rises, and the prisoner's flesh swells and his skin stretches to the point of breaking. Sometimes the prisoner

---

58 Associated Press, 'Condemned Man's Mask Bursts Into Flames During Execution', New York Times, March 26, 1997, B9.

59 Rick Bragg, 'Florida's Messy Executions Put the Electric Chair on Trial', New York Times, Nov. 18, 1999, A14.

60 Carl S. Kaplan, 'Execution Debate is Broadened by Photos on Web', New York Times, Oct. 29, 1999, http://movies2.nytimes.com/1999/10/29/technology/29law.html. The pictures were posted as an appendage to a dissent in *Provenzano v. Moore*, 744 So. 2d 413 (Fla. 1999), a Florida Supreme Court decision that upheld the electric chair against a claim that it was 'cruel and unusual' under the Eighth Amendment. In dissent, Justice Leander J. Shaw, Jr. claimed that the pictures of Allen Lee Davis 'depict a man who—for all appearances—was brutally tortured to death by the citizens of Florida.' Ibid., 440 (Shaw, J., dissenting).

61 Ron Word, 'Flawed Execution Prompts Florida to Study Method', South Coast Today, March 26, 1997, https://www.southcoasttoday.com/apps/pbcs.dll/article?AID=/19970326/NEWS/303269969.

catches on fire, particularly if he perspires excessively. Witnesses hear a loud and sustained sound like bacon frying, and the sickly sweet smell of burning flesh permeates the chamber.[62]

Of course, this is not how death by electrocution was initially advertised. Early proponents of this execution method promised that it would bring death in 'the most humane, practical and painless manner.'[63] It only later became apparent that none of that was true.

The promotion of new and improved methods of execution as humane, painless alternatives to their existing counterparts, followed by the realization that they are nothing of the sort, would become a theme. The gas chamber, which followed the electric chair, was initially hailed as a 'swift and painless' method of execution, 'the most merciful form yet devised.'[64] It turned out to be the single most painful and inhumane execution method of modern times. Death by poisonous gas causes gasping, retching, vomiting, drooling, and violent convulsions, which morph into involuntary twitches as the dying process comes to an end.[65] And unlike the electric chair, which kills relatively quickly, executions by lethal gas are agonizingly slow, averaging eight to ten minutes or longer, and leaving little doubt about whether the condemned suffered during that time.[66]

The latest chapter in this story is lethal injection, touted as 'humane as any form of death you can find.'[67] Yet it is hard to know whether that is true because the standard three-drug protocol paralyzes inmates so they cannot speak or move, making it nearly impossible to tell whether an execution went smoothly or whether it just looked that way because the inmate was chemically entombed. A growing body of data suggests the latter. Autopsies performed

---

62 *Glass v. Louisiana*, 471 U.S. 1080, 1087–88 (1985) (Brennan, J., dissenting from denial of certiorari).

63 New York (State) Commissioners on Capital Punishment, *Report of the Commission to Investigate and Report the Most Humane and Practical Method of Carrying Into Effect Sentence of Death in Capital Cases* (Troy, N.Y.; Troy Press Company, 1888), 89.

64 L. Kay Gillespie, *Inside the Death Chamber: Exploring Executions* (New York: Pearson, 2003), 64. Indeed, the legislation adopting the gas chamber in Nevada in 1921 was called the 'Humane Death Bill.' See Hugo Adam Bedau, *The Death Penalty in America* (Oxford: Oxford University Press, 1998), 16.

65 *Gomez v. U.S. Dist. Court for Northern Dist. of California*, 503 U.S. 653, 655–56 (1992) (Stevens, J., dissenting).

66 Ibid., 655 (Stevens, J., dissenting).

67 Jonathon I. Groner, 'The Hippocratic Paradox: The Role of the Medical Profession in Capital Punishment in the United States' (2008) 35 Fordham Urban Law Journal 883, 891 (quoting a Texas prison chaplain).

on several Florida inmates who were executed by lethal injection without apparent incident revealed lungs heavy with fluids, a sure sign of slow death and prolonged struggle.[68] In the end, lethal injection may be no less painful than other execution methods; it might just be better at hiding it.

Killing is violent, and violence brings pain. This is the nature of the beast. Cortada's depiction of *Proffitt* forces us to face this reality, to see pain as an intrinsic part of the execution process. Cortada forces us to acknowledge both the person *and* the pain.

Yet pain in the death penalty context comes from more than just executions. It also comes from the conditions under which the condemned live while waiting to die, bringing us to two more of Bacon's themes: Imprisonment and isolation. In the death penalty, they go together, inescapably intertwined. Bacon's *Pope* depicts a pontiff trapped and isolated, sitting in a cage in some dark void. Cortada likewise depicts his subject alone in the dark, writing in his artist's statement, 'He sits in a vacuum, waiting for one of us to pull the switch.'[69]

Pulling the switch is one moment in time and it is the focus of Cortada's work. But the waiting, the isolation, the imprisonment—the cage—draw the mind quite vividly to another moment in time: the anguished existence of solitary confinement on death row. In virtually every death-penalty state, condemned inmates are housed in a separate unit from the mainstream prison population, where they spend at least twenty-two hours each day, sometimes twenty-three, in a windowless cell the size of a standard parking lot space.[70] They are fed through slots in doors, monitored by cameras, and spoken to through intercoms.[71] These are the standard conditions of solitary confinement on death row, and the condemned are subject to its hallmarks—extreme isolation and forced idleness—for agonizingly long periods of time. From arrival to execution, the average stay on death row is just over fifteen years.[72]

---

68   Sarah Whites-Koditschek, 'Cruel and Unusual The Question Before Federal Court in Second Execution Hearing' Arkansas Public Media, Apr. 10, 2017, https://www.arkansaspublicmedia.org/post/cruel-and-unusual-question-federal-court-second-execution-hearing.

69   Artist's Statement.

70   Craig Haney, 'Mental Health Issues in Long-Term Solitary and "Supermax" Confinement' (2003) 49 Crime & Delinquency 125, 127, 146. Death Row inmates are typically allowed one hour of exercise each day, which takes place in caged pens akin to a dog run. Ibid., 126.

71   Ibid.; American Civil Liberties Union, 'A Death Before Dying: Solitary Confinement on Death Row' (2013), 4, at https://www.aclu.org/report/death-dying-solitary-confinement-death-row.

72   U.S. Dept. of Justice, Capital Punishment, 2013—Statistical Tables 14 (2014) https://deathpenaltyinfo.org/files/pdf/cp13st.pdf (reporting average time between sentencing and execution in 2013 at 186 months, or 15.5 years).

Research has shown that such solitary confinement is not only unnecessary,[73] but also particularly bad for human health and wellbeing. Studies show that even a few days of solitary confinement will cause a shift in EEG patterns indicative of cerebral dysfunction,[74] and over time the effects are debilitating, causing a condition known as 'death row syndrome.'[75] Long-term solitary confinement causes maladies ranging from severe anxiety and hypersensitivity to stimuli, to perceptual distortions and hallucinations, to paranoia and confused thought processes, to suicidal ideations and behavior.[76] The damage is similar to that suffered by victims of severe sensory deprivation torture techniques,[77] and many condemned inmates find it too much to bear. Some go insane. Some commit suicide. And some drop their appeals and ask to be executed. Just over ten percent of those executed are so-called 'volunteers.'[78]

Cortada envisioned a pope being electrocuted in the painting that inspired him, but Bacon's *Pope* is every bit as evocative of the agonizing existence that precedes that moment in time. The utter isolation. The literal application of the cage metaphor. And the darkness that both surrounds death row inmates and consumes them. These are all unmistakable aspects of solitary confinement on death row. Cortada looked to Bacon's *Pope* in creating his depiction of *Proffitt*, but the source of his inspiration had even more to offer as a comment on the death penalty than Cortada's moment in time—electrocution—could show.

The same is true of the final theme that Bacon's *Pope* explored—the covering that comes with the veil. We can see Bacon's screaming pope, but we cannot see him clearly; he is obscured, covered by a thin veil. So it is with the death penalty as well.

One way that this is true has already been discussed: our formulaic approach to deciding death obscures the profoundly moral choice of the life-or-death decision. Guided-discretion statutes provide a covering of sorts—a legal pretense for a moral choice. They mask the decision-making process so we cannot see it clearly; like the veil in Bacon's *Pope*, they provide a degree of detachment from what is taking place. The event is happening inside the veil; we are on the outside.

---

73 Marah Stith McLeod, 'Does the Death Penalty Require Death Row? The Harm of Legislative Silence' (2017) 77 Ohio State Law Journal 525.
74 Stuart Grassian, 'Psychiatric Effects of Solitary Confinement' (2006) 22 Washington University Journal of Law & Policy 331.
75 Haney, 'Mental Health', 134–37.
76 Ibid., 125, 130–31, 137.
77 Ibid., 132.
78 Ibid.; American Civil Liberties Union, 'A Death Before Dying', 8.

So viewed, one might surmise why Cortada did not incorporate the veil into his own work of art in some way. Cortada's project is all about cutting through this thinly veiled reality. It is about pulling back the curtain and forcing us to face what we see.

A second way that the veil analogy applies to the death penalty is in the state's covering and obfuscation of the execution process. Lethal injection is the most explicit example of this phenomenon. It is designed to make it look as if the state were not even killing; condemned inmates simply go to sleep and fade away. With lethal injection, the veil is not just metaphorical. States literally use a veil—a chemical veil in the form of a paralytic—to conceal from public view whatever the condemned inmate experiences. As one attorney lamented, the paralytic that states use 'hides the real fact of what [i]s going on behind the artificial chemical curtain.'[79] Indeed, this is its very point.

The veil also is reflected in the decision by executing states in the mid-nineteenth century to move executions from the public to private sphere. A sense of repugnance at the violence of executions led to the move,[80] and this too was a conscious, concerted effort to hide reality. Those executions were still violent; they were just no longer in public view.

Executions are the ultimate expression of the death penalty; they are where the rubber meets the road. They are also where the state works hardest to hide what is actually happening. The various veils that states use to hide the violence of executions allow us to think about the death penalty abstractly, in a way that does not entail thinking about what it actually looks like to take a life, and that in turn allows us to think a whole lot less about the death penalty overall. To borrow again from Cortada's articulation of the point, these veils are yet another way that the state 'de-emotionalizes the death penalty so that it can be carried out.' What is happening is on the inside of the veil; we are on the outside.

Thus far, the discussion of the veil analogy has focused on the beginning of the death penalty process (death sentencing) and the end (executions). But the entire system of constitutional regulation of capital punishment serves as a veil of sorts, giving the false impression that death cases are carefully circumscribed and diligently supervised when in fact they are not.[81] As

---

79   http://www.wkyc.com/video/news/allen-bohnert-on-ronald-phillips-execution/95-2671712 (statement of capital defender Allen Bohnert on the execution of Ronald Phillips).
80   Stuart Banner, *The Death Penalty: An American History* (Cambridge: Harvard University Press, 2003), 144–168 (detailing the privatization of executions in the mid-nineteenth century and the forces driving it).
81   *Callins v. Collins*, 510 U.S. 1141, 1145 (1994) (Blackmun, J., dissenting from denial of certiorari) ('Having virtually conceded that both fairness and rationality cannot be achieved

Carol and Jordan Steiker have observed, the Supreme Court's regulatory project is largely a façade, with lots of cases but little substantive protection, and that façade obscures a much more uncomfortable reality.[82] From beginning to end and everywhere in between, the veil is a metaphor custom-made for state-sanctioned death.

Having noted how the themes in Bacon's *Pope* illuminate various points about the death penalty, the discussion would be remiss if it ended without a comment on the nature of Bacon's project itself. Cortada was inspired by Bacon's painting, but that painting was itself a deliberate distortion of another work of art. Bacon's *Pope* is a work in gross distortion. It is a comment about an idealized conception of one thing that is in actuality something else—something dark, ugly, disturbing, and unmistakably anguished.

Welcome to the world of the death penalty. Our idealized conception of the death penalty is sanitized and pristine. In this idealized world, the death penalty is reserved for the worst of the worst offenders and imposed only after the benefit of a panoply of protections designed to ensure that it is fairly administered and accurately imposed. In the real world, the death penalty is none of these things. It is imposed arbitrarily, capriciously, and in a racially discriminatory manner.[83] It is imposed upon those who have grossly incompetent lawyers.[84] And it is imposed upon the innocent. To date, there have been 170 exonerations from death row.[85]

---

in the administration of the death penalty, the Court has chosen to deregulate the entire enterprise, replacing, it would seem, substantive constitutional requirements with mere esthetics....').

82   Carol S. Steiker and Jordan M. Steiker, 'Sober Second Thoughts: Reflections on Two Decades of Constitutional Regulation of Capital Punishment' (1995) 109 Harvard Law Review 355, 433–437.

83   United States General Accounting Office, 'Death Penalty Sentencing', 5 ('In 82 percent of the studies, race of victim was found to influence the likelihood of being charged with capital murder or receiving the death penalty, i.e., those who murdered whites were found to be more likely to be sentenced to death than those who murdered blacks. This finding was remarkably consistent across data sets, states, data collection methods, and analytic techniques.').

84   For the most famous account, see Stephen B. Bright, 'Counsel for the Poor: The Death Sentence Not for the Worst Crime but for the Worst Lawyer' (1994) 103 Yale Law Journal 1837. For a more recent version, see Robert J. Smith, 'The Worst Lawyers', Slate, November 4, 2015, https://slate.com/news-and-politics/2015/11/the-worst-defense-lawyers-for-death-penalty-cases-in-arizona-florida-louisiana.html.

85   Innocence and the Death Penalty', Death Penalty Information Center (as of July 15, 2020), at https://deathpenaltyinfo.org/innocence-and-death-penalty. I credit Allison Tait for noting the irony that the object of Bacon's distortion is a portrait of Pope Innocent.

Cortada's depiction of *Proffitt v. Florida* could not possibly capture all of these distortions. But what it does capture is perhaps most important distortion of all—the humanity that is lost when we let legal formulas dictate the decision between life and death. That is the decision that most matters; it is the decision that triggers the machinery of death. Cortada forces us to see this decision more clearly. For that we can all be grateful, for as he poignantly notes in the closing line of his artist's statement, 'in the end, it's all of us who have a firm grip on that switch.'

Recommended Reading

Bentele, Ursula and William J. Bowers. 'How Jurors Decide on Death: Guilt is Overwhelming; Aggravation Requires Death; and Mitigation Is No Excuse.' *Brooklyn Law Review* 66 (2001): 1011–1041.

Bowers, William J. 'The Capital Jury Project: Rationale, Design, and Preview of Early Findings.' *Indiana Law Journal* 70 (1995): 1043–1094.

Eisenberg, Theodore, Stephen P. Garvey, and Martin T. Wells. 'Jury Responsibility in Capital Sentencing: An Empirical Study.' *Buffalo Law Review* 44 (1996): 339–360.

Geimer, William S. and Jonathan Amsterdam. 'Why Jurors Vote Life or Death: Operative Factors in Ten Florida Death Penalty Cases.' *American Journal of Criminal Law* 15 (1988): 1–25.

Haney, Craig, Lorelei Sontag, and Sally Costanzo. 'Deciding to Take a Life: Capital Juries, Sentencing Instructions, and the Jurisprudence of Death.' *Journal of Social Issues* 50 (1994): 149–166.

Haney, Craig. 'Mental Health Issues in Long-Term Solitary and "Supermax" Confinement.' *Crime & Delinquency* 49 (2003): 125–2.

Hidalgo v. Arizona, 138 S. Ct. 1054 (2018) (statement accompanying denial of certiorari).

Hoffman, Joseph L. 'Where's the Buck?—Juror Misperception of Sentencing Responsibility in Death Penalty Cases.' *Indiana Law Journal* 70 (1995): 1137–2.

Lain, Corinna Barrett. '*Furman* Fundamentals.' Washington Law Review 82 (2007): 1–74.

Luginbuhl, James and Julie Howe. 'Discretion in Capital Sentencing Instructions: Guided or Misguided?' *Indiana Law Journal* 70 (1995): 1161–1174.

Steiker, Carol S. and Jordan M. Steiker. 'Sober Second Thoughts: Reflections on Two Decades of Constitutional Regulation of Capital Punishment.' *Harvard Law Review* 109 (1995): 355–438.

Sylvester, David. *Looking Back at Francis Bacon*. London: Thames & Hudson, 2000.

Weisberg, Robert. 'Deregulating Death.' *The Supreme Court Review* 1983 (1983): 305–395.

Palmore v. Sidoti, 466 U.S. 429 (1984)

Xavier Cortada

In the backdrop we see eyes. Blue eyes in a sea of Caucasian skin. You can almost hear them gossiping. Talking about her, the traitor. Protecting the man whom she divorced.

Eyes, can't believe what they are seeing, that she has hooked up with Palmore, a 'black man.'

Eyes, bewildered that she could marry someone of another race.

Eyes, horrified that she's taken her daughter—one of their own—to live with him.

Eyes, choosing sides in an otherwise resolved custody battle, trying to tip the balance.

At the trial level, they succeeded. Their profound racism was given weight by the court, agreeing that the child would be more vulnerable to social stigmatization in a racially mixed household. The mother lost custody of her child.

She appealed. A unanimous Supreme Court saw things her way—*Palmore v. Sidoti*, 466 U.S. 429 (1984). The private prejudices of others may be something the state can't control, but it certainly shouldn't give them effect. Removing the kid from her Mom was wrong.

Discrimination is always wrong. Pure and simple.

Let's never lose sight of that.

FIGURE 8.1   Xavier Cortada, *Palmore v. Sidoti*, 466 U.S. 429 (1984), 48" × 36", acrylic on canvas, 2004
PHOTO: ZENAIDA PIRRI, MIAMI, FLORIDA

CHAPTER 8

Palmore v. Sidoti
The Troubling Effects of 'Private Biases'

Linda C. McClain

Eyes are a central motif in Xavier Cortada's artistic portrayal of *Palmore v. Sidoti*, and appropriately so. The disembodied and disapproving eyes, in (as Cortada puts it) 'a sea of Caucasian skin,' surround the three figures forming a family tableau at the center of the painting: Linda Sidoti Palmore, a white mother holding onto her young daughter, Melanie, also white, who in turn holds the hand of Clarence Palmore, a Black man, who became Linda's new husband and, for a brief period, Melanie's stepfather. This interracial family tableau so alarmed Linda's ex-husband (and Melanie's father), Anthony Sidoti, that in 1982 he succeeded in persuading a state court judge in Tampa, Florida, where they all resided, to transfer custody of five-year-old Melanie from her mother to him. Two years later, a unanimous Supreme Court of the United States reversed that ruling, agreeing with Linda Sidoti Palmore that it violated the Constitution to remove her child from her because of her interracial marriage. It was unusual for a custody determination, typically the province of state courts, to reach the Supreme Court. But, as Chief Justice Burger explained in his opinion for the Court, the state court's reliance on 'what it regarded as the damaging impact on [Melanie] from remaining in a racially mixed household' as a reason for transferring custody away from the mother raised 'important federal concerns arising from the Constitution's commitment to eradicating discrimination based on race.'[1]

Palmore is famous for two very different views about whether the effects of racial prejudice—or 'private bias'—are a proper basis for judicial decision-making about custody: one expressed by Hillsborough County Circuit Court Judge Morison Buck in ruling for Anthony Sidoti, the other by the Supreme Court in ruling for Linda Sidoti Palmore. Those two views reflect different reactions to those many eyes looming in the background of Cortada's family portrait. The Supreme Court's rejection of Judge Buck's view set an important

---

1 *Palmore v. Sidoti*, 466 U.S. 429, 432 (1984). This chapter capitalizes 'Black' when referring to people of African ancestry unless it is quoting historical sources that use 'black.' Nancy Coleman, 'Times Insider: Why We're Capitalizing Black', New York Times, July 5, 2020, A2.

precedent about the role of race in family law cases, but it has had more far-reaching effects in understanding the limits to public endorsement of private prejudice and discrimination.

The reported case, however, tells only part of the story of Linda Sidoti Palmore's effort to regain custody of Melanie. Although, as Cortada observes in the label for his painting, 'a unanimous Supreme Court saw things her way,' she never regained custody of her daughter. Her case vindicated an important principle, but she went without a remedy. Indeed, she, Clarence, and Melanie formed a family tableau only briefly. It was not just those judgmental eyes—those of her ex-husband and state court judges—that doomed this interracial family almost from the start. It was also the blind eye the Supreme Court turned to Linda's requests for emergency relief to have her daughter returned to her while she pursued her constitutional claim before the Court and then after she prevailed. Similarly, state court judges in Florida and Texas failed to heed her pleas and instead aided the legal maneuverings by her ex-husband, determined to keep custody of Melanie. It is a truism in property law that 'possession is nine tenths of the law.' While a child is not a parent's 'possession,' it is a similar truism in custody law that continuity and stability are paramount in determining the 'best interests of the child.' Through his initial legal action dispossessing Linda of custody of her child and through his strategic use of the state court system, Anthony kept Melanie with him even after the nation's highest court ruled that he had obtained custody on an unconstitutional ground.

This tragic dimension of *Palmore*—a wrong unremedied despite a landmark Supreme Court ruling—also could be captured with imagery of eyes. Cortada portrays Linda holding and gazing lovingly at Melanie as Melanie holds her hand and the hand of Clarence, who stands next to Linda. But the more typical portrait of this family during Linda's legal ordeal is of she and Clarence seated together, without Melanie; Linda's eyes are focused on a framed photograph of her daughter. Melanie's absence from Linda's life was nearly constant during those years, with occasional, too brief, chances for Linda to see or even to speak to her daughter. No wonder Florida newspaper headlines of that time referred to the 'cost' or 'price' paid by Linda for her marriage to Clarence. As she put it in one story, after her initial loss of custody: 'They are denying me the right to choose to marry who I want to. I'm being persecuted by society because I do something out of the ordinary.'[2]

---

2 Frank DeLoache, 'Interracial Couple Says Race Cost Them Custody of Daughter', Tampa Bay Times, Feb. 7, 1983.

Understandably, Linda Sidoti Palmore believed she had a right to marry without punishment. More than a decade earlier, the Supreme Court in *Loving v. Virginia* declared invalid Virginia's antimiscegenation law—and that of sixteen other states, including Florida—because it unconstitutionally used a racial classification to determine who may and may not marry.[3] *Palmore* is a significant companion to *Loving*, taking up some of *Loving*'s unfinished business. But unlike Mildred Jeter and Richard Loving, whose love story and legal victory in the aptly named case have become iconic cultural references, *Palmore* did not produce a similar happy ending for Linda and her family.

This essay is not, however, unrelentingly bleak. The social and legal landscape today is different for interracial—or multiracial—families. Public opinion is more favorable toward interracial marriage than it was in the 1980s, when these events unfolded. The share of intermarried couples has grown steadily since 1980, when just three percent of married people had a spouse of a different race or ethnicity. One in six new marriages in the United States now crosses racial or ethnic lines, although the white-Black line is crossed less frequently than other lines, such as white-Asian, white-Latinx, or other combinations.[4] Due to cases like *Loving* and *Palmore*, the legal landscape is more protective of such family ties.

This chapter proceeds in four parts. The first part discusses the state court proceedings and how a Hillsborough County court gave credence to private prejudice, as depicted in Cortada's portrait of hovering eyes. The second part discusses the Supreme Court's reversal of the state court and the limits it set on public officials, such as judges, 'giving effect' to private prejudice. The third part describes how the Court turned a blind eye—or deaf ear—to Linda's requests to restore custody to her, contributing to the stark disparity between her legal victory and her continuing deprivation of her daughter during years of state court proceedings. These first three parts draw on contemporary media coverage of the case. The fourth part moves forward in time to consider the significance of *Palmore* in the present day. *Palmore* continues to inform custody law, when judges must determine the best interests of the child. Judges, however, read *Palmore* differently, with some interpreting it to require 'colorblindness' (or not taking race into account in any way) and others interpreting it to allow some 'race-conscious' decision-making.

---

3 *Loving v. Virginia*, 388 U.S. 1 (1967).
4 Gretchen Livingston and Anna Brown, 'Intermarriage in the U.S. 50 Years After *Loving v. Virginia*', Pew Research Center, May 18, 2017.

1   The Florida Court: The Inevitability of 'Social Stigmatization' Due to an Interracial Household

When Linda and Anthony Sidoti, both white, divorced in May 1980, the court awarded Linda custody of their three-year-old daughter, Melanie.[5] Awarding custody to the mother with visitation by the father was fairly typical for the time. (Years later, as states became less hostile to joint custody, Florida would adopt a legal presumption in favor of shared parental responsibility, unless it would be detrimental to a child.) At some point after her divorce, Linda met Clarence Palmore, a truck driver, at Tampa College, a business school where she worked as a secretary and took classes. They had a 'casual relationship' for nearly a year before he moved in with her.[6] In September 1981, her ex-husband filed a petition to modify custody because of 'changed conditions' since the original custody order: '[t]he change was that the child's mother was then cohabiting with a Negro, Clarence Palmore, Jr., whom she married two months later.'[7] He also alleged that Linda had not properly cared for Melanie, asserting that Melanie 'had head lice on two occasions and was sent to school in mildewed clothing.'[8] But one news account quotes Linda, by then Linda Sidoti Palmore, as stating that, 'We were divorced more than a year and there had never been a word about custody. There was no indication Tony wanted any responsibility—until he saw a black man in my kitchen hanging curtains.'[9] After a hearing before Judge Buck and an investigation by a social worker, the judge ordered a transfer of custody to the father. He made no findings about the father's allegations of inadequate care. To the contrary, he made a finding that 'there is no issue as to either party's devotion to the child, adequacy of housing, or respectability of the new spouse of either parent.' (By the time he filed his petition, Anthony had remarried, to a white woman.) Instead, the crux of Judge Buck's ruling was Linda's interracial marriage and its, in his view, inevitable harmful effect on Melanie. In the following passage, Judge Buck offered

---

5   *Palmore,* 466 U.S. at 430. The legal facts in this section are drawn from the Supreme Court's statement of the case, unless otherwise indicated. I draw the portrait of the parties from various newspaper and magazine stories about the state court and then Supreme Court phases of the case.
6   'Woman Takes Claim for Child to Nation's Highest Court', Galveston Daily News, Feb. 26, 1984, 32.
7   *Palmore,* 466 U.S. at 430.
8   The details of these allegations are mentioned in the later state court case, *Palmore v. Sidoti,* 472 So. 2d 843, 844 (Fla. Dist. Ct. App. 1985). Many news reports mention these allegations, as well.
9   'Woman Takes Claim for Child to Nation's Highest Court', 32.

his rationale for concluding that it was in the best interests of Melanie to award custody to her father:

> The father's evident resentment of the mother's choice of a black partner is not sufficient to wrest custody from the mother. It is of some significance, however, that the mother did see fit to bring a man into her home and carry on a sexual relationship with him without being married to him. Such action tended to place gratification of her own desires ahead of her concern for the child's future welfare.[10]

So far, the court's reasoning might seem to rest solely on the mother's perceived immorality in cohabiting. At that time, in a number of states, a divorced parent's nonmarital sexual conduct (particularly that of a mother) could disadvantage them in any custody proceeding. (Until 2016, nonmarital cohabitation was a crime in Florida.) But by the time the court issued its ruling, Linda had married Clarence, whom the court described as a 'respectable' spouse. Instead, in a key passage quoted frequently in news coverage of the case, Judge Buck made clear that it was the racial composition of the household and its perception by the outside world that was at the core of his ruling:

> This Court feels that despite the strides that have been made in bettering relations between the races in this country, it is inevitable that Melanie will, if allowed to remain in her present situation and attains school age and thus more vulnerable to peer pressures, suffer from the social stigmatization that is sure to come.[11]

Melanie, in other words, will be vulnerable to the disapproving eyes of her peers. Why would she suffer such social stigma? As if Judge Buck's race-based reasoning were not clear enough from the above passage, he also referred to the court counselor's recommendation that custody be changed to the father because 'the wife [Linda] has chosen for herself and for her child, a life-style unacceptable to the father and to society. ... The child ... is, or at school age will be, subject to environmental pressures not of choice.'[12]

Society generates social stigma. An interracial marriage in Tampa, Florida, in the early 1980s was, on this view, an 'unacceptable' lifestyle. The Palmore marriage was legal in Florida following *Loving*'s rejection of anti-miscegenation

---

10   *Palmore,* 466 U.S. at 431 (quoting Appendix to Petition for Certiorari, 26–27).
11   Ibid.
12   Ibid., 430–31.

laws; that did not mean it was socially acceptable. In 1982, Ernest Porterfield, author of one of the first ethnographic studies of Black-white marriages, observed that 'no other [intermarriage] mixture touches off such widespread condemnation as black-white race mixing.'[13] News coverage of the time reveals that even as the number of such 'mixed' couples was on the rise, problems of prejudice and lack of acceptance–particularly by the white community–had not decreased.[14]

Judge Buck was remarkably candid in his race-conscious reasoning. In the years between *Loving* and *Palmore*, a number of white women lost custody after entering into interracial romances, although courts often tried to mask the role played by the racial element.[15] In one case from Oklahoma, where a white mother lost custody after she started an interracial sexual relationship with an African-American man, the trial and appellate courts insisted that the issue was the immorality of cohabitation, rather than the race of her partner: whether the mother's 'swain' was 'white, yellow, red, brown or black,' she had allowed her child to live in a 'home environment society currently considers immoral'[16] When a white mother prevailed in court despite an interracial relationship, the opinions suggested 'continuing disapprobation of interracial romance,' even a decade or more after *Loving*. A Louisiana trial court granted custody to the white mother, even as it spoke of the 'scandal and gossip in the community' caused by her interracial, adulterous relationship, adding that such conduct was 'particularly scandalous and offensive to the sensibilities of the local community in that her lover was of another race.'[17] The reviewing court reversed, stressing the mother's 'open and public adultery.' Although the reviewing court did not mention the interracial dimension of this conduct, it seems likely the court had that in mind in referring to the mother's 'disregard of the embarrassment and injuries which might be sustained by the children.'[18]

By comparison, Judge Buck made his race-conscious reasoning clear. Following the ruling, Linda observed in *Florida Today*: 'The first time I was before

---

13 Ernest Porterfield, 'Black-White American Intermarriage in the United States' (1982) 1 Marriage & Family Review 17, 17. His study is Ernest Porterfield, *Black and White Mixed Marriages: An Ethnographic Study of Black-White Families* (Chicago: Nelson-Hall, 1978).
14 Ricki Furman, 'Mixed Couples on Increase, and So Are Their Problems', Chicago Tribune, Oct. 12, 1980.
15 Melissa Murray, 'The Regulation of Sex and Sexuality' (2017) 86 Fordham Law Review 2671 (discussing cases).
16 Ibid., 2687 (quoting *Brim v. Brim*, 532 P.2d 1403 (Okla. Civ. App. 1975)).
17 Ibid. (quoting *Schexnayder v. Schexnayder*, 364 So. 1318, 1318 n.1 (La. Ct. App. 1978), *rev'd*, 371 So. 2d 769 (La. 1979)).
18 Ibid., 2688 (quoting *Schexnayder v. Schexnayder*, 371 S. 2d 769, 772–773 (La. 1979)).

Judge Buck he thought I was a terrific lady. Then his whole opinion changed and I was not good. It was because I loved a black man. I hadn't changed. Neither had my love for my daughter.'[19] In another story, she commented: 'They treat my husband like he was nonhuman. I realize now just a little bit of what the black race has gone through.'[20] Linda's association across racial lines and assumptions about the impact it would have on Melanie triggered Anthony's custody petition and Judge Buck's ruling.

The Florida appellate court affirmed Judge Buck's ruling without a written opinion. Facing a deadline of February 8, 1983, when she was to surrender Melanie to her father's custody, Linda made an emergency appeal to Justice Powell (the Justice assigned to hear such appeals from Florida), asking the Court to allow her to keep Melanie while she pursued her appeal to the Supreme Court.[21] Her attorney argued that she sought to avoid 'destroying the stability essential to the well being of a child'; the child would suffer by 'being bounced back and forth between parents' should Linda prevail before the Supreme Court.[22] But Justice Powell denied her request—a denial that would prove consequential.[23] Although Linda quickly reapplied for a stay to Justice Marshall (as the Court's rules permitted) and her second request 'piqued greater interest' on the Court, by the time the Court considered and voted to deny her request, Melanie was back in Anthony's custody.[24] This made her request, as lawyers say, 'moot.'[25]

The Court granted certiorari in October 1983. Anthony Sidoti had urged the Court not to take the case, arguing that 'in acknowledging the realities of contemporary American life'–evidently the 'social stigmatization' to which Judge Buck referred–'the state of Florida does not necessarily violate the constitutional strictures against racial discrimination.'[26] A *New York Times* story observed that the case was 'an unusual one' for the Court to hear, since it had been 'reluctant' to be involved in 'the large number of domestic disputes that arrive steadily from the state courts'; a few years earlier, the Justices refused to review a case of a mother who lost custody because she lived with a man to

---

19 Pat Leisner, 'Racial Custody Fight Reaches High Court', Florida Today, Feb. 19, 1984.
20 Frank DeLoache, 'Interracial Couple Says Race Cost Them Custody of Daughter', Tampa Bay Times, Feb. 7, 1983.
21 Richard Bockman, 'High Court Rejects Woman's Plea in Custody Fight', Tampa Tribune, Feb. 3, 1983.
22 Ibid.; 'Custody Plea Goes to Justice', Florida Today, Feb. 2, 1983, 4B.
23 Bockman, 'High Court Rejects Woman's Plea'.
24 Katie Eyer, 'Constitutional Colorblindness and the Family' (2014) 162 University of Pennsylvania Law Review 537, 559–62.
25 Ibid., 561.
26 'Justices to Review Use of Race in a Custody Case', New York Times, Oct. 18, 1983, A18.

whom she was not married.²⁷ Linda Palmore Sidoti's attorney, Robert Shapiro, argued that the Court should take the case to clarify that it was unconstitutional to rely on a parent's subsequent interracial marriage as a basis for ordering a change of custody. 'No modern decision of this court has sustained a racial classification which burdens or stigmatizes black citizens upon the basis of race'; yet, he argued, Judge Buck's 'decision ... exacts a terrible price from petitioner because her new husband is black.'²⁸ Linda was already paying that 'price,' because Melanie was in the custody of her father, who was living in Mulberry, Florida and would soon move with Melanie to Texas.

2   The U.S. Supreme Court: The Law Cannot Give Effect to 'Private Biases,' Even if It Can't Reach Them

The Supreme Court phase of Linda Sidoti Palmore's custody battle generated considerable interest—many eyes were on the case. Media reports about the case frequently quoted Judge Buck's statement about Melanie's inevitable 'social stigmatization' despite 'strides' in bettering race relations. Columnist William Raspberry pondered the Florida judge's reasoning, asking whether the judge would toss a coin if Melanie's father married a Black woman or if a Chinese wife or stepmother would bring less 'stigmatization' than a Black one. In the alternative, if the father married a 'certifiably white woman,' what stigmatizing trait or combination of traits–such as being a 'certifiable drug addict, bigot, gossip, atheist, exhibitionist, loudmouth ... [or] alcoholic'–would be 'sufficient to tip the scales of custody in favor of a mixed-race couple?'²⁹

Several leading civil rights organizations filed *amicus curiae* briefs on Linda's behalf, including the American Civil Liberties Union Foundation, the NAACP Legal Defense and Education Fund, and the National Organization for Women Legal Defense and Education Fund. So, too, did the United States, in a brief filed by the Reagan Department of Justice ('DOJ'). These briefs expressed sharp opposition to Judge Buck's view about how to respond to the problem of persisting racial prejudice and the constitutional limits on capitulating to such disapproval.

---

27   Ibid.
28   Pat Leisner, 'Racial Custody Fight Reaches High Court', Florida Today, Feb. 19, 1984; DeLoache, 'Interracial Couple'.
29   William Raspberry, 'Plot Too Mixed Even for Shakespeare', Austin-American Statesman, Oct. 21, 1983, 24.

The DOJ brief, for example, granted that 'racial prejudice still exists in our society and that children subjected to such prejudice may be adversely affected.' But 'this Court has made it clear in a variety of contexts that bowing to popular prejudice, whether to protect the potential victims of such prejudice or to avoid racial unrest generally, cannot constitute a sufficient justification for departing from the constitutional command of equal protection.'[30] The brief cited cases in which the Court rejected claims that maintaining racially segregated facilities or stalling on desegregation of public spaces was necessary to 'prevent interracial disturbances, violence, riots, and community confusion and turmoil.'[31]

While Florida law appropriately uses 'best interests of the child' as the lodestar for custody matters, the DOJ brief added, other states, using this same standard, had made clear that racial considerations should be irrelevant to determining best interests. What of the disapproving eyes of society? In the words of the Iowa Supreme Court in a different case: 'community prejudice, even when shown to exist, cannot be permitted to control the makeup of families.'[32]

Some briefs turned to the rhetoric of bigotry to describe the societal disapproval that may not shape custody decisions. The American Civil Liberties Union reminded the Court of its numerous civil rights-era cases in which it had 'refused to hold constitutional values hostage to racial bigotry in any form' or be 'pressured into race conscious decisions by the reprehensible actions of a small minority of bigots.'[33] A noteworthy brief filed by Leigh Earls, a white child raised in an interracial home, spoke of the positive effects from her experience being raised by her white mother and Black stepfather. She expressed her concern that if courts were allowed 'to presume that an interracial home is detrimental to the interests of a white child, she could [have been] taken from her home.'[34] Earls's brief, joined by several civil rights and children's rights

---

30   Brief for the United States as Amicus Curiae Supporting Petitioner, *Palmore v. Sidoti*, 466 U.S. 429 (1984), No. 82–1734, 1983 U.S. S. Ct. Briefs LEXIS 1179, *15.

31   Ibid., *16 (citing *Watson v. City of Memphis*, 373 U.S. 526, 535 (1963)).

32   *Ibid.*, *17 (citing *Commonwealth ex rel. Myers v. Myers*, 360 A.2d 587, 591 (Pa. 1976), and *In re Marriage of Kramer*, 297 N.W.2d 359, 361 (Iowa 1980)).

33   Brief Amici Curiae of the American Civil Liberties Union Foundation, the American Jewish Committee, and the National Association for the Advancement of Colored People in Support of Petitioner, *Palmore v. Sidoti*, 466 U.S. 429 (1984), No. 82–1734, *19-*20 (citing *Cooper v. Aaron*, 358 U.S. 1 (1958) (responding to Little Rock school board's attempt to postpone integration)).

34   Brief *Amici Curiae* of Leigh Earls, The Washington Lawyers' Committee for Civil Rights Under Law, the Children's Defense Fund, the Anti-Defamation League of B'Nai Brith and the American Jewish Congress in Support of Petitioner, *Palmore v. Sidoti*, 466 U.S. 429 (1984), No. 82–1734, 2.

organizations, discussed family law cases rejecting Judge Buck's reliance on the assumed prejudice and stigma Melanie would encounter: '"a court must never *yield* to prejudice because it cannot *prevent* prejudice." '[35] Earls cited a California case from 1968 for the proposition that "[w]hile the Constitution cannot prevent bigotry, it can prevent an individual from involving the State, through its Courts, in such bigotry."[36] The Supreme Court's eventual opinion would mirror this declaration, although substituting 'private bias' and 'prejudice' for 'bigotry.'

At oral argument, Shapiro similarly argued that the Court should not bow to 'racial hatred and prejudice', or give the 'racial bias of [the] few the force of law'—as Judge Buck had done. Shapiro also challenged Judge Buck's premise that 'social stigmatization' was inevitable, arguing that 'there is not one scintilla of evidence, nor is there a finding of fact that there is any adverse effect as a result of the interracial marriage.'[37] Shapiro argued that Linda, like the couple in *Loving*, was 'being punished for having exercised her right to marry a person, without regard to race.' It made no difference that the interracial marriage in *Loving* triggered the 'penalty of imprisonment,' while for Linda 'the interracial marriage itself triggered the forfeiture of the child, with no facts to justify the penalty.'[38]

The Justices asked Shapiro far fewer questions than they asked Anthony's attorney, but one issue on the minds of some Justices concerned adoption: Could a state 'consider the biological characteristics of the adoptive parents in an effort to place the child in a family with similar characteristics of the baby or child being placed?' Shapiro conceded that adoption was a different case than custody, which involves a biological parent, and that, provided no 'racial slur' was involved in doing so, the state 'may take race into consideration.'[39]

By comparison, the Justices peppered Anthony's attorney, John Hawtrey, with questions; news reports described the questions as 'tough' and even 'unusually harsh.'[40] Hawtrey faced the formidable task of arguing that Judge Buck's ruling did not rest on an impermissible racial classification—or at least not solely on that basis. He attempted to shift the focus from Linda's interracial

---

35 Ibid., 12 (citing *In re Custody of Temos*, 450 A.2d 111, 120 (Pa. 1982)) (emphasis in original).
36 Ibid. (citing *DeLander v. DeLander*, 37 U.S.L.W. 2139 (Calif. Super. Ct. 1968)).
37 Transcript of Oral Argument, *Palmore v. Sidoti*, 466 U.S. 429 (1984), No. 82–1734, 7.
38 Ibid., 10.
39 Ibid., 8. The papers of the justices indicate some were concerned about a ruling that would prohibit the practice of considering race in adoption placements. Eyer, 'Constitutional Colorblindness', 572–79.
40 Paul Anderson, 'High Court Hears Case on Interracial Custody', Austin-American Statesman, Feb. 23, 1984, D21.

marriage to the impact that it had on her relationship with her daughter. In response to questions about whether there were 'nonracial grounds' for leaving custody with the father, he attempted to interpret Judge Buck's words as referring to the judge's 'primary feeling' that 'the mother couldn't cope with the new relationship' with Clarence, in terms of her 'incapability' of handling the impact of that relationship on Melanie and her 'inability to relate to her child.' But he conceded that the supposed inability to relate was connected to a 'racial matter'—the effects of an interracial marriage.[41] Asked by Justice Marshall to put a number between one and ten on the importance of race 'in this case,' Hawtrey said five, but insisted that the state's concern was with the impact the parent's new marriage had on the quality or quantity of the parent-child relationship. Hawtrey made weak attempts to distinguish the criminal penalties in *Loving*, leading one Justice to ask if he were suggesting that taking a mother's child away from her was not akin to a penalty. He also seemed to argue that if Judge Buck had made a racially based decision, it could be approved because of present societal attitudes about interracial marriages.[42]

Press coverage of the oral argument focused on the Justices' skepticism about Hawtrey's arguments. Stories noted both that Linda and her husband, as well as 'black community leaders in Tampa,' viewed Judge Buck's decision as racist and that Anthony complained that news coverage of the case 'unfairly branded him a racist.'[43] One story quoted Anthony saying 'I think interracial marriage has a great effect on a child and I think the judge should be able to consider that to do his job ... (but) my own feelings on interracial marriage have nothing to do with this case.'[44]

Meanwhile, Melanie continued to live with her father in Texas. Starkly contrasting photographs of the parties appeared in the press. In one, Anthony smiles and relaxes on a sofa, eyes looking off to the side, while Melanie sits in front of him, looking straight at the camera with her hand propped under her chin. In a photo of the Palmores in their Florida home, as the *Jet* magazine caption aptly described the scene: 'Linda and Clarence Palmore view portrait of daughter Melanie.'[45] Their family portrait remained one of painful absence rather than presence.

---

41   Transcript of Oral Argument, 18–22.
42   *Id.* at 22–29.
43   Paul Anderson, 'High Court', 49; Al Christopher, 'Supreme Court Told that Racism "Tainted" Child Custody Ruling', Tampa Tribune, Feb. 23, 1984, 112.
44   'Woman Takes Claim for Child to Nation's Highest Court', Galveston Daily News, Feb. 26, 1984.
45   Anderson, 'High Court', 49; 'Mr. & Mrs. -- High Court Hears Florida Child Custody Battle', Jet, Mar. 12, 1984.

The Court announced its decision in *Palmore* on April 25, 1984. Chief Justice Burger, writing for a unanimous Court, reversed the Florida appellate court's affirmance of Judge Buck's custody order. Echoing the briefs of Linda and her amici, the Court rejected Judge Buck's view of the effect that racial prejudice should have on custody decisions. The Court had 'little difficulty' concluding that 'the reality of private biases and the possible injury they might inflict' are not 'permissible considerations for removal of an infant child from the custody of its natural mother.' The Court cited its own precedent rejecting the appeal to 'acknowledged racial prejudice' to justify racial classifications. For example, in *Buchanan v. Warley*, the Court declared invalid a Kentucky law forbidding 'colored people' from buying homes in white neighborhoods (and vice versa) that had been justified as 'promot[ing] the public peace by preventing race conflicts.' Burger wrote: 'Whatever problems racially mixed households may pose for children in 1984 can no more support a denial of constitutional rights than could the stresses that residential integration was thought to entail in 1917.'[46]

Notably, the Chief Justice did not draw on *Loving* for the idea that Linda was being punished for exercising the right to marry the person of her choice. Nonetheless, he cited *Loving* to explain that racial classifications are 'subject to the most exacting scrutiny' because such classifications are 'more likely to reflect racial prejudice than legitimate public concerns.'[47]

The opinion grants the state's 'substantial governmental interest' in determining custody based on the 'best interests of the child.' It further acknowledges the present-day persistence of prejudice and that such prejudice could impact a child in an interracial household:

> It would ignore reality to suggest that racial and ethnic prejudices do not exist or that all manifestations of those prejudices have been eliminated. There is a risk that a child living with a stepparent of a different race may be subject to a variety of pressures and stresses not present if the child were living with parents not of the same racial or ethnic origin.[48]

But Burger concluded that such considerations were an 'impermissible' basis on which to take custody from Linda. In a passage frequently quoted in media reports about the decision, Burger stated:

---

46   *Palmore v. Sidoti*, 466 U.S. 429, 434 (citing *Buchanan v. Warley*, 245 U.S. 60 (1917)).
47   Ibid., 432.
48   Ibid., 433.

> The Constitution cannot control such prejudices but neither can it tolerate them. Private biases may be outside the reach of the law, but the law cannot, directly or indirectly, give them effect.[49]

With these words, the Court rejected Judge Buck's vision about the effect that the hovering cloud of eyes bearing down on Mrs. Palmore's interracial family should have on her parental rights.

To be sure, the Court's unanimous opinion was a significant victory for Linda Sidoti Palmore. And its language about law not giving effect to 'private biases' has played a significant role in other constitutional struggles, including for LGBTQ rights. In reversing the Florida courts, however, the Court did not order that custody be restored to Linda to reconstitute the family disrupted by Judge Buck's unconstitutional ruling. Instead, the Court's reversal led to a remand of the case to the trial court, presumably so it could rule on Anthony's motion to change custody in a constitutional manner—that is, without basing a decision on the alleged social consequences of Linda's marriage and her racially mixed household.

3   The Less Visible Aftermath of a Canonical Case

The rest of the tale is a sobering example of how constitutional rights may be vindicated in what becomes a canonical case, but the individual wrong that spurred that case may persist. Here, I tell of an aftermath not visible in Cortada's portrait of Linda, Clarence, and Melanie.

Just a day after the Court's ruling, Anthony persuaded a Texas court to issue a temporary restraining order prohibiting Linda from removing Melanie from her father's custody in Texas during the 25-day waiting period he had to seek a rehearing by the Supreme Court. As with Linda's request for emergency relief to avoid giving up her child while the case was pending, the Supreme Court denied her emergency request to stop Texas courts from intervening in her attempt to regain custody in the Florida court.[50] A turf war ensued between the Florida and Texas courts over jurisdiction over Melanie. Judge Manuel Menendez, Jr., the Florida judge assigned to the case, declined to order that Melanie be returned to her mother, despite the Supreme Court's ruling, saying he 'wanted time to study the dispute'; instead, he awarded Linda temporary

---

49   Ibid.
50   'Judge: Keep Melanie Sidoti With Father', Florida Today, Apr. 28, 1984, 1A; 'Texas Can Act In Custody Case', Paris News, May 3, 1084, 1.

visitation rights.[51] In mid-August, 1984, during the procedural wrangling, news stories reported that Linda was 'ecstatic' and 'thrilled' that she was able to see her daughter for the first time in nearly two years.[52] A few months later, Judge Menendez agreed to allow the Texas court to determine custody, since Texas was now Melanie's home state.[53] Linda vowed to continue to fight to be reunited with her daughter.

By December 1984, Linda's marriage took a disturbing turn, her family life departing most starkly from the seeming harmony between the couple portrayed in Cortada's portrait. News reports indicated that she filed for divorce from Clarence and was granted a temporary restraining order against him, based on her complaint that he physically abused her several times during their three years of marriage. The judge granting that order was Judge Menendez, who had yielded jurisdiction over the custody case to the Texas courts.[54] Several months later, a more shocking story appeared: Clarence Palmore was in the hospital after being stabbed in a 'domestic fight.' 'Mrs. Palmore denied stabbing her husband' and accused him of 'bruising her wrist.' Each signed a waiver, declining to prosecute the other.[55] One news account referred to Linda's allegation in her divorce filings of physical violence by Clarence. In asserting that '[t]he marriage to Palmore cost Mrs. Palmore custody of her daughter by a previous marriage,' such account almost seemed a morality tale of the heavy toll of her marriage, ignoring the causal role of her ex-husband's legal maneuverings in dispossessing her of such custody.[56]

In July, 1985, Linda lost her appeal of Judge Menendez's ruling. Although Anthony had violated a court order in moving Melanie to Texas without prior approval, the Florida appellate court concluded that he probably would have received approval had he asked, since his move was for 'business reasons'—a 'valid' purpose—and not for 'child snatching.' The court claimed to express no views on the merits of who should receive custody, insisting that the Texas court must be allowed to make a full consideration of the custody issue since the Supreme Court did not order reinstatement of the original custody order.[57]

---

51 'Mom Allowed to See Child, Judge Rules', Fort Lauderdale News, Aug. 15, 1984, 10.
52 Charles Reid, 'Palmore Gets Visitation Rights for Daughter', Tampa Tribune, Aug. 16, 1984, 126; 'Woman Gets Temporary Custody of Daughter', Victoria Advocate, Aug. 16, 1984, 5.
53 'Texas Court Gets Custody Case', Tampa Tribune, Oct. 16, 1984, 26.
54 Barry Klein, 'Woman Seeks to End Interracial Marriage That Sparked Custody Dispute', Tampa Bay Times, Dec. 28, 1984; 'Palmores May Divorce', United Press International, Dec. 27, 1984; 'New Event May Change Palmore Custody Case', Tampa Tribune, Dec. 27, 1984.
55 'Interracial Custody Couple Involved in Stabbing', AP, Apr. 23, 1985; 'Husband in Hospital After Domestic Fight' Fort Lauderdale News, Apr. 23, 1985, 11.
56 'Interracial Custody Couple Involved in Stabbing'.
57 Palmore v. Sidoti, 472 So. 2d 843, 846 (Fla. Dist. Ct. App. 1985).

The court indicated that Linda had not established that it was in Melanie's 'best interests' to order her returned to Linda; instead, '[w]e cannot disagree [with Judge Menendez] that it appears to be in the best interests of Melanie that she continue in the status quo at least for the time being until the custody issue is finally resolved.'[58] The court did not refer to the recent problems in Linda's marriage, her filing for divorce, or the impact those new events might have on the merits of her custody case. It observed, however, that 'we have no knowledge from the record of any relevant events which might have occurred during the relatively long period subsequent to [Judge Buck's 1982] order which was the basis for the appeal to the Supreme Court.'[59]

Continuity and stability again worked against Linda, who had tried to keep Melanie with her to preserve continuity in her life after the original custody order. The Florida appellate court details the shifting household arrangements that Melanie has already experienced over the course of the various legal proceedings, concluding that the 'eight-year-old child appears to have had substantial upheavals of her life, and we find no compelling reason at this point to add a further upheaval.' It ends its opinion by admonishing, 'A child custody suit is not a game to be played for the benefit of either parent,' ignoring Anthony's tactical success in (as it were) gaming the state court systems for the last three years.[60] By August 1985, Linda Sidoti Palmore and Clarence Palmore were divorced, with Melanie's custody case pending in Texas.

In contrast to this troubling demise of the Palmore marriage, one year later NBC produced a docu-drama, *A Fight for Jenny*, loosely based on the still-ongoing custody battle between Linda and Anthony and featuring a glamorous cast. Reviews of the film offered occasion again to quote Judge Buck and Chief Justice Burger's sharply contrasting views about how law should deal with the reality of ongoing racial prejudice.[61] Some reviews noted that, in 1986, interracial relationships were still seldom and 'gingerly' depicted on television; perhaps for that reason, the film went into 'contortions' to make the interracial couple 'acceptable' to as many viewers as possible, painting 'David' (the Black husband) as a 'saint' and 'model stepfather,' and 'Kelsey' (the white wife and mother) as a 'loving and totally dedicated mother.'[62] On October 8, 1986, a

---

58 Ibid., 847.
59 Ibid., 846.
60 Ibid., 847.
61 John J. O'Connor, 'NBC's "Fight for Jenny"', New York Times, Oct. 6, 1986. Leslie Ann Warren played 'Kelsey' (based on Linda Palmore) and Philip Michael Thomas played 'David' (based on Clarence Palmore).
62 Ibid.

newspaper reported that Mrs. Palmore was expected to sign papers within the next month giving custody of Melanie to Anthony Sidoti but leaving her with visitation rights. The story quotes the attorney appointed to represent Melanie in the custody proceedings as saying that the last time she spoke to Melanie, Melanie indicated she wanted to live with her father.[63]

From a distance of more than thirty years, it is impossible to know what strains Melanie's absence, the long and ultimately futile battle for her return, or the 'private biases' toward interracial families placed on Linda, on Clarence, and on their brief marriage. On first viewing, Cortada's portrait seems to foreground Linda, Clarence, and Melanie with their backs to the hovering eyes, poised to step forward confidently and strongly—even moving off the canvas to get on with their family life, aided by the Court's ruling limiting the power of prejudice to thwart such a life. But another interpretation of Cortada's portrait is that he alludes to the eye motif in the swirls he depicts in Linda's dress and in circular swirls on Linda's and Clarence's arms and legs. Linda's gaze is not wholly triumphant, but watchful and anxious. If that interpretation is fair, then the portrait may suggest that the menace of the disapproving and watchful eyes could be internalized by the interracial couple themselves, so that the 'private biases' of society had their effect.

4   Gazing on Multiracial Families as a 'Reflection' of Modern Society?

The Court's famous declaration (included in Cortada's label for the painting) about the law not giving effect to private bias and prejudice has had a long afterlife in many battles against discrimination, including against LGBTQ persons.[64] Within custody law, *Palmore*'s legacy is murkier. Some courts have read it as requiring colorblindness: Courts may not consider race at all in deciding with whom children should live. On another reading, courts may consider race—be race-conscious—so long as race is not the sole factor.[65] Solangel

---

63   'Movie Tinselizes Story of a Family', Galveston Daily News, Oct. 8, 1986, 27. I could not find any record of an official ruling on custody by the Texas court, so perhaps these papers were a settlement the two parents reached to establish a visitation schedule with Melanie.

64   E.g. *Goodridge v. Department of Public Health*, 798 N.E.2d 941, 968 (Mass. 2003) (quoting *Palmore*'s language about 'private biases' in a ruling that the Massachusetts constitution requires that same-sex couples be allowed to marry); Linda C. McClain, *Who's the Bigot? Learning from Conflicts over Marriage and Civil Rights Law* (Oxford: Oxford University Press, 2020), 154–70 (discussing invocation of Palmore in Supreme Court litigation over LGBTQ rights).

65   David D. Meyer, 'Palmore Comes of Age: The Place of Race in the Placement of Children' (2007) 18 University of Florida Journal of Law and Public Policy 183.

Maldonado's review of custody cases finds courts taking both approaches, concluding that a colorblind approach, where 'racial, ethnic, or cultural differences are not acknowledged, is *more* likely to result in biased decisions.' For when courts do not think they are taking race into account, their implicit racial, ethnic, and cultural biases influence their decisions. By contrast, while judges should not rely on racial or ethnic stereotypes, custody determinations should be allowed to consider how parents would address a child's multiracial identity, particularly since such children are more likely to experience challenges not experienced by monoracial individuals, such as social exclusion and disapproval from extended family members.[66]

What about the social landscape? Has the weather changed for multiracial families—and perceptions of them—since the cloud of disapproving eyes depicted in Xavier Cortada's portrait? One possible ray of hope is, as mentioned at the outset of this essay, that families in the United States are becoming more multiracial and multiethnic and that a growing number of people believe that intermarriage is good for society. The gaze cast on such families is more approving than in the past, although not uniformly so. The percentage who would oppose a close relative marrying someone of a different race has also fallen, while the percentage of people who say intermarriage is good for society has increased.[67]

Consider also glimmers of a more positive gaze in the world of advertising, where portrayals of multiracial families are more common. A recent Honey-Maid graham cracker advertisement featured a (Black-white) multiracial family, with the slogan, 'This is wholesome.'[68] Such depictions may reflect 'activist advertising,' where marketers seek to shatter stereotypes, be more inclusive, and help to bring about positive change. But marketers must connect to consumers, so marketing campaigns for products are prudent in portraying the diversity of the consumers they want to reach.[69] Unfortunately, some ads have generated backlash. A 2013 Cheerios commercial depicting an interracial couple and their bi-racial daughter received so much racist vitriol online that the YouTube channel for comments on the ad was closed. But Cheerios also received an outpouring of support and ran a sequel during the 2014 Super

---

66 Solangel Maldonado, 'Bias in the Family: Race, Ethnicity, and Culture in Custody Disputes' (2017) 55 Family Court Review 213, 214–216.
67 Livingston and Brown, 'Intermarriage', 26–28.
68 Joanne Kaufman, 'Marketers Turn to Multiracial Families to Project a Modern Image', New York Times, June 4, 2018, B4.
69 Enrica N. Ruggs, Jennifer Ames Stuart, and Linyun W. Yang, 'The Effect of Traditionally Marginalized Groups on Consumer Response' (2018) 29 Marketing Letters 319, 319–20.

Bowl.[70] The dramatic increase in ads portraying multiracial couples and families is (in the words of one ad executive) 'a reflection of modern society'; people increasingly demand that the media they consume portray the diversity of their lives.[71] Undeniably, private bias and prejudice remain. But this shift inspires hope of more acceptance and appreciation of such diversity in family life and in society.

Recommended Reading

Eyer, Katie. 'Constitutional Colorblindness and the Family.' *University of Pennsylvania Law Review* 162 (2014): 537–603.

Kennedy, Randall. *Interracial Intimacies: Sex, Marriage, Identity, and Adoption.* New York: Pantheon Books, 2003.

Maldonado, Solangel. 'Bias in the Family: Race, Ethnicity, and Culture in Custody Disputes.' *Family Court Review* 55 (2017): 213–242.

Meyer, David D. 'Palmore Comes of Age: The Place of Race in the Placement of Children.' *University of Florida Journal of Law & Public Policy* 18 (2007):183–207.

Moran, Rachel F. *Interracial Intimacy: The Regulation of Race and Romance.* Chicago: University of Chicago Press, 2001.

Murray, Melissa. 'Loving's Legacy: Decriminalization and the Regulation of Sex and Sexuality.' *Fordham Law Review* 86 (2018): 2671–2700.

Onwuachi-Willig, Angela, and Jacob Willig-Onwuachi. 'A House Divided: The Invisibility of the Multiracial Family.' *Harvard Civil Rights-Civil Liberties Law Review* 44 (2009): 231–253.

---

70   Kaufman, 'Marketers'.
71   Ibid.

*Church of the Lukumi Babalu Aye, Inc.
v. City of Hialeah*, 508 U.S. 520 (1993)

Xavier Cortada

Every day my exercise routine takes me through the spoil islands connecting Miami to Key Biscayne. It's a free beach, so folks come by, park their cars at the beach head, and picnic away. I really have to watch where I'm stepping—I could land on a stranded jelly fish, the excretions of someone's dog, a used condom, or on someone's leftover KFC chicken wings being devoured by an army of red ants.

Every now and then, I also see groupings of Turkey Vultures feasting. It's an eerie sight. Dressed in black they gather around a circle, pecking away at someone else's ritual, usually a goat or chicken carcass. These are the sacrificial animals of the Santeria religion, offerings placed at the water's edge.

Santeria Beach, I call it. I could as easily call it KFC Beach. I guess Santeria sounds more sensational because of the animal sacrifice. It shouldn't. At the end of the day, some choose to pray before killing, cooking, and eating. Others prefer to pray between the cooking and the eating parts. And all of us waste, and thereby needlessly cause animals to be killed.

In *Church of the Lukumi Babalu Aye v. City of Hialeah*, the Supreme Court found that the animal sacrifice ordinances had more to do with stopping Santeria than promoting animal rights.

In the painting I created to represent the case, we have a goat wrapped in some purple sheet, hanging in a butcher shop and chopped into select cuts of meats. Perhaps for a non-traditional Christmas Roast. At the base are two dogs, which could be patiently waiting for some gristle to drop. The two crutches are ambiguous, maybe the butcher is limping because he dropped a cleaver on his foot.

The Hialeah ordinance would have had no problem with the activity depicted in the painting, unless you imbued it with meaning: Unless the meats had something to do with worshiping Babalu.

Babalu—or known more commonly by the syncretic name of San Lazaro—is always depicted wearing a cape, on crutches, and with two dogs at his feet. If that goat was being carved up for Babalu instead of 'Bob' or 'Lou' or either of their dogs, the City would have made it illegal. The Court killed the ordinance, and gave life to the free exercise of religion.

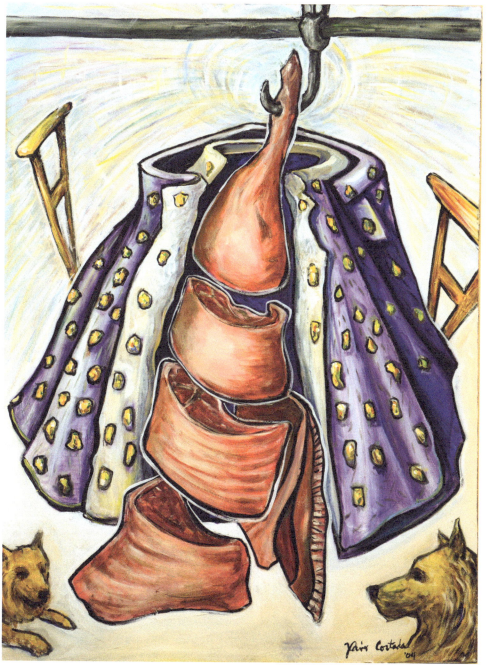

FIGURE 9.1 Xavier Cortada, *Church of the Lukumi Babalu Aye, Inc. v. City of Hialeah*, 508 U.S. 520 (1993), 48" × 36", acrylic on canvas, 2004.
PHOTO: ZENAIDA PIRRI, MIAMI, FLORIDA

CHAPTER 9

Church of the Lukumi Babalu Aye, Inc. v. City of Hialeah

The Meaning of Free Exercise: Equality and Beyond

Kathleen A. Brady

A purple cape. Cuts of goat meat ready to be cooked. A pair of crutches and two dogs. A collection of items without any apparent meaning. Perhaps, as Xavier Cortada suggests of his painting, it is a nontraditional Christmas roast hanging in a butcher shop. The butcher has injured his foot. The dogs, maybe his dogs, are waiting for some gristle to drop. But that explanation for this assortment seems unlikely.

A different, more sensible meaning would be immediately apparent to the viewer if she were a practitioner of Santería, an Afro-Cuban religion brought to the United States by immigrants from Cuba in the wake of the revolution of 1959. Many, probably most, viewers will miss this meaning because Santería is practiced largely in private. Secrecy became an integral part of the faith when hundreds of thousands of Yoruba people from West Africa were brought to Cuba as slaves and forced to adopt their captors' Catholic faith. Catholicism and African religious practices intertwined over time, and Catholic saints became the public faces of African spiritual entities known as orishas. The orisha tradition from Nigeria and the popular folk piety of Cuban Catholicism together became Santería, Spanish for 'the way of the saints.'

Cortada's painting depicts the symbols of the orisha Babalú-Ayé, identified with Saint Lazarus. Babalú-Ayé is the orisha of illness and healing, with the power to cause and to cure sickness. He is represented in Santería as infirm and lame. He wears sackcloth and is accompanied by two dogs reminiscent of the dogs who licked the sores of the beggar Lazarus in the Gospel of Luke. Babalú-Ayé's favored color is purple. As with all orishas, Babalú-Ayé's power is strengthened by nonanimal sacrifices such as tobacco, rum, and toasted corn and animal sacrifices such as doves, poultry, and goats.

When the Church of the Lukumi Babalu Aye announced its public opening in 1987, its plan to make the practice of Santería more visible met fierce resistance from the local community of Hialeah, Florida. Residents of other faiths and animal-rights advocates condemned the practice of animal sacrifice, and the city council passed a series of ordinances designed to prohibit it.

The ensuing litigation reached the Supreme Court of the United States, and in 1993 in *Church of the Lukumi Babalu Aye, Inc. v. City of Hialeah*, the Court agreed with the church that the ordinances violated the Free Exercise Clause of the First Amendment.[1] *Lukumi* 'killed' the ordinances, Cortada writes, and 'gave life to the free exercise of religion.' The decision made clear that the Free Exercise Clause retains important protections for religious practice even after the Court had substantially narrowed its reach a few years earlier. Lower courts and scholars have disagreed about how much life *Lukumi* offers, but a close examination of the case reveals that it could be great indeed.

1   The Santería Faith

Babalú-Ayé and the other orishas in the Santería tradition are not immortal. They were created by the almighty God Olodumare, the source and ground of all being, and they are manifestations of the different aspects of the divine power, ashé, that sustains all life. The orishas protect and guide their followers, but they require sacrifice to strengthen their ashé. For the greatest problems, an animal sacrifice may be necessary, and the orishas are fed blood poured from the sacrificial animal onto stones that represent them in a symbolic and real sense. Kept in tureens, these sacred stones, or otanes, are fed during ceremonies, feasts, and initiations of the Santería faith.

The relationship between the orishas and their human followers is central to Santería. The priests of the religion, known as santeros (santeras if they are female), communicate with the orishas through divination systems that reveal the source of human problems and their solutions. When an individual consults a santero, the answer to their problems may be a ritual cleansing, an herbal remedy, or an offering of food. The high priests of Santería, known as babalawos, employ additional forms of divination for the most difficult problems. The orishas' answers allow individuals to understand and to realize their destiny from Olodumare. When an individual becomes a santero, he undergoes a form of rebirth. He becomes a child of the orisha in whose mysteries he is initiated, and the orisha becomes 'seated' in his 'head.' The most direct way that the orishas become present to the community occurs during tambors or bembes, when rhythmic drumbeats and dances coax the orishas to descend and possess individual santeros and santeras, allowing direct conversation between members of the community and the orisha.

---

1   *Church of the Lukumi Babalu Aye, Inc. v. City of Hialeah*, 508 U.S. 520, 524, 547 (1993).

Substantial numbers Santería followers live in South Florida and other regions where Cuban immigrants settled in large numbers, such as New York and Los Angeles. Santería in America has gained a following among Puerto Ricans, other Latin American groups, African-Americans, and whites. Many of its followers come from poor and modest backgrounds, although it also has attracted educated and more affluent followers.

But Santería remains invisible to most Americans. One reason is Santería's tradition of secrecy. For most of its history, Santería has been a largely oral tradition with initiation as the path to greater knowledge of its mysteries; successive initiations bring additional knowledge. Santería is also largely decentralized and lacks the typical institutional structures and fixtures of America's more familiar faiths. The basic unit of the worshipping community is the ilé or casa de santo. The activities of the ilé occur at the home of a santero, and the ilé includes the santero and the spiritual children whom he or she has initiated in the mysteries of Santería. The ilé is a spiritual family. There are loose connections between different ilés but no centralized authority and, until recently, no public congregations like churches or church buildings.

2 The Conflict over Animal Sacrifice in Hialeah

When Santería came to America, it encountered a culture that celebrates religious freedom but retains significant religious prejudice. It also entered a cultural climate in which individualism in religion thrives and pioneers chart new paths in many disciplines.

Perhaps it was not surprising when Ernesto Pichardo, who had been part of the first wave of exiles to South Florida following the Cuban revolution, announced in 1987 that he was opening a church that would serve the Santería community and also provide outreach and education to the public. Religious ceremonies would include animal sacrifice. Pichardo and several family members had founded the Church of the Lukumi Babalu Aye more than a decade earlier, seeking to purify and institutionalize the faith. The lack of centralization in Santería allowed misinformation and charlatanism to spread within the community; Pichardo's solution was standardization and controls. Pichardo also sought to return Santería to its African roots. He viewed the religion's Catholic aspects as unnecessary accretions, an uncommon view at the time, though more prevalent today. Many santeros in South Florida resisted Pichardo's claims to authority and his efforts to shed Catholic features. Pichardo was on the margins of his religious tradition. But he fit the mold of the religious pioneer who has thrived in the context of American freedom.

Pichardo and the other founders planned to open the church in the City of Hialeah, a small community north of Miami. The pushback was quick and strong and came from multiple quarters. White Cubans were politically powerful in Hialeah and often negatively associated Santería with the uneducated and lower classes. Religious leaders from many other faith communities in the city were repulsed by the practice of animal sacrifice, denouncing it as an 'abomination,' 'sinful,' and 'barbaric.'[2] For Pichardo, the orishas were real spiritual beings and sacrifices to strengthen their power were an essential part of the process of exchange through which humans receive their protection and help. The symbolism in Cortada's painting reveals a religious reality that is true and beneficial. For other religious leaders in Hialeah, the religious meaning associated with animal sacrifice made the practice especially repugnant. For these opponents, the symbolism in Cortada's painting points to harmful and false religious teaching.

Animal-rights groups opposed the church's plan to conduct animal sacrifice and had sparred over the practice in communities across the country. For them, practitioners of Santería were free to believe whatever they wanted, but they could not be permitted to treat animals cruelly. They did not care about the truth or falsity of Santería's belief system. What mattered was the treatment of animals, and it mattered for secular reasons—a goat hanging in a butcher shop that has been killed through humane methods of slaughter was different from one killed during a Santería ceremony.

During the summer and fall of 1987, the Hialeah City Council passed a number of resolutions and ordinances condemning animal sacrifice and designed to prohibit it. The first resolution, in June, expressed the community's concern 'that certain religions may propose to engage in practices which are inconsistent with public morals, peace or safety,' and 'reiterate[d] [the city's] commitment to a prohibition against any and all acts of any and all religious groups which are inconsistent with public morals, peace or safety.'[3] The resolution was coupled with an ordinance incorporating Florida's animal cruelty law, which prohibited, among other things, the 'unnecessary' killing of animals.[4] In July, the Florida attorney general construed state law to ban ritual animal sacrifice for purposes other than food consumption and indicated that Hialeah could pass additional legislation banning animal sacrifice consistently with state

---

2 David M. O'Brien, *Animal Sacrifice and Religious Freedom: Church of the Lukumi Babalu Aye v. City of Hialeah* (Lawrence: University Press of Kansas, 2004), 35, 42–43.
3 City of Hialeah, Florida, Resolution 87-66, June 9, 1987.
4 City of Hialeah, Florida, Ordinance 87-40, June 9, 1987.

law.[5] In August, the city council passed a resolution announcing city policy to prosecute anyone seeking to practice ritual animal sacrifice.[6]

In September, the city followed with three additional ordinances. One prohibited the possession of animals for slaughter or sacrifice within the city. It defined sacrifice as 'to unnecessarily kill, torment, torture, or mutilate an animal in a public or private ritual or ceremony not for the primary purpose of food consumption.' Slaughter was defined as 'the killing of animals for food.' It prohibited any person from 'own[ing], keep[ing] or otherwise possess[ing], sacrific[ing], or slaughter[ing]' any animal intending to use the animal for food purposes, and it stated that this prohibition applied to 'any group or individual that kills, slaughters or sacrifices animals for any type of ritual, regardless of whether or not the flesh or blood of the animal is to be consumed.' There was an exemption for licensed establishments that slaughter animals for food purposes in accordance with the requirements of state and local law.[7]

Reiterating that animal sacrifice undermines 'the public health, safety, welfare and morals of the community,' the second ordinance prohibited any person or group from sacrificing an animal in the city.[8] The third ordinance prohibited the slaughter of animals outside of premises zoned as slaughterhouses, with an exemption for 'any person, group or organization that slaughters, or processes for sale, small numbers of hogs and/or cattle per week in accordance with an exemption provided by state law.'[9]

Shortly after the city adopted the ordinances, the church sued in the United States District Court for the Southern District of Florida, alleging a violation of the First Amendment's protections for religious freedom. The following year, Judge Eugene Spellman declared that all the rules were constitutional.[10] He found that the ordinances served a number of compelling secular purposes. Animal sacrifice endangered the public health and welfare because animals that were not eaten often were disposed of in public places with the risk of spreading disease and because ritual sacrifices resulted in the consumption of uninspected meat.[11] It endangered the psychological well-being of children exposed to the practice,[12] and the method used to sacrifice animals did not

---

5   Fla. Op. Att'y Gen. 87-56, *Annual Report of the Attorney General* (1988), 146.
6   City of Hialeah, Florida, Resolution 87-90, Aug. 11, 1987.
7   City of Hialeah, Florida, Ordinance 87-52, Sept. 8, 1987.
8   City of Hialeah, Florida, Ordinance 87-71, Sept. 22, 1987.
9   City of Hialeah, Florida, Ordinance 87-72, Sept. 22, 1987.
10   *Church of the Lukumi Babalu Aye, Inc. v. City of Hialeah*, 723 F. Supp. 1467 (S.D. Fla. 1989).
11   Ibid., 1485.
12   Ibid., 1485–86.

guarantee that animals would be sacrificed humanely.¹³ Judge Spellman credited expert testimony that the methods used in Santería rituals were unreliable and that animals suffered fear and stress while awaiting sacrifice.¹⁴ Additionally, botánicas selling animals and other religious goods often kept animals in overcrowded conditions without adequate food and water.¹⁵ Protections for religious liberty are not absolute, observed Judge Spellman, pointing to an example from the free speech field: 'No one for a moment would espouse the view that freedom of speech would allow an individual to shout 'Fire' in a crowded theater.'¹⁶

In June 1991, the United States Court of Appeals for the Eleventh Circuit affirmed the district court's decision in a short unpublished opinion.¹⁷ The church sought review from the Supreme Court of the United States, which granted certiorari in March 1992.

3 Free Exercise before *Lukumi*

While religious liberty is one of America's most cherished values, what religious freedom entails has been the subject of great debate and, for the Supreme Court, an ongoing process of doctrinal development shaped by conflicts between government and the nation's minority religions. The defining feature of America's religious landscape is its pluralism, and the cases that have reached the Court have reflected the breadth of this pluralism. The Court has heard cases involving religions brought to America by the country's immigrants, homegrown faiths, belief systems that predate the arrival of Europeans, and recently, more mainstream faiths whose power in American life has been waning with the rise of unaffiliated forms of spirituality and secularism. Doctrinal protections for religious practices have ebbed and flowed. When the Court agreed to hear the church's appeal, its jurisprudence had recently undergone a dramatic shift that curtailed the reach of the First Amendment's Free Exercise Clause.

The First Amendment forbids government from 'prohibiting the free exercise' of religion.¹⁸ *Reynolds v. United States*, the Court's first case construing the

---

13 Ibid., 1486.
14 Ibid., 1472–73, 1486.
15 Ibid., 1474.
16 Ibid., 1482–83.
17 *Church of Lukumi v. City of Hialeah*, 936 F.2d 586 (1991) (table) (referring to unpublished per curiam opinion).
18 U.S. Const. amend. I.

Free Exercise Clause, distinguished between religious belief and action and rejected the argument that religious duty excuses believers from the requirements of valid laws serving legitimate public purposes.[19] George Reynolds, a Mormon, had sought to avoid conviction under federal antipolygamy legislation on the ground that his faith required polygamy when feasible.[20] While laws may not interfere with religious opinion, they can interfere with religious practices;[21] an exemption such as the one Reynolds sought would 'make the professed doctrines of religious belief superior to the law of the land, and in effect to permit every citizen to become a law unto himself.'[22]

In the 1940s, the Court expanded the reach of the Free Exercise Clause. The First Amendment protects both religious belief and conduct, although protections for religious practice cannot be absolute.[23] The Court recognized that at least in some circumstances, the Free Exercise Clause affords relief where burdens on religious practice are the result of neutral, nondiscriminatory laws.[24]

In *Sherbert v. Verner*,[25] the Court articulated the rule that where a law substantially burdens religious practice, the believer is entitled to an exemption unless the government can demonstrate that the application of the law to the believer is the least restrictive means of achieving a compelling state interest.[26] That is, the law must serve an interest of the highest order, and applying the law to the believer must be necessary to that purpose. The plaintiff in *Sherbert* was a Seventh-day Adventist who had lost her job and been denied state unemployment benefits because she would not work on Saturdays, her Sabbath day.[27] According to the Court, the South Carolina Employment Security Commission's determination that Sherbert had 'failed, without good cause ... to accept available suitable work'[28] placed a substantial burden on her religious practice because it put her to a choice of following her faith and losing unemployment benefits or violating her beliefs and accepting Saturday work.[29] The Court found that the state had not met its burden of proving that

---

19 *Reynolds v. United States*, 98 U.S. 145 (1879).
20 Ibid., 161–62.
21 Ibid., 163–64, 166.
22 Ibid., 167.
23 *Cantwell v. Connecticut*, 310 U.S. 296, 303–04 (1940); *Murdock v. Pennsylvania*, 319 U.S. 105, 109–10 (1943).
24 *Murdock*, 319 U.S. at 115.
25 374 U.S. 398 (1963).
26 Ibid., 406–08.
27 Ibid., 399–401.
28 Ibid., 401 (quoting from South Carolina's Unemployment Compensation Act).
29 Ibid., 404.

its denial of benefits was necessary to achieve a compelling state interest.[30] The Court followed this approach in a number of subsequent cases, including one in 1989.[31]

Employment Division v. Smith, decided in 1990, two years before the Court agreed to hear the Church of the Lukumi's appeal, turned Free Exercise jurisprudence on its head. Holding that the Free Exercise Clause does not prohibit a state from applying its criminal drug laws to religiously inspired peyote use at ceremonies of the Native American Church, the Court denied that the First Amendment requires exemptions from valid legislation serving legitimate public purposes.[32] Free Exercise prohibits the government from interfering with religious beliefs, but religious practice is different.[33] The Clause would likely prohibit the state from regulating conduct because of its religious inspiration or only when it is engaged in for religious reasons,[34] but it does not afford relief when burdens on religious practice are the incidental result of neutral, generally applicable laws that are otherwise valid.[35] The Court distinguished *Sherbert* on the ground that South Carolina had put in place a system for making individualized assessments of the reasons for an applicant's unemployment, including whether there was good cause for any failure to accept suitable work.[36] Where such a system of individual exemptions exists, the government cannot reject a claim of religious hardship without a compelling state interest.[37] The Court also noted that prior cases had granted relief in 'hybrid situations,' in which Free Exercise claims combined with claims of other constitutional violations.[38] Otherwise, the Free Exercise Clause does not require exemptions from neutral, generally applicable laws.

Smith recalled *Reynolds*. Constitutionally required exemptions from neutral laws of general applicability allow the religious objector to 'become a law unto himself,'[39] the Court repeated, an interpretation of the First Amendment inviting chaos.[40] It is also problematic for courts to balance the significance of

---

30   Ibid., 406-07.
31   *Frazee v. Illinois Department of Employment Security*, 489 U.S. 829 (1989) was decided the year before *Employment Division v. Smith*, 494 U.S. 872 (1990).
32   *Smith*, 494 U.S. at 878–79.
33   Ibid., 877.
34   Ibid., 877–78.
35   Ibid., 878–79.
36   Ibid., 884.
37   Ibid.
38   Ibid., 881–82.
39   Ibid., 879, 885 (quoting *Reynolds v. United States*, 98 U.S. 145, 167 (1879)).
40   Ibid., 888.

religious practices against the importance of state interests.[41] Legislatures may make exceptions from their laws and can be expected to do so in a nation that values religious liberty.[42] But the right of exemption recognized in *Sherbert* is a 'luxury' that cannot be afforded in a deeply pluralistic country.[43] Leaving the accommodation of religious practice to the political process might disadvantage religious minorities, but this 'unavoidable consequence' is preferable to 'a system in which each conscience is a law unto itself or in which judges weigh the social importance of all laws against the centrality of all religious beliefs.'[44]

4   *Lukumi* and the Meaning of Neutrality and General Applicability

When the Court agreed to review *Lukumi*, constitutional protection for religious practice was much narrower than it had been a few years earlier. Some observers feared that the 'unpleasant' facts of animal sacrifice risked a decision that would further narrow religious freedom.[45] At the same time, some hoped that the Court might reconsider *Smith* and return to a more protective construction of the Clause's safeguards.

The Court did neither. All the Justices agreed that Hialeah's ordinances were unconstitutional. And three Justices wrote or joined concurring opinions arguing that *Smith* should be reexamined[46] or abandoned.[47] But a majority affirmed *Smith* and declared the laws invalid under that narrower standard. Justice Kennedy wrote for the Court that Hialeah's actions violated the 'fundamental nonpersecution principle of the First Amendment'[48] and its ordinances were neither neutral nor generally applicable.[49]

Lukumi was about what remained of the Free Exercise Clause under *Smith*. The Court did not revisit its prior holding that Free Exercise does not afford relief when burdens on religious practice are the result of neutral, generally applicable laws. Instead, it elaborated upon the concepts of neutrality and

---

41 Ibid., 889 n.5.
42 Ibid., 890.
43 Ibid., 888.
44 Ibid., 890.
45 O'Brien, *Animal Sacrifice*, 103 (quoting Michael W. McConnell).
46 *Church of the Lukumi Babalu Aye, Inc. v. City of Hialeah*, 508 U.S. 520, 559 (1993) (Souter, J., concurring in part and concurring in the judgment).
47 Ibid., 577–78 (Blackmun, J., with O'Connor, J., concurring in the judgment).
48 Ibid., 523 (majority opinion).
49 Ibid., 524.

general applicability and how the Free Exercise Clause is implicated when laws fail to meet these standards.

The Court first addressed neutrality and held that laws are not neutral when they restrict conduct because of its religious motivation.[50] Hialeah's ordinances were not neutral because their purpose was to target and to suppress Santería religious practice.[51] While religious discrimination was not clear from the face of the laws because their references to ritual animal sacrifice did not necessarily have a religious meaning,[52] the ordinances reached Santería animal sacrifice and little else.[53] Narrowly tailored proscriptions coupled with secular exceptions 'singled out' Santería practice for discriminatory treatment.[54] The ordinances also prohibited more conduct than was necessary to achieve the city's interests. For example, the risk of disease from improper disposal of animal carcasses could be addressed with regulations regarding disposal, rather than an outright ban on all animal sacrifice.[55] The city's interest in preventing animal cruelty could have been addressed by regulating the conditions under which animals were kept and by requiring santeros to use humane methods of sacrifice.[56]

Furthermore, when Hialeah incorporated Florida's prohibition against the unnecessary killing of animals, it adopted a system for individually assessing the reasons for killings and 'devalue[d]' religious justifications.[57] The city permitted many types of killings as necessary—such as hunting, pest control, and euthanasia[58]—but rejected Santería's religious justifications, 'judging them to be of lesser import than nonreligious reasons.'[59]

Finally, Justice Kennedy drew on the historical background and legislative history of the city's enactments, including statements at city council meetings condemning Santería religious practice, although only one other justice joined this part of the opinion.[60] Justice Scalia, in a concurrence joined by Chief Justice Rehnquist, rejected consideration of the subjective motivations of lawmakers,[61] but agreed that the ordinances evidenced religious animosity.[62]

---

50   Ibid., 533.
51   Ibid., 534–40, 542.
52   Ibid., 533–34.
53   Ibid., 535–38.
54   Ibid., 538.
55   Ibid., 538–39.
56   Ibid., 539.
57   Ibid., 537–38.
58   Ibid., 537.
59   Ibid., 537–38.
60   Ibid., 540–42 (Kennedy, J., joined by Stevens, J.).
61   Ibid., 558–59 (Scalia, J., concurring in part and concurring in the judgment).
62   Ibid., 542, 547 (majority opinion).

The Court's discussion of general applicability considered factors similar to those in its discussion of neutrality and recognized that these concepts are interrelated.[63] The Court found it unnecessary to 'define with precision' the standard for general applicability because Hialeah's ordinances 'f[e]ll well below the minimum standard necessary to protect First Amendment rights.'[64] In enacting its ordinances, Hialeah pursued its interests in public health and the prevention of animal cruelty 'only against' conduct motivated by religious belief.[65] The ordinances were underinclusive because they 'fail[ed] to prohibit nonreligious conduct that endanger[ed] [its] interests in a similar or greater degree than Santeria sacrifice d[id],' and this underinclusiveness was 'substantial, not inconsequential.'[66] Few killings were prohibited in Hialeah aside from religious animal sacrifice,[67] and many instances of improper disposal of animal carcasses went unaddressed, including the improper disposal of garbage from restaurants.[68] Hunters and fishermen could eat uninspected meat, but practitioners of Santería could not.[69] Small numbers of hogs and cattle could be slaughtered outside of slaughterhouses, but Santería sacrifice, classified as slaughter, was forbidden.[70] In sum, these 'ordinances 'ha[ve] every appearance of a prohibition that society is prepared to impose upon [Santeria worshippers] but not upon itself,'[71] and '[t]his precise evil is what the requirement of general applicability is designed to prevent.'[72]

When a law is not neutral or generally applicable, it 'must undergo the most rigorous of scrutiny.'[73] The Court held that the ordinances failed a demanding version of the compelling state interest test.[74] A government's interest cannot be compelling when the laws leave unrestricted so much conduct that undermines this interest.[75] Even if Hialeah's interests were compelling, its ordinances were not narrowly tailored to achieve those ends.[76] Hialeah's laws burdened

---

63   Ibid., 531.
64   Ibid., 543.
65   Ibid., 542–43, 545.
66   Ibid., 543.
67   Ibid., 543–44.
68   Ibid., 544–45.
69   Ibid., 545.
70   Ibid.
71   Ibid. (quoting *Florida Star v. B.J.F.*, 491 U.S. 524, 542 (1989) (Scalia, J., concurring in part and concurring in the judgment)).
72   Ibid., 545–46.
73   Ibid., 546.
74   Ibid., 546–47.
75   Ibid.
76   Ibid., 546.

Santería practice to a greater degree than necessary to achieve its interests in public health and prevention of animal cruelty, while leaving unregulated nonreligious conduct that threatened these interests as much as Santería's rituals.[77] Both substantially underinclusive and overbroad, the ordinances were not the least restrictive means of achieving its purposes.[78]

The Court did not discuss the city's interest in child welfare or the role that animal-rights groups had played in urging and defending the ban on animal sacrifice. The latter omission was especially significant. While many Hialeah residents were actively hostile to the Santería faith, the animal-rights groups who joined the fray had secular reasons for supporting the ordinances. The religious nature of animal sacrifice was irrelevant to them, except insofar as Santería's traditions included troubling instances of inhumane treatment of animals. Had the Court discussed their role, however, it would have identified the same problematic features of the laws. The ordinances only pursued the state's interest in preventing animal cruelty against Santería's religious rituals, although secular conduct posed similar threats. The city prohibited more conduct than necessary to prevent the inhumane treatment of animals, creating a 'religious gerrymander.'[79]

Perhaps the animal-rights activists viewed these laws as a step in the right direction, so they piggybacked on the city's hostility toward Santería for a greater purpose. But the Free Exercise Clause does not allow the state to pursue its goals only against religious groups when nonreligious conduct present similar dangers. In a concurrence favoring a return to the Court's approach from *Sherbert*, Justices Blackmun and O'Connor wrote that the prevention of animal cruelty 'is not a concern to be treated lightly,' but Hialeah's discriminatory ordinances were not the 'harder case' of 'a generally applicable anticruelty law.'[80]

5 Illustrations of Inequality

The Court focused on Hialeah's unequal treatment of religious and nonreligious conduct, not on the unpleasant facts of animal sacrifice. Cortada's painting and commentary illustrate this inequality and how extensive it was.

---

77   Ibid.
78   Ibid..
79   Ibid., 535 (quoting *Walz v. Tax Comm'n*, 397 U.S. 664, 696 (1970) (Harlan, J., concurring)); see also ibid., 542.
80   Ibid., 580 (Blackmun, J., concurring in the judgment).

As Cortada observes, and followers of Santería appreciate, animals are frequently killed to support human life. Cortada's image of cuts of meat hanging uncooked is jarring, reflecting the viewer's uneasiness when confronted with the reality behind a diet that includes meat. It is unpleasant—as unpleasant as the facts of animal sacrifice. Most of the animals sacrificed in Santería rituals are eaten, as are animals slaughtered for food. Practitioners of Santería also believe that the orishas consume the animal's blood as it is poured over the sacred stones. The orishas are 'fed' to strengthen their power to help their human followers. Animal sacrifice supports life in Santería, as secular slaughter supports the lives of those who consume meat. Some sacrificial animals are not eaten. For example, animals sacrificed in ritual cleansings are not consumed but disposed of as prescribed by the orishas through divination. But even this sacrifice is viewed as life-giving, as the ritual passes the negative energy from the person to the animal.

Perhaps, Cortada writes, the goat in his painting hangs in a butcher shop for a nontraditional Christmas roast and an injured butcher limping on crutches has prepared it for sale. Perhaps it was carved up for Bob or Lou or either of their dogs. Any of these scenarios would have been legal in Hialeah. But if the goat was sacrificed for Babalú-Ayé, it would have been unlawful. But an animal was killed and consumed either way.

Nor would a Christmas roast have lacked religious meaning. At a Christmas feast, prayers may be offered after the goat is cooked and before it is eaten; at a Santería ceremony, prayers precede the killing, cooking, and eating of the animal. But while Hialeah saw value in the killing of the goat for the Christmas feast, it saw no value in sacrificing the animal at a Santería ceremony. Preparing the goat for Bob or Lou, or even for their dogs, had value, but Santería sacrifice, unlike these other activities, was unnecessary.

Animal-rights advocates were concerned with the inhumane and unreliable method of sacrificing animals in Santería rituals and the treatment of animals prior to sacrifice, points with which the district court agreed. But Hialeah did not need to prohibit animal sacrifice altogether to address these problems. It could have regulated the conditions under which animals were held before being killed and prohibited unreliable forms of killing. Its choice of a flat ban on animal sacrifice evidenced its discriminatory purpose.

Likewise, the city pursued its interests in public health against Santería sacrifice while permitting other activities that equally undermined this interest. In his statement regarding the picture, Cortada describes an animal carcass from a Santería ritual on the beach, sitting along the water's edge surrounded by turkey vultures. The offering has probably been made to Yemayá, the orisha of motherhood associated with the power of the sea. As Cortada walks, he must be careful to avoid stepping on other detritus—a stranded jellyfish, used condom, dog feces, or leftover KFC chicken wings devoured by an army of red ants. The beach is a popular picnic spot. These items would be considered litter, and allowing dogs to defecate on the beach is undoubtedly illegal. Some of this abandoned garbage could spread disease. But ritual animal sacrifice bears a unique burden. Unlike picnicking on the beach, the preparing and consuming of fried chicken, or walking one's dog, it is completely banned. Hialeah did not have to ban sacrifice to address the community's concerns and it did not proscribe other activities causing comparable harms. Targeting Santería's rituals and leaving comparable activities untouched, Hialeah violated the First Amendment.

6   *Lukumi* and the Life of the Free Exercise Clause

Cortada writes that as the *Lukumi* Court 'killed' Hialeah's ordinances, it 'gave life to the free exercise of religion.' But scholars and lower courts have debated and disagreed over how much life *Lukumi* offers. The facts presented a rare instance of blatant religious persecution. The city deliberately and directly sought to suppress the unpopular religious practice of a minority faith; in pursuing legitimate interests in public health and animal protection, it singled out that religious practice for unique burdens while allowing other conduct that equally burdened the city's ends. Few animal killings besides Santería sacrifice were prohibited, and the improper disposal of animal carcasses and the consumption of uninspected meat remained a problem associated with other activities, including hunting, fishing, and the operation of restaurants.

But what about the less extreme case? What if Hialeah had prohibited ritual animal sacrifice but also prohibited hunting and the use of rodent poison in one's yard as well? The Court's test for neutrality focused on whether the government restricted a practice because of its religious motivation. Perhaps the city's object in such a scenario was to suppress Santería rituals while simultaneously addressing other concerns of the animal-rights community. Or the city may have added more restrictions to mask its religious hostility. Proving an impermissible purpose may be difficult if courts cannot examine historical background and legislative history for evidence of legislative intent. Justice Kennedy considered such evidence in *Lukumi*, but this part of his opinion was joined by only one other justice and was rejected in Justice Scalia's concurrence.

In its 2018 decision in *Masterpiece Cakeshop, Ltd. v. Colorado Civil Rights Commission*,[81] the Court appeared open to this evidence. *Masterpiece Cakeshop* held that the Colorado Civil Rights Commission had failed to consider a Christian baker's refusal to design a cake for a same-sex wedding with the neutrality required by the Free Exercise Clause.[82] Drawing on Justice Kennedy's analysis from *Lukumi*, the Court identified expressions of religious hostility by some commissioners and the Commission's disparate treatment of other bakers with conscientious objections to baking cakes with messages opposing same-sex marriage.[83] The Court recognized that the Justices in *Lukumi* had disagreed about considering lawmakers' statements when evaluating the neutrality of legislation, but it distinguished this case's adjudicative context.[84] The Court also emphasized that the First Amendment's requirement of neutrality 'must be strictly observed,'[85] and it repeated the statement in *Lukumi* that '[t]he Free Exercise Clause bars even "subtle departures from neutrality" on matters of religion.'[86]

The current debate over the reach of *Lukumi* focuses primarily on the meaning of 'general applicability.' Some lower courts and scholars have suggested that a law is not generally applicable only if there is evidence of religious hostility or disfavor,[87] an approach that conflates general applicability with neutrality. A second, more plausible interpretation holds that only laws that single out religious practice for unique burdens cease to be generally applicable.[88] The Court described Hialeah's ordinances in these terms, but it also stated that it was unnecessary to define precisely the meaning of general

---

81   *Masterpiece Cakeshop, Ltd. v. Colorado Civil Rights Comm'n*, 138 S. Ct. 1719 (2018).
82   Ibid., 1729–32.
83   Ibid., 1731–32.
84   Ibid., 1730.
85   Ibid., 1732.
86   Ibid., 1731 (quoting *Lukumi*, 508 U.S. at 534).
87   *Little Sisters of the Poor Home for the Aged v. Burwell*, 794 F.3d 1151, 1197–98 (10th Cir. 2015), *vacated on other grounds and remanded*, *Zubik v. Burwell*, 136 S. Ct. 1557 (2016); *Thomas v. Anchorage Equal Rights Comm'n*, 165 F.3d 692, 701–02 (9th Cir. 1999), *vacated on other grounds on reh'g en banc*, 220 F.3d 1134 (9th Cir. 2000); *O'Brien v. U.S. Dep't of Health & Human Servs.*, 894 F. Supp.2d 1149, 1161–62 (E.D. Mo. 2012), *rev'd in part, vacated in part, and remanded*, 766 F.3d 862 (8th Cir. 2014); James M. Oleske, Jr., '*Lukumi* at Twenty: A Legacy of Uncertainty for Religious Liberty and Animal Welfare Laws' (2013) 19 Animal Law Review 295, 330, 335–37.
88   *Mich. Catholic Conference v. Burwell*, 755 F.3d 372, 394 (6th Cir. 2014), *cert. granted, vacated, and remanded*, 575 U.S. 981 (2015), *reissued and reaff'd*, 807 F.3d 738 (6th Cir. 2015), *cert. granted, judgment vacated on other grounds, and case remanded*, 136 S. Ct. 2450 (2016); Frederick Mark Gedicks, 'The Normalized Free Exercise Clause: Three Abnormalities' (2000) 75 Indiana Law Journal 77, 114.

applicability because Hialeah's 'ordinances f[e]ll well below the minimum standard necessary to protect First Amendment rights.'[89] Thus, the Court suggested that laws singling out religious practice for unique burdens are not the only type of non-general legislation. The Court also described Hialeah's ordinances as 'substantially' underinclusive because the government failed to regulate a substantial amount of nonreligious conduct endangering its interests to at least the same degree as Santería animal sacrifice. A law written to prohibit broadly the killing of animals with exceptions for hunting, fishing, and pest control also would be substantially underinclusive. So would a law prohibiting only ritual animal sacrifice, hunting, and the use of rodent poisons in one's yard, but leaving fishing and other pest control unregulated. In both cases, the government would permit many instances of animal killing, undermining its interests in public health and the prevention of cruelty to animals to at least the same degree as animal sacrifice. A number of lower courts look for such substantial underinclusiveness when evaluating general applicability.[90]

For some, a single secular exemption or single category of comparable nonreligious conduct left unregulated renders a law not generally applicable.[91] Justice Alito adopted this position while on the United States Court of Appeals for the Third Circuit and he tied it to *Lukumi*'s discussion of individualized exemptions.[92] When Hialeah incorporated Florida's prohibition on the unnecessary killing of animals, it adopted a system for making individualized assessments of the reasons for killing, and its failure to permit religious animal sacrifice when many other forms of killing were deemed necessary 'devalue[d] religious reasons for killing by judging them to be of lesser import than nonreligious reasons.'[93] Then-Judge Alito extended this reasoning in *Fraternal Order of Police Newark Lodge No. 12 v. City of Newark*. He argued that when a law

---

89 *Church of the Lukumi Babalu Aye, Inc. v. City of Hialeah*, 508 U.S. 520, 543 (1993).
90 *Blackhawk v. Pennsylvania*, 381 F.3d 202, 209, 211 (3d Cir. 2004); *Mitchell Cnty. v. Zimmerman*, 810 N.W.2d 1, 11–12, 16 (Iowa 2012); *Stormans, Inc. v. Wiesman*, 794 F.3d 1064, 1079 (9th Cir. 2015), cert. denied, 136 S. Ct. 2433 (2016).
91 *Fraternal Order of Police Newark Lodge No. 12 v. City of Newark*, 170 F.3d 359, 365–66 (3d Cir. 1999); *Midrash Sephardi, Inc. v. Town of Surfside*, 366 F.3d 1214, 1234–35 (11th Cir. 2004); Douglas Laycock and Steven T. Collis, 'Generally Applicable Law and the Free Exercise of Religion' (2016) 95 Nebraska Law Review 1, 21; Douglas Laycock, 'Religious Liberty and the Culture Wars' (2014) 2014 University of Illinois Law Review 839, 843; Thomas C. Berg, 'The Permissible Scope of Legal Limitations on the Freedom of Religion or Belief in the United States' (2005) 19 Emory International Law Review 1277, 1294–95.
92 *Newark*, 170 F.3d at 365.
93 *Lukumi*, 508 U.S. at 537–38.

provides a secular exemption for nonreligious conduct, the failure to offer a similar exemption for religious conduct with no greater effect on the government's goal devalues the religious justifications for engaging in that conduct.[94] The government is 'deciding that secular motivations are more important than religious motivations.'[95] *Newark* declared invalid a police department policy prohibiting officers from wearing beards while making exceptions for medical reasons and undercover officers but not for religious reasons.[96] While allowing undercover officers to wear beards did not undermine the department's interest in fostering a uniform appearance, that interest would be undermined as much by the permitted medical exception as by the religious exemption sought by Muslim officers.[97] To make a medical exception but not a religious exception, when both undermine the government's purposes, entailed 'a value judgment in favor of secular motivations.'[98] Other courts and commentators have drawn on Justice Alito's reasoning.[99]

If general applicability is read broadly, *Lukumi* gives the Free Exercise Clause much life. Secular exceptions are common in legislation and many regulatory regimes leave substantial categories of relevant conduct untouched. Justice Alito, joined by Chief Justice Roberts and Justice Thomas, advocated a robust interpretation of the requirements of neutrality and general applicability in their 2016 dissent from the denial of certiorari in *Stormans, Inc. v. Wiesman*.[100] The case involved state regulations requiring pharmacies to stock and sell emergency contraceptives; the regulations contained a number of secular exceptions but none for religious or moral objections to emergency contraception. Looking to the enforcement as well as the text of the rules and to evidence of discriminatory intent during their adoption, these Justices saw the same type of religious targeting and underinclusiveness present in *Lukumi*.[101] As the composition of the Supreme Court shifts, it becomes more likely that a majority will read *Lukumi* expansively in the future. If so, it will not just be a

---

94 *Newark*, 170 F.3d at 365–66.
95 Ibid., 365.
96 Ibid., 360.
97 Ibid., 366.
98 Ibid.
99 *Midrash Sephardi, Inc. v. Town of Surfside*, 366 F.3d 1214, 1234–35 (11th Cir. 2004); *Mitchell Cnty. v. Zimmerman*, 810 N.W.2d 1, 11–13 (Iowa 2012); Douglas Laycock, 'The Supreme Court and Religious Liberty' (2000) 40 Catholic Lawyer 25, 35; Laycock and Collis, 'Generally Applicable Law,' 23; Berg, 'The Permissible Scope,' 1294–95.
100 *Stormans, Inc. v. Wiesman*, 136 S. Ct. 2433 (2016) (Alito, J., dissenting from denial of certiorari).
101 Ibid., 2436–40.

precedent about a rare case of religious persecution but a case about equality of treatment more broadly.

Even read expansively, however, *Lukumi* remains limited. When a neutral regulation contains no exceptions for comparable secular conduct, *Lukumi* offers no relief, even if the burden on religious practice is great. Had Hialeah banned the killing of animals in the city without exception, practitioners of Santería would have been unable to point to more favorable treatment of secular conduct. That law, motivated by genuine concern about animal cruelty, would have been neutral and generally applicable under any reading of *Lukumi*. And under *Smith*, the First Amendment would not have guaranteed the church an exemption. *Smith* and *Lukumi* envision the Free Exercise Clause as protecting against religious discrimination, not as a guarantee of affirmative rights in the face of nondiscriminatory state action. At its broadest, *Lukumi* is no substitute for the Court's pre-*Smith* case law.

But if we look harder and dig deeper, *Lukumi* may offer more life. When Hialeah treated most animal killings as necessary under the state's animal cruelty statute but prohibited Santería sacrifice, it devalued these religious justifications. The Court's reasoning assumed that religious practice has a value with which we should be concerned. Governments frequently value some secular concerns over others when developing regulatory regimes. Hialeah could have valued hunting over fishing by deeming the former necessary and the latter unnecessary or by passing a law prohibiting all animal killings with an exception for hunting but not fishing. Interpreting the Free Exercise Clause to require that the government give equal weight to religious concerns when it makes secular exceptions to its rules recognizes that religious practice is an important human activity protected in special ways by the First Amendment. This recognition informed the Court's pre-*Smith* jurisprudence. In *Sherbert*, the Court viewed religious liberty as a fundamental aspect of human freedom; Justice Brennan, who wrote *Sherbert,* later called it a 'precious liberty.'[102] To the extent that *Lukumi* recognizes this value, even if only implicitly, it contains the seeds of further life, a path towards affirmative First Amendment protections for religious practice.

Smith was initially unpopular, prompting a wave of legislative responses. The year the Court decided *Lukumi*, Congress enacted the Religious Freedom Restoration Act (RFRA), which was designed to restore the compelling state interest test where state action substantially burdens religious conduct.[103] In

---

102   *Goldman v. Weinberger*, 475 U.S. 503, 523 (1986) (Brennan, J., dissenting).
103   42 U.S.C. §§ 2000bb-2000bb-4 (2012).

1997, the Supreme Court declared RFRA invalid as applied to state and local law,[104] but it still applies to federal law. Twenty-one states have enacted state-law RFRAs.[105] In 2000, Congress enacted the Religious Land Use and Institutionalized Persons Act (RLUIPA), which applies to state and local law and restores the compelling state interest test to conflicts involving individuals residing in or confined to government institutions, such as prisons, and to cases involving land use regulations.[106]

But support for state RFRAs has dropped in recent years, as has support among academics for returning to the Court's pre-*Smith* jurisprudence. Religious liberty has become enmeshed in the culture wars. The most visible claims for protection come from conservative religious groups seeking exemptions from laws reflecting rapidly changing norms regarding marriage, family, and sexuality, making religious accommodations more controversial. *Smith* generated shock and outrage, but many scholars now disagree with the balance struck in *Sherbert*. The compelling state interest test affords too little weight to government interests, they argue, and weak interpretations that were once criticized are now offered as models for construing federal and state RFRAs.

Scholars began to question the fairness of affording religious exercise special protections not long after *Smith*.[107] Increasingly they embrace *Smith* for using nondiscrimination as the touchstone for the protection of religious practice. There is nothing unique about religious exercise that entitles it to more protection than the demands of secular conscience. The Free Exercise Clause guarantees religious believers equality of treatment, but no more.

But let us take another look at Cortada's painting, now in light of additional background about the Santería faith. The painting illustrates how religious and secular conduct overlap, but it also discloses how they differ. A goat carved up for Bob or Lou feeds the physical body, but a goat sacrificed to Babalú-Ayé feeds a god-like being. It is part of the exchange through which the divine power manifest in the orishas is strengthened and shared with humanity. The orishas are present in their sacred stones, when they are seated in the heads of santeros and when they descend to possess santeros during the music and dances

---

104   *City of Boerne v. Flores*, 521 U.S. 507 (1997).
105   'State Religious Freedom Restoration Acts,' National Conference of State Legislatures, May 4, 2017, http://www.ncsl.org/research/civil-and-criminal-justice/state-rfra-statutes.aspx.
106   42 U.S.C. §§ 2000cc-2000cc-5 (2012).
107   Kathleen A. Brady, *The Distinctiveness of Religion in American Law: Rethinking Religion Clause Jurisprudence* (Cambridge: Cambridge University Press, 2015), 24–25.

of the tambors. In Santería, as in all religions, the human and divine meet. At the heart of religious faith is the human desire to engage the divine power that underlies all reality, to draw life from it, and to draw close to it. Religion arises from the human experience of finitude in the face of the infinite and finds salvation in a divine-human relationship. Disagreement over the sacred ignited the controversy in Hialeah; the events that followed demonstrated the importance of religious practice to believers and how varied understandings of the path to God can be.

Given these features, equal treatment of religious and secular concerns does not provide sufficient protection for the free exercise of religion. The human desire to reach out to the divine is rooted in human nature. Religious faith is not universal. But it appears in different forms across human cultures, and when it appears, it is a matter of supreme importance for adherents. It is through religious practice that the divine-human relationship—promising salvation, liberation, or fulfillment—is pursued and lived. When practitioners of Santería feed the sacred stones of the orishas, as during the rituals and practices of other faiths, humanity touches the divine and the sacred becomes part of human life. For religious believers, nothing can be more important. A society that does not respect the religious impulse in human culture is neither stable nor liberal. The leaders of other faiths in Hialeah missed that Pichardo and his church sought the same freedom that protects their own practices. Religious freedom protects all faiths or it risks protecting none. Anyone can be in the minority depending on time and place; in a deeply pluralistic community, the religious landscape is constantly shifting.

Returning to something like the Court's pre-*Smith* jurisprudence would not mean eliminating all constraints on religious practice. Even under *Sherbert*, burdens on religious practice can be justified by a compelling state interest. As Justices Blackmun and O'Connor recognized in their *Lukumi* concurrence, the prevention of cruelty to animals 'is not a concern to be treated lightly.'[108] Nor are many of the secular interests at stake in today's fights over religious liberty. But the nature of religious faith and practice requires that the protection of religious exercise weigh heavily in any balance.

Without constitutional protection, religious minorities are vulnerable to burdens from neutral laws of general applicability. The more unorthodox the faith and the more public its practices, the more likely conflicts over such rules are to arise. When religious practices entail unusual conduct out of step with

---

108   *Church of the Lukumi Babalu Aye, Inc. v. City of Hialeah*, 508 U.S. 520, 580 (1993) (Blackmun, J., concurring in the judgment).

majoritarian norms, there may be no secular exemptions for religious believers to piggyback on to obtain relief. The more unpopular a religion, the less likely legislators and administrators are to accommodate its practices. *Smith* argued that a robust right of exemption such as that recognized in *Sherbert* is a luxury that a pluralistic society cannot afford. But if we remember what religious faith entails for believers, perhaps we cannot afford anything less. *Lukumi* may help us to see that.

The Court may clarify the reach of *Lukumi* during its October Term 2020. In *Fulton v. City of Philadelphia*, the Court will review a case brought by a Catholic organization challenging a municipal requirement that foster care programs certify same-sex couples as foster parents.[109] Catholic Social Services argues that Philadelphia's requirement would force it to endorse relationships that violate its religious teaching about marriage[110] and that its policies are neither neutral nor generally applicable.[111] The questions presented to the Court also include an invitation to revisit *Smith*. In 2019 Justice Alito, joined by Justices Thomas, Gorsuch and Kavanaugh, suggested a willingness to do so.[112] Justice Alito was joined by Chief Justice Roberts and Justice Thomas in his robust reading of *Lukumi* in his dissent from the denial of certiorari in *Stormans*. Regardless of which party prevails in *Fulton*, the Court may breathe substantial life into *Lukumi* or even roll back *Smith*. If the Court does the latter and returns to a framework of affirmative protections for religious practice, the path may well go through *Lukumi*.

7 Conclusion

In the years since Ernesto Pichardo and a few others founded the Church of the Lukumi, Santería has become more public. Students and followers of Santería have written books for insiders and outsiders; what was once an oral tradition increasingly takes written forms. As practitioners reach out to inform and to educate those outside the faith, Santería's tradition of secrecy has diminished. With these changes come disagreements about doctrine and authority, including disagreements over the continued value of Santería's Catholic forms. For most Americans, however, Santería remains largely invisible; the religious

---

109 140 S. Ct. 1104 (2020) (granting petition for writ of certiorari).
110 *Fulton v. City of Philadelphia*, 922 F.3d 140, 160 (2019), *cert. granted*, 140 S. Ct. 1104 (2020).
111 Ibid., 153.
112 *Kennedy v. Bremerton Sch. Dist.*, 139 S. Ct. 634, 637 (2019) (Alito, J., respecting denial of certiorari).

symbolism depicted in Cortada's painting would be missed without his clarifying commentary.

Not long after the Supreme Court decided *Lukumi*, Pichardo disavowed public animal sacrifices. Perhaps he believed that Americans from other backgrounds were not ready yet. Fortunately, the Constitution was.

Recommended Reading

Brandon, George. *Santeria from Africa to the New World: The Dead Sell Memories.* Bloomington: Indiana University Press, 1993.

Church of the Lukumi Babalu Aye, Inc. v. City of Hialeah, 508 U.S. 520 (1993).

De La Torre, Miguel A. *Santería: The Beliefs and Rituals of a Growing Religion in America.* Grand Rapids: William B. Eerdmans Publishing Company, 2004.

Duncan, Richard F. 'Free Exercise is Dead, Long Live Free Exercise: *Smith*, *Lukumi* and the General Applicability Requirement.' *University of Pennsylvania Journal of Constitutional Law* 3 (2001): 850–84.

Employment Division v. Smith, 494 U.S. 872 (1990).

González-Wippler, Migene. *Santería: The Religion, Faith, Rites, Magic.* Second edition. Woodbury: Llewellyn Publications, 2018.

Laycock, Douglas and Steven T. Collis. 'Generally Applicable Law and the Free Exercise of Religion,' *Nebraska Law Review* 95 (2016): 1–27.

Murphy, Joseph M. *Santería: African Spirits in America.* Boston: Beacon Press, 1993.

O'Brien, David M. *Animal Sacrifice and Religious Freedom: Church of the Lukumi Babalu Aye v. City of Hialeah.* Lawrence: University Press of Kansas, 2004.

Oleske, James M., Jr. '*Lukumi* at Twenty: A Legacy of Uncertainty for Religious Liberty and Animal Welfare Laws.' *Animal Law* 19 (2013): 295–346.

Sherbert v. Verner, 374 U.S. 398 (1963).

Stormans, Inc. v. Wiesman, 136 S. Ct. 2433 (2016) (Alito, J., dissenting from the denial of certiorari).

Seminole Tribe of Florida v. Florida,
517 U.S. 44 (1996)

Xavier Cortada

∴

Back in law school, I remember my Constitutional Law professor warning us to look out for Eleventh Amendment cases. They were the new ones to watch in the legal landscape.

Five years after I graduated, the Supreme Court handed down *Seminole Tribe v. Florida*, 517 U.S. 44 (1996), an important Eleventh Amendment ruling regarding all states as sovereign entities. I thought to paint it.

In this case, the Seminole Tribe (represented by the green Seminole jacket) brought suit before the federal court (represented by the American flag) against the State of Florida for violating a requirement of the Indian Gaming Regulatory Act. The act allowed the tribe to engage in gaming (i.e., casino gambling, slot machines). The case worked its way up the Supreme Court, which held that sovereignty under the Eleventh Amendment (depicted by the two vertical tears created on the jacket) inherently implies that states may not be sued by parties without their consent.

The ripped jacket reveals the façade of a slot machine—showing three rows of repetitive symbols. Jackpot! And the winner is ... The Sovereign State of Florida.

As an aside: It is no secret that the drafters of the Eleventh Amendment had no love lost for Native Americans, who have historically been exploited and undermined by the majority population. How ironic that a couple of centuries later the words they wrote are interpreted to further restrict native people.

FIGURE 10.1 Xavier Cortada, *Seminole Tribe of Florida v. Florida,* 517 U.S. 44 (1996), 48" × 36", acrylic on canvas, 2004.
PHOTO: ZENAIDA PIRRI, MIAMI, FLORIDA

CHAPTER 10

Seminole Tribe of Florida v. Florida
Sovereignty and the Eleventh Amendment Imag(in)ed

James E. Pfander

1   Introduction

Symbols abound in the work of artist Xavier Cortada. In his painting of the Supreme Court decision *Seminole Tribe v. Florida*,[1] Cortada depicts three different governments. The flag of the United States waves in the background, all red, white, and blue. In the foreground, Cortada places a Native American jacket, pieced together from leather, with complex stitching and decorative beadwork. We see the jacket from the back, set against the backdrop of the U.S. flag, as a depiction of the Seminole Tribe of Florida. Embedded in the jacket, Cortada places symbolic representations of the state of Florida. A map of the state appears along with the state flag and the state's initials, FL. These state markers have been arrayed as if they were the images in a slot machine. In the lottery that has just played out on the back of the Seminole jacket, and the indigenous people it represents, the state of Florida has come up a winner.

In portraying the three governments involved in *Seminole Tribe*, Cortada invites us to consider the nature of sovereignty and the way the Constitution of the United States structures and limits government power. Cortada's use of a slot machine reflects that the litigation between the tribe and the state arose from the Indian Gaming Regulatory Act (IGRA),[2] a federal statute that provides for tribes and states to bargain in good faith over the siting of tribal casinos. As part of that legislation, Congress authorized the tribes to sue the states for breach of that bargaining duty. When negotiations over a new casino broke down, the Seminole Tribe brought suit against Florida to enforce the good-faith bargaining obligation under federal law. In defending against that suit, Florida invoked the Constitution's Eleventh Amendment,[3] which limits the power of federal courts to hear certain suits against the states. Embracing

---

1   *Seminole Tribe of Fla. v. Florida*, 517 U.S. 44 (1996).
2   Indian Gaming Regulatory Act of 1988, Pub. L. 100–497, 25 U.S.C. § 2701 *et seq.*
3   U.S. Const. amend. XI (1798).

the state's argument, the Supreme Court upheld Florida's claim to sovereign immunity, dismissing both the bargaining-duty claim of the Seminole Tribe and the federal government's claim, under the Indian Commerce Clause, to regulatory power over relations with Native tribes.

Cortada represents the decision as an act of violence against Native people. The federal Constitution appears in his painting as two parallel strips torn from the back of the native jacket. Those two strips create holes that form the shape of an eleven, symbolizing the Court's conclusion that the Eleventh Amendment prohibits Congress from allowing the Seminole Tribe to sue the state of Florida. Cortada thus forces us to reckon with the many acts of violence that the federal and state governments have directed at Native people over the years. Waving in the background of Cortada's painting, the U.S. flag calls to mind the federal government's claim to plenary power over Native affairs and then-General Andrew Jackson's incursion into Spanish Florida some two hundred years ago to chastise the Seminole people and destabilize Spanish rule. We are reminded that tribes have sometimes sought protection from state depredations in the federal courts, only to be turned away as 'domestic dependent nations.'[4] Above all, the painting forces us to reckon with conflicting ideas of sovereignty, a status that will strike many as wholly out of place in a government of and by the people, but one to which all three governments depicted in the painting—federal, state, and tribal—have long laid claim.

This chapter on Cortada's evocative painting begins with an overview of the history of those conflicting claims to sovereignty. After tracing the fraught relations among tribes, states, and nations during the War for Independence from Great Britain, the chapter describes a growing national deference to state incursions on tribal rights. The Seminole people, attacked in Florida and deported in part to reservations in Oklahoma, were no strangers to the genocidal impulses of European settlers. The remarkable modern renaissance of Native life, both in Florida and throughout Indian country, provides the backdrop for the introduction of Indian gaming and the dispute among Congress, the tribes, the states, and the Supreme Court that lies at the center of Cortada's painting. After placing the dispute over state and tribal sovereign immunity into historical context, the chapter concludes with a reflection on the painting's hopeful implication. Perhaps with time and careful stitching, Native people might bind

---

4 On the status of Native tribes in Marshall's jurisprudence, see *Cherokee Nation v. Georgia*, 30 U.S. (5 Pet.) 1 (1831) (describing Native tribes as domestic dependent nations, rather than foreign nations, and refusing on that basis to exercise original jurisdiction over an action brought by the Cherokee tribe to enjoin Georgia from taking native land and expelling native people).

up their wounds and repair the twin strips that have been torn, but not removed, from the jacket's back.

2   Sovereignty and the War for Independence

Sovereignty was a slippery concept for those who steered the people of British North America from their status as dependent subjects of Great Britain to that as citizens of the 'free and independent states' proclaimed in the Declaration of Independence. Sovereignty was associated with the British King and sovereign immunity with the idea that the King can do no wrong. But in the geopolitics of the late eighteenth century, it was only too apparent to the patriots in North America that the King could repeatedly do wrong. The Declaration offered a litany of the 'long train of abuses and usurpations' that the people of North America had suffered at the hands of the 'tyrant' King. To speak of the sovereign in the Declaration of Independence was to speak of an exceedingly error-prone human being, King George III. In proclaiming that the colonies were absolved of all allegiance to the British Crown, the Declaration rejected claims to sovereignty.

But in rejecting sovereignty, the patriots had in mind the powers exercised by a distant monarch. Home-grown notions of sovereignty were more congenial. States claimed the powers of newly sovereign and independent governments and sought to protect their autonomy from the United States, in Congress assembled. In working up the Articles of Confederation in 1778—the new nation's first constitution—the states were careful to decree that they retained all "sovereignty, freedom and independence and every power, jurisdiction, and right" that was not expressly delegated to the United States, in Congress assembled. Without a monarch to lead the new government(s), the United States were claiming sovereignty without a sovereign.

Native American tribes enjoyed but little of the formal sovereignty that the states now claimed for themselves. Camped on the edge of a constantly expanding European population, the Native tribes fared poorly in the aftermath of independence. Numbering perhaps 150,000 members, the tribes were scattered north and south and had few traditions of inter-tribal confederation on which to draw in resisting European expansion. By contrast, the colonies had upwards of 2.4 million people at the outbreak of hostilities with Britain, a figure that would grow to 4 million by the time of the first census in 1790. Outnumbered and standing between the settlers and a beckoning western frontier, the Native tribes had much to lose from the overthrow of British authority in the new world. After winning the French and Indian Wars, Great Britain had imposed the Proclamation Line of 1763 as a boundary between English settlement and Native American lands in the transalpine West. Honored in the breach, the Line had little holding power in the face of a flood of European immigrants who flocked to the western lands in search of fertile farms and a new life. Facilitating this flow of new migrants, speculators acquired vast tracts of land by means both legal and dubious and raced to plant new settlers on the land.

Facing the pressure of expansion, Native tribes allied themselves with the British policy of preserving the Proclamation Line and ensuring a more orderly form of western expansion. One can see that alliance recapitulated in the Declaration's criticism of Crown policy:

> He has excited domestic insurrections amongst us, and has endeavored to bring on the inhabitants of our frontiers, the merciless Indian Savages, whose known rule of warfare, is an undistinguished destruction of all ages, sexes and conditions.

The war for independence from Great Britain also triggered war with Native tribes, driven by the expansionary desires of the patriots on the frontier and abetted by the states who claimed sovereign authority to dispose of property within their metes and bounds. The resolution of the conflict with Great Britain, and the Treaty of Peace in 1783 ceding to the United States all territory from the old Proclamation Line to the Mississippi River, marked the beginning of the end for Native tribes in the East.

Following the peace with Great Britain, state sovereignty under the Articles of Confederation (1783 to 1788) meant uncoordinated and harsh policies toward Native tribes. At least fifteen treaties were signed with tribes in a twelve-year period from Independence to the demise of the Articles, creating a bountiful harvest of conflicting land claims. The United States through Congress took the position that, having conquered the Native tribes alongside the British, the new nation had acquired all of the Native land ceded in the 1783 Treaty of Peace. But the United States could not make that claim stick. The British retained a military presence in the old Northwest and continued their alliance with Native tribes. Indian leaders secured support from Britain and Spain (which controlled Spanish Florida) and pressed for a pan-Indian confederacy to resist the wave of new American settlers. In 1786 and 1787, Native war parties armed by the Spanish drove settlers out of disputed areas in Georgia and Tennessee. In 1790, the Ohio Indians defeated American armies in the field.

The Americans therefore changed course. Under the leadership of such Federalist leaders as Henry Knox (who would serve as Secretary of War under

President Washington), a new policy of negotiation and conciliation replaced the policy of demands. Partly this new policy reflected the Americans' conception of themselves as a chosen people; they could scarcely set an example to an enlightened world if their treatment of the Native people mirrored the practices of the Spanish.[5] Partly the new approach reflected a growing perception that Indian policy, like so much else, was not best left in the hands of states along the frontier. The cession of the western lands, which created a national domain within the oversight and control of the national government, played a role in shifting the locus of control over Indian affairs from the periphery to the center. The Northwest Ordinance of 1787 consolidated national control over the western lands, just as the Federalists gathered to dicker about how to form a more perfect union in Philadelphia.

3 Sovereignty, Federalism, and the New Constitution

The new Constitution transferred power from the states to the national government in keeping with the Federalist project of greater centralized authority. One can see the shift in the provisions governing congressional power over Indian affairs. Under the Articles of Confederation, to be sure, Congress had 'sole and exclusive right and power of … regulating the trade and managing all affairs with the Indians.' But the grant of power was qualified in two important respects: the national government could exercise authority over only those Indians who were not members of any state and the legislative rights of the states, within their own limits, could not be infringed. These restrictions led to conflicts of authority as the state and national governments vied to lead negotiations with tribal leaders. James Madison proposed language late in the Philadelphia convention to remove the two restrictions. Eventually, some text was added that empowered Congress to regulate Commerce 'with foreign nations, and among the several states, *and with the Indian Tribes*.' Madison celebrated the language of the so-called 'Indian Commerce Clause' in Federalist No. 42 for having eliminated the caveats that had spawned claims about reserved state power.

The new Constitution transferred additional powers to Congress. Rather than proclaiming the 'sovereignty' and independence of the states, the

---

[5] Richard Ross, *The Rule of Law in British America: Thinking with Indians While Comparing to Spaniards* (unpublished manuscript on file with author) (noting the ways in which British colonists distinguished their treatment of indigenous people from that of Spanish colonists).

Constitution omitted any reference to the states as sovereign. It similarly omitted any requirement that delegations of power to Congress be express. Instead, under Article 1, section 8, Congress was empowered to enact laws 'necessary and proper' to carry the other powers—including that over commerce with the Indian tribes—into effect. That basic structure was preserved and restated in the Tenth Amendment, which reserves power to the states, respectively, or to the people, unless 'delegated' to the United States. Efforts to model the provision after the Articles, by limiting federal power to that *expressly* delegated, were turned aside. The Necessary-and-Proper Clause (or the sweeping clause, as it was known) thus neatly reverses the Articles' rule of strict construction for the style of loose construction that the Federalists would later apply in defining the scope of congressional power.

Other sources of federal power augmented that assigned in the Indian Commerce Clause. In treating with the tribes in the 1790s under the terms of the Indian Trade and Intercourse Act, the Washington Administration claimed federal exclusivity and traced federal authority to the national powers over war, peace, and treaty formation. In keeping with this conception that war and peace were central to the claim of national regulatory power, Indian affairs were managed by Knox and the War Department. Meanwhile, the Constitution deprived the States of both treaty-making and war-making powers; states lost those predicates for any claim to retained power over Indian affairs (although their control over state militias survived). Along with this shift of power to the center, the Federalists increasingly viewed negotiations with Native tribes as a matter informed, if not quite fully governed, by the law of nations.

In embracing a law-of-nations predicate for its interactions with Native tribes, the Washington Administration abandoned claims of conquest and acknowledged tribal rights to the soil and the proper role of diplomacy, treaties, and purchase in the lawful acquisition of Native land. But even this somewhat-broadened conception of indigenous control of land was thought to include an important caveat: the United States recognized only itself as a legitimate purchaser of Native land. Other nations (Great Britain, Spain, and France) were barred from treating with Natives in the United States and from acquiring Native land. Natives were quick to point out that the preemptive right of the United States to negotiate for Native land ran afoul of the law of nations, but that did not change administration policy. Here then lies the root of Chief Justice John Marshall's view of Native tribes as 'domestic dependent nations,' hybrid nations with some claim to their territory and to some, but certainly not all, of the attributes of sovereignty.

4 Democrats and National Expansion

The growth of European America during the antebellum period was little short of astonishing and corresponded to a series of calamities for Native people. Land acquisition was the rage—at the national level with the Louisiana Purchase and at the state and local level, where settlers forcibly expelled Native people from their land and brought it under till. States such as Georgia were impatient with the pace at which new lands became available, leading to frontier conflicts and battles. President Jefferson, when he thought about Native issues at all, focused on the transfer of tribal members to new federal land across the Mississippi. In effect, the federal government adopted a practice of ethnic cleansing, symbolized most starkly by the Trail of Tears, the forced march of the Cherokee from their tribal lands in Georgia to new lands out west.

Something similar occurred in the Seminole tribal lands of Florida. Well before he became President, Andrew Jackson was a leading author of this new chapter in Native American relations. In 1818–19, General Jackson led members of the U.S. Army and local militias from Georgia and Tennessee on a filibustering expedition into Spanish Florida with the stated intention of chastising the Seminole Indians. One stated grievance was long-standing: runaway slaves from Georgia plantations headed south (instead of north), seeking refuge on Spanish soil and in some cases taking up new lives with Native people. Jackson based his right to intervene in part on the Spanish government's inability to bring law and order to the region and to return runaway slaves. In addition, the United States had an outstanding set of economic claims against the Spanish government. Despite these bases for intervention, many people, including some in President Monroe's cabinet, believed that Jackson's foray into Spanish territory violated the law of nations. Jackson's own military campaign undercut his claim that the Native people were his object. He assaulted and captured two Spanish forts in Northern Florida and summarily executed two British subjects suspected of arming Natives and encouraging hostilities. Jackson, and many others, believed that Spain was too weak to retain its American colonies; as with later filibustering expeditions throughout Spanish America, he acted to pry territory from its tenuous grip.

The Adams-Onis Treaty of 1819 ratified the transfer of the Florida territory that Jackson had set in motion but did not bring peace to the Seminole nation. Before Florida attained statehood in 1845, a second Seminole war erupted. This round of hostilities stemmed from U.S. military enforcement of the Indian Removal Act of 1830, which called for the transfer of the Seminole people to Oklahoma. Over the next several years, many Seminoles were relocated, many were killed, and a small number hid in the Florida swamps. Today's Seminole Tribe of Florida traces its origins to these hardy survivors, with two thousand members living on six reservations in the state. The Seminole Tribe of Florida and Seminole Tribe of Oklahoma received a $12 million payment from the Indian Claims Commission in 1957 to compensate the tribes for Native lands taken by the government during the relocation campaign. Around the time it received this award, the Seminole Tribe sought to establish a framework for modern governance. Its constitution, vesting power in a tribal council and establishing tribal courts, dates from the 1950s. The Tribe also created the Seminole Tribe of Florida, Inc., a corporation to manage the tribe's commercial relations.

The flag of the state of Florida, as emblazoned on the back of the jacket in Cortada's painting, nicely, if somewhat elliptically, summarizes this history. The Florida flag consists of the state's seal, firmly planted in the middle of a white field, with two red stripes running diagonally across the middle in the form of a cross. Official website accounts of the red cross emphasize its similarity to the Spanish colonial flags that flew over Florida before its acquisition by the United States. But an alternative interpretation emerges from the timing of the red cross's addition to the flag. The original state flag featured only a white field and a state seal. Florida Governor Francis Fleming called for the addition of the red cross, or saltire, to ward off any suggestion that the flag was meant to convey a message of surrender. Florida voters approved the change in 1900, when strident white supremacy was remaking flags throughout the South. Five years earlier, Alabama had altered its state flag to incorporate the stars and bars of the Confederate flag. As a veteran of the Civil War who fought for the Confederacy, Governor Fleming surely noticed that his proposed addition of a red saltire to the Florida flag tracked the geometry of the Confederate standard. Florida's flag thus evokes the Seminole people (represented on the state's seal as a Native woman spreading flowers), Spanish colonialism, slavery, the Civil War, and the Lost Cause ideology that sprung up in its aftermath and helped to institutionalize Jim Crow segregation in the South. Few flags better capture their state's history.

5   Native Tribes and Gaming

The Seminole Tribe of Florida has been a leader in developing a business model to support tribal activities. In 1977, it was among the first to sell tax-free cigarettes on reservation lands and the first to offer gambling (bingo) on the reservation. As other tribes emulated these business plans, state authorities began to impose taxes and other forms of regulation on the revenue that tribes were raising through reservation gaming. States were motivated by at least two concerns: protecting their own gambling enterprises from Native competition and collecting taxes on the sizable income generated by Native gaming. But the Supreme Court concluded that such state intervention was incompatible with the sovereignty of the tribes reflected in federal statutes limiting the states to the enforcement of criminal laws on the reservation. In *Bryan v. Itasca County*,[6] the Court invalidated a state tax imposed on property owned on reservation land.

Tribes invoked *Itasca County*, which assured a measure of Native autonomy from state regulation and taxation, as they pressed to expand reservation gambling. California and Florida tribes took advantage of the new immunity from state regulation, instituting bingo and poker gaming on reservation land. When California sought to shut down such activities as violations of state criminal laws, the Court in *California v. Cabazon Band of Mission Indians*[7] invalidated the state's action as an impermissible form of tribal regulation. So long as California (and other states) allowed off-reservation forms of gambling (such as a state lottery), they could not use criminal laws to prohibit the tribes from conducting gaming activities on tribal lands.

State leaders asked Congress to intervene, setting the stage for the adoption of the Indian Gaming Regulatory Act of 1988. IGRA authorizes tribes to conduct Class I gaming, such as traditional ceremonial and social gaming within the tribe, without regulatory oversight. It places Class II gaming, such as bingo and table-stakes poker, within tribal control, at least so long as the state permits such gaming on non-reservation sites. The law subjects Class III gaming (casino-style gaming such as slot machines, bank craps, blackjack, and the like) to greater regulation. Tribes can offer such gaming only if the state permits similar forms of gambling off the reservation and only after negotiating a tribal-state compact to govern the siting of the casinos. IGRA requires both sides to bargain in good faith with a view toward reaching agreement on a compact, and provides for additional regulatory oversight at the national level if the tribe and the state fail to reach agreement. IGRA also authorized the tribes to sue the state for breach of its duty to bargain in good faith.

6   *Seminole Tribe v. Florida*

IGRA's provision for suits brought by the tribes against the states gave rise to the Supreme Court's landmark decision in *Seminole Tribe v. Florida*.[8] The Seminole Tribe of Florida sued Florida and its governor in 1991, arguing that the state

---

6   426 U.S. 373 (1976).
7   480 U.S. 202 (1987).
8   517 U.S. 44 (1996).

had declined to enter into good-faith negotiations to site a Class III casino on tribal land. Florida invoked its immunity from suit in federal court, an attribute of state sovereignty that was said to inhere in the Eleventh Amendment to the Constitution. While Florida's argument failed in the federal district court, the United States Court of Appeals for the Eleventh Circuit accepted the state's claim of immunity. Seeking further review, the Tribe happened to present an issue of sovereign immunity on which a five-Justice majority on the Supreme Court had been yearning to make new law. In a sweeping decision, the Court rejected the Tribe's suit and with it the power of Congress to authorize parties to bring suit against the states to enforce federal obligations rooted in the regulatory powers conferred on Congress in the original Constitution of 1788. That meant that Congress lacked power under Article I to authorize suits against the states in the course of regulating interstate commerce and commerce with the Indian tribes.

Several aspects of the decision reflect the Court's desire to make broad new law. Chief Justice William Rehnquist viewed the case as a vehicle to impose an important new restriction on the power of Congress. Rehnquist had been among the chief architects of the Court's 'new federalism' of the 1970s and 1980s, a series of decisions establishing important limits on congressional power. One of those restrictions—on the power of Congress to regulate the states as states by subjecting them to federal regulatory schemes such as the Fair Labor Standards Act—had been overruled in a decision that emphasized the political (as opposed to judicial) safeguards of federalism.[9] Rehnquist dissented vehemently from that retreat from judicial enforcement and vowed that he would work to restore the doctrine of judicial limits.[10] *Seminole Tribe* represents Rehnquist's attempt to deliver on that promise. Instead of barring all regulation of states under the Commerce Clause, however, *Seminole Tribe* restricts the manner in which the beneficiaries of the statute may enforce the regulations. While the rules remain binding on the states, *Seminole Tribe* eliminates private civil litigation against the state itself as an enforcement mechanism.

---

9   Compare *National League of Cities v. Usery*, 426 U.S. 823 (1976) (invalidating extension of fair labor standards to state employees on the ground that it improperly regulated the states as states) with *Garcia v. San Antonio Metro. Transit Auth.*, 469 U.S. 528 (1985) (overruling *Usery* and relying on the political safeguards of federalism to protect the states from burdensome congressional regulation).

10 *Garcia*, 469 U.S. at 580 (Rehnquist, J., dissenting) (expressing confidence that the principle in *Usery* would one day again command a majority of the Court).

A second revealing feature of the decision was its rejection of a companion claim against Florida Governor Lawton Chiles. A separate doctrine, associated with the Court's decision in *Ex parte Young*,[11] permitted individuals to enforce federal laws against the state by suing the state official charged with enforcing the challenged state law. While the state might claim immunity from suit if sued in its own name, state officials enjoyed no such immunity. But *Seminole Tribe* waved aside the argument of the federal government, appearing in defense of IGRA and the tribe's right to sue, that *Ex parte Young* allowed the Tribe to enforce the statute against Florida's officials. It concluded that IGRA had impliedly displaced the *Ex parte Young* action by providing an alternative remedial framework: when coupled with the Court's holding on state immunity from suit, the decision deprived the tribe of any judicial remedy to enforce the state's duty to bargain.

The Court struggled to explain its handling of prior cases. On one hand, it reaffirmed its view that Congress enjoys power to subject the states to suit in the exercise of other non-Article I grants of legislative power, such as that conferred in section 5 of the Fourteenth Amendment. On the other hand, it overruled precedent upholding the power of Congress to subject states to suit in the exercise of its commerce power.[12] In accounting for this differential treatment of its earlier decisions, the Court explained that the Eleventh Amendment (ratified in the 1790s) had qualified all congressional grants of authority then on the books, including the interstate and tribal commerce powers. Sources of legislative power that had been added to the Constitution after the 1790s, such as those conferred in the Reconstruction Amendments, limited the Eleventh Amendment, restoring power to Congress to subject the states to suit. Among the gravest obstacles to this position was the inconvenient fact that the text of the Eleventh Amendment speaks of the 'judicial power of the United States' under Article III of the Constitution but says absolutely nothing about the legislative power.

The outcome of *Seminole Tribe* thus had everything to do with the urgent desire of a five-Justice majority to shield the states from congressional power and very little to do with the historical terms and purpose of the Eleventh Amendment or with the specific claims of the Seminole Tribe against Florida. The Court lumped together two sources of congressional power—over 'commerce among the several states' and over commerce 'with the Indian tribes'—and treated them the same for purposes of assessing the right to sue. That lumping-together enabled the Court to avoid any discussion of difficult questions about how the nature of tribal and state sovereignty differ under the

---

11   209 U.S. 123 (1908).
12   *Seminole Tribe*, 517 U.S. at 66 (overruling *Pennsylvania v. Union Gas Co.*, 491 U.S. 1 (1989)).

Constitution and how those differences might inform the right of the parties to sue and be sued. Instead of reading and interpreting the Eleventh Amendment for clues to such questions, the Court ignored the text of the provision and focused on its decision in *Hans v. Louisiana*.[13] Like *Seminole Tribe*, *Hans* broadly interpreted and applied the Eleventh Amendment to protect states from suit on grounds of sovereign immunity, without regard to the limited text and apparent purpose of the Amendment.

7   Sovereignty, Immunity, and the Origins of the Eleventh Amendment

If one were to ponder the questions of sovereignty and sovereign immunity that *Seminole Tribe* and *Hans* largely ignored, one might begin by looking to the decision that led to the proposal and ratification of the Eleventh Amendment, *Chisholm v. Georgia*.[14] Four of the five Justices who participated in the decision voted to uphold the right of an individual from South Carolina to bring suit against the state of Georgia in federal court. The opinions of the Justices in the majority reflect a variety of themes. Most referred to the text of Article III, which specifically provides for the exercise of federal jurisdiction over controversies between a state and a variety of opposing parties, including another state, a foreign country, and a citizen or subject of another state or country. Coupled with the provision in Article III conferring original jurisdiction on the Supreme Court in state-party matters, the extension of the judicial power to these proceedings did much to persuade the Court that the states were subject to suit in federal court. After all, in a controversy between two states, one state must appear as a defendant.

Of those in the majority, Justice James Wilson wrote the longest and one of the most intriguing opinions. Wilson devoted much of his opinion to the meaning of sovereignty under the newly minted Constitution. For Wilson, among the most learned of the lawyers at the Philadelphia Constitutional Convention and a member of the Convention's important Committee of Detail, it was clear that the states had no rightful claim to sovereignty and no claim to immunity from suit. The Constitution specified (in language that he had helped to write in 1787) that it was ordained and established by the action of the people of the United States, rather than by the states themselves. Toasts

---

13   134 U.S. 1 (1890).
14   2 U.S. (2 Dall.) 419 (1793).

offered to the United States were not, Wilson emphasized in language that anticipated modern usage, 'politically correct.' Such toasts were properly offered instead to the 'people of the United States.'

Wilson's radical populism mirrored that of other members of the Founding generation and represented a clean break with Great Britain, where the Crown enjoyed the sovereign's immunity from suit in the superior courts. Even in Britain, moreover, the courts had long since worked around the problems associated with the aphorism that the King can do no wrong. In its most straightforward terms, sovereign immunity meant that the Crown was not subject, as such, to suit in the courts of England. But that simple statement of sovereign immunity did not get things quite right. Although nominally a matter of grace, the petition of right was available in the Court of Chancery to litigants with property claims against the Crown. What's more, suits against the Crown's officers had long proceeded on the assumption that they did not share the Crown's immunity from suit. Indeed, in the opinion of such respectable jurists as William Blackstone, the King could do no wrong precisely because the King's courts would ensure redress for government misconduct by entertaining appropriate proceedings against the King's men. Following Blackstone, A.V. Dicey, the great British student of constitutional law, described the suability of government officials as the very root of British constitutionalism and the rule of law.[15]

Wilson's idea of popular sovereignty carried with it an idea of jural equality: individuals, groups, associations, and governments all should stand on equal footing before the courts of the United States. Born and educated in Scotland, Wilson may have hit upon this conception of jural equality as a reflection of practice in the Scottish Court of Session, where the Crown was a proper defendant in suits for declaratory relief. Wilson saw jural equality in Article III, which provides for states to sue and be sued in federal court, like other parties to litigation. Others joined Wilson in rejecting the idea of sovereign immunity that the states had invoked in opposing the Court's jurisdiction in *Chisholm*. In his separate opinion, Chief Justice John Jay likened the City of Philadelphia (which was subject to suit as a corporate entity) to the State of Delaware, noting that they had roughly comparable populations. Individuals injured by the wrongs of such government entities were equally entitled to a forum for adjudication of their claims.

Viewed in light of *Chisholm*, one has trouble seeing the states' claim to sovereign immunity as reflecting the overriding consensus view of Founding

---

15   James E. Pfander, 'Dicey's Nightmare: An Essay on the Rule of Law' (2019) 107 California Law Review 108 (describing Dicey's account of the British constitution).

Era understandings of constitutional meaning. Justice James Iredell alone dissented, basing his argument on the view that Congress had not acted with the clarity necessary to subject the states to suit on claims that pre-dated the ratification of the Constitution. Iredell argued that the common law writ of assumpsit did not run against the states as such, leaving claims for money to be addressed as petitions to the Georgia legislature for appropriation bills. Iredell also observed that the All Writs Act, a source of judicial authority to fashion writs necessary for the exercise of federal jurisdiction, incorporated existing forms of action. Iredell would have defused what he correctly saw as a looming crisis over the threat of judicially enforced repayment of state war debts by assigning responsibility to Congress. He mentioned in passing that he had his doubts about the scope of congressional power, but reserved decision on that point. In short, Iredell's disagreement with the majority was not based on his view that the states enjoyed a constitutional immunity from suit.

Given the debate among the Justices, it bears noting that the language of the Eleventh Amendment tracks the language of Article III and does not proclaim an all-encompassing principle of state sovereign immunity. Thus, the Amendment declares that the judicial power of the United States shall not be construed to extend to 'any suit in law or equity, commenced or prosecuted against one of the United States by Citizens of another State, or by Citizens or Subjects of any Foreign State.' It echoes Article III's provision for jurisdiction over 'controversies ... between a State and the Citizens of another State.' As scholars have long argued, and as Justice David Souter emphasized in his *Seminole Tribe* dissent, these words do not proclaim a rule of state sovereign immunity from suit. Instead, they foreclose the exercise of judicial power over two of the diverse-party controversies that Article III had assigned to federal court. One might best read the provision, in short, as curtailing jurisdiction on the basis of party alignment, but as leaving untouched all jurisdiction over claims against states based on federal law. Party-alignment suits were controversial in part because they authorized individuals to pursue money claims on legal obligations that predated the Constitution's ratification and thus threatened the states with retrospective liability. Federal-law claims, by contrast, would operate only on state actions taken after ratification of the new Constitution.

8   Tribal Sovereignty and Immunity

Fitting Native tribes into the scheme of sovereignty and sovereign immunity that has emerged in the last century poses a graver challenge than making sense of the text of the Eleventh Amendment. On one hand, we have it on good authority that Native tribes enjoy immunity from suits brought by both individuals and the states themselves. In *Michigan v. Bay Mills Indian Community*,[16] the Supreme Court reaffirmed several features of the existing law of tribal sovereign immunity. It reaffirmed the status of tribes as domestic dependent nations with a claim to immunity from suit commensurate with their sovereign status and subject to the plenary control of Congress. It explained that the suit in question, seeking to enjoin the tribe from conducting a gambling operation off its reservation, did not fall within the scope of IGRA, allowing states to bring some but not all such injunctive proceedings. Finally, the Court confirmed that both individuals and states can work around the tribe's immunity by suing a responsible tribal official under *Ex parte Young*.

What sense any of this makes may be fairly debated. States, the people of which voluntarily ratified the Constitution and entered the Union subject to its terms, enjoy a constitutionalized form of sovereign immunity that has little textual support in the Eleventh Amendment. Tribes, by contrast, were incorporated into the United States by dint of the treaty and war powers, transforming tribal nations into the domestic dependent nations they have become. Under the law of nations, which framed the early interactions between the Washington Administration and the tribes, foreign nations enjoyed sovereign immunity from suit in the courts of the United States.[17] One might argue, therefore, that the tribal claim to immunity from suit has a stronger historical predicate than a state claim to immunity.

But time has run away with tribal claims to immunity from suit by reference to the law of nations, just as the states' entry into the Union curtailed any immunity they once enjoyed as sovereigns under the law of nations. In 1924, Congress by statute conferred citizenship on all Native Americans, including those who remained on the reservations. Even if one were to regard tribal citizens as members of a separate nation, the immunity accorded foreign nations has eroded over time. Under the restrictive theory on which Congress based the Foreign Sovereign Immunity Act, foreign governments may be subject to suit in the courts of the United States to enforce commercial obligations. By subjecting tribes to suit to enforce commercial obligations, Congress brought tribal immunity mostly in line with that accorded foreign nations.

Arguments from jural equality have had some impact on the right of tribes to sue states in federal court, although they have ironically operated to

---

16   134 S. Ct. 2024 (2014).
17   E.g., *Schooner Exchange v. McFaddon*, 11 U.S. (7 Cranch) 116 (1812) (upholding French vessel's immunity from suit).

broaden state immunity. In *Blatchford v. Native Village of Noatak*,[18] the Court held that an arm of the state of Alaska enjoyed immunity from a suit by a tribe seeking to compel payment of revenue-sharing monies allegedly due to the tribe. The tribe argued that Congress had abrogated the state's immunity, an argument that the Court dodged by concluding that the statute failed to specify the states' suability with the requisite clarity. (Six years later, *Seminole Tribe* rejected the abrogation premise of the tribe's argument when faced with a clear declaration of state suability in IGRA.) The tribe also argued that the states surrendered their immunity to suit in the plan of the convention by agreeing to provisions in Article III that subjected them to suit at the instance of sovereign entities such as states, foreign nations, and Indian tribes. The Court rejected this argument out of hand, concluding that an earlier decision refusing to allow foreign nations to sue the states in federal courts was dispositive.[19] Arguments from jural equality depend on a mutual surrender of immunity, and the Court pointed out that its previous decisions had upheld the immunity of the tribes from unconsented suits by states. Jural equality thus required a symmetric state immunity from suits brought, without state consent, by the tribes.

One can fairly ask if *Seminole Tribe* upsets that symmetrical balance. Congress retains broad power to manage the immunity of the tribes and can subject them to suit in the circumstances it deems appropriate. Thus, no one on the *Bay Mills* Court questioned the power of Congress to subject the tribe to suit; the only issue was whether Congress had done so for the kind of claim presented. *Seminole Tribe*, by contrast, holds that Congress lacks similar authority over the states' amenability to suit. By depriving Congress of power to manage the immunity of the states, *Seminole Tribe* places the states' sovereign immunity from suit on questions of tribal relations beyond the abrogation authority of Congress.

9   Eleventh Amendment Symbolism

Today, the Eleventh Amendment operates as a symbol of state sovereignty, a monument to the successful efforts of the states to gain a measure of protection against federal judicial enforcement of their legal obligations. Those who pressed for the proposal and ratification of the Eleventh Amendment in the

---

18   501 U.S. 775 (1991).
19   Ibid., 780 (citing *Monaco v. Mississippi*, 292 313 (1934)).

1790s sought to protect the states from judicial resolution of disputes over the ownership of land and payment of debts contracted during the Revolutionary War. While those old disputes were interred with the ratification of the Amendment, the symbol of state sovereignty embodied in the Amendment has played a growing and disruptive role in our constitutional jurisprudence. Aimed at common law obligations, the Amendment has been expanded by judicial interpretation to encompass the states' obligation to comply with federal law. Other than in exceptional circumstances, neither individuals, nor foreign nations, nor the domestic dependent nations we know as Indian tribes can sue the states when they violate their legal obligations. The Court supports these results not with the text of the Amendment itself, but with an idea of state dignity that it regards the Amendment as having come to symbolize. How fitting that Cortada has used symbols of his own to contest the symbolism of state sovereignty that the Court has projected onto the Eleventh Amendment.

10 Conclusion

The artistic rendition of the vindication of state sovereignty at the center of this chapter's rumination about *Seminole Tribe* evokes these discordant messages. Cortada captures the connection to IGRA in his depiction of the slot machine-like alignment of Florida icons on the back of the Native jacket. He shows us that Florida emerged as the winner, successfully invoking its immunity from suit as a bar to the enforcement of a federal statute that sought to level the playing field between the tribes and the states. Finally, Cortada suggests that by attributing a free-floating conception of state sovereign immunity to the words of the Eleventh Amendment, the Court has torn away a piece of the fabric of Native life. The Court's conception of the states as 'sovereign, free, and independent' returns us not to the early Republic, when state suability was debated and the Eleventh Amendment was drafted and ratified, but to the era of the Articles of Confederation. And that, as we have seen, was a time when the states dealt harshly with the native people along their western and southern frontiers.

Native people no longer occupy the margins of frontier life. Taking charge of their own affairs and building a commercial foundation for tribal life, they do not depend on federal largesse. Native people have built houses, schools, and government buildings, not the least of which house tribal courts with a growing docket of legal matters arising in Indian country. Tribal claims to jural equality with the state and national governments follow naturally from the growth and success of Native self-government. Perhaps in due course, the practice of tribal sovereignty and independence will occasion a reconsideration of the tribal role in federal adjudication.

Or to put the matter in terms of Cortada's painting—with patient handicraft and artistry, tribes might restore the strips torn from the back of the jacket of the Seminole people.

Recommended Reading

Ablavsky, Gregory. 'Beyond the Indian Commerce Clause.' *Yale Law Journal* 124 (2015): 1012.

Articles of Confederation (1778).

Blatchford v. Native Village of Noatak, 501 U.S. 775 (1991).

Bryan v. Itasca County, 426 U.S. 373 (1976).

California v. Cabazon Band of Mission Indians, 480 U.S. 202 (1987).

Chisholm v. Georgia, 2 U.S. (2 Dall.) 419 (1793).

Cherokee Nation v. Georgia, 30 U.S. 1 (1830).

Declaration of Independence (1776).

Ex parte Young, 209 U.S. 123 (1908).

Hans v. Louisiana, 134 U.S. 1 (1890).

Indian Gaming Regulatory Act of 1988, (Pub. L. 100–497, 25 U.S.C. § 2701 *et seq.*).

Johnson v. McIntosh, 21 U.S. (8 Wheat.) 543 (1823).

Merrell, James H. 'Declarations of Independence: Indian-White Relations.' In *The American Revolution: Its Character and Limits*, edited by Jack P. Greene. New York: New York University Press, 1987.

Michigan v. Bay Mills Indian Community, 134 S. Ct. 2024 (2014).

Perkins, Samuel. *General Jackson's Conduct in the Seminole War, Delineated in a History of That Period, Affording Conclusive Reasons Why He Should Not be President*. Farming Hills: Gale, 2012.

Pfander, James E. 'History and State Suability: An "Explanatory" Account of the Eleventh Amendment.' Cornell Law Review 83 (1998): 1269.

Pfander, James E. 'Rethinking the Supreme Court's Original Jurisdiction in State-Party Cases.' *California Law Review* 82 (1994): 555.

Pfander, James E. 'Sovereign Immunity and the Right to Petition: Toward a First Amendment Right to Pursue Judicial Claims Against the Government.' *Northwestern University Law Review* 91 (1997): 899.

Pfander, James E. 'Waiver of Sovereign Immunity in the "Plan of the Convention."' *Georgetown Journal of Law & Public Policy* 1 (2002): 13.

Pfander, James E. and Jessica Dwinell. 'A Declaratory Theory of State Accountability.' *Virginia Law Review* 102 (2016): 153.

Rosen, Deborah A. *Border Law: The First Seminole War and American Nationhood*. Cambridge: Harvard University Press, 2015.

Seminole Tribe of Fla. v. Florida, 517 U.S. 44 (1996).

U.S. Constitution (1788).

Worcester v. Georgia, 31 U.S. (6 Pet.) 515 (1832).

Bush v. Gore, 531 U.S. 98 (2000)

Xavier Cortada

..

In painting the hourglass at the center of the work, I wanted capture the crucial element of time as it applied to the 2000 presidential election. Time ran out to count all the ballots in Florida (the state whose electors would decide the outcome between Bush and Gore). So the Supreme Court chose to tally nine ballots instead: Theirs.

The hourglass with ballots swirling inside captures that moment, but it also serves as an instrument to measure the passage of time as American democracy continues to (d)evolve. The hourglass is the perfect metaphor for the chaos to come. A nation that grows more and more polarized, a democracy that becomes more fragile with the passage of time.

In my painting, the hourglass also highlights what can happen when you attempt to measure the strength of American democracy—the resolve of its people—in a vacuum. Outside the hourglass-turned-ballot-box chamber is a world that isn't part of the vote-counting calculus. There is a sea of votes casts—hanging chads, butterfly ballots, votes that will never be counted. But these ballots don't matter.

All that matters is what is inside the chamber of the hourglass—its constricting (disappearing) middle cleaves it into two. Two partisan chambers, each intent in upturning the other's world in order to achieve domination and control.

Here two Supreme Court Justices, each standing by and branding the colors of their partisanship, are looking to a universe of ballots that were cast in Florida on November 7, 2000. Both know that imperfections in the voting process make any result other than hand counting every single ballot suspect.

The state courts, charged with overseeing the election, had an option of how to make sure that all votes are counted. Those who disagreed with their decision felt the outcome is predetermined.

The arbiters of truth were tasked with making a decision. In *Bush v. Gore*, the five Republicans on the Supreme Court decided that the clock had run out on the vote counting in Florida. They effectively selected the Republican nominee as the 43rd president of the United States. With only nine votes in the chamber, the tally was easier to count. It was 5 to 4, along party lines.

FIGURE 11.1 Xavier Cortada, *Bush v. Gore*, 531 U.S. 98 (2000), 48" × 36", acrylic on canvas, 2017.
PHOTO: ZENAIDA PIRRI, MIAMI, FLORIDA

CHAPTER 11

Bush v. Gore
Haste Makes Mistakes

Erwin Chemerinsky

After President John F. Kennedy was assassinated, cartoonist Bill Mauldin drew a picture of Abraham Lincoln crying. If I could draw, my picture to illustrate *Bush v. Gore* would be of Chief Justice John Marshall weeping. The Supreme Court in *Bush v. Gore* abandoned basic principles of constitutional law to determine, for the first time in American history, the outcome of a presidential election.

Xavier Cortada's picture is quite different. It features an hourglass at its center, conveying the sense of time pressure surrounding *Bush v. Gore*. And it shows two justices, one seeming to side with Bush, the other with Gore. These elements capture the two fundamental problems with the decision. The perception of a need for an immediate decision led the Court to ignore justiciability problems and to prevent Florida courts from deciding controlling issues of Florida law. And although the Justices were divided, it was not an even split. The five most conservative justices—all appointed by Republican Presidents—ruled in favor of Bush and effectively decided the presidential election in his favor.

In this essay, I want to argue that it is precisely what Cortada depicts with his hourglass—time pressure—that caused the Court to go wrong. Part I reviews what occurred in November and December 2000. Part II describes the Court's decision in *Bush v. Gore*. Part III discusses what went wrong because of the false perception of time pressure depicted by Cortada.

1   What Happened?

The presidential election of Tuesday, November 7, 2000, was one of the closest in American history. By early Wednesday morning it was clear that the Democratic candidate, Vice President Al Gore, won the national popular vote but that the outcome of the electoral vote was uncertain. The presidency turned on Florida and its 25 electoral votes. Early on election night, the television networks called Gore the winner in Florida, only to retract their prediction later in the evening. In the early hours of Wednesday, November 8, the networks declared Bush the winner of Florida and the presidency, only to recant that a short time later and to conclude that the outcome in Florida, and thus of the national election, was too close to call.

On November 8, the Florida Division of Elections reported that Bush had received 2,909,135 votes and Gore had received 2,907,351 votes. Florida law provides for a recount of votes if the election is decided by less than one-half of a percent of the votes cast.[1] Because the difference in votes between the two candidates was less than one-half of a percent, Gore asked for a machine recount of the tally of votes in four counties: Volusia, Palm Beach, Broward, and Miami-Dade. On November 9, Florida Secretary of State Katherine Harris declined to extend the statutory deadline for counties to submit vote totals beyond November 14. By this point the machine recount had narrowed Bush's lead to a mere 327 votes.

Upon learning of the close margin between him and Bush, Gore petitioned and received permission to have a hand recount in the four counties in question. On Saturday, November 11, Bush sued in federal district court to block the manual recount, but his request was denied.

Nevertheless, Harris declared that she would enforce the November 14 deadline and that she would not accept late recounts from counties. She said that the Florida election statute required counties to report their votes within one week of the election, unless one of the statutory exceptions was met. These exceptions included 'proof of fraud that affects the outcome of the election', 'substantial noncompliance with statutory election procedures, and a reasonable doubt exists as to whether the certified results expressed the will of the voters', or where compliance with the deadline is 'prevented as a result of an act of God, or extenuating circumstances beyond their control'. Each of the four counties responded and requested acceptance of late completion of totals; Harris denied each. A suit was brought against Harris in Florida court to compel her to extend the time for the reporting of the results. On Friday, November 17, the Florida trial court ruled in favor of Harris. On Monday, November 20, the Supreme Court of Florida held a nationally televised hearing. On Tuesday night, November 21, the court unanimously reversed and ordered that the secretary of state accept hand recounts from the four counties if they

---

1   Fla. Stat. §102.141(4) ('If the returns for any office reflect that a candidate was defeated or eliminated by one-half of a percent or less of the votes cast for such office ... the board responsible for certifying the results of the vote on such race or measure shall order a recount of the votes cast with respect to such office or measure.')

were completed by 5 p.m. on Sunday, November 26, or Monday morning if the secretary of state was not open for business on Sunday afternoon.

The state court ruled that Florida's secretary of state abused her discretion in refusing to extend the deadline for certifying elections so as to provide the needed time for the recounts. The court said that it was confronted with a conflict between two statutes. One statute, Fla. Stat. §102.111, providing that local election canvassing boards must submit their results 'by 5:00 of the seventh day following an election,' provided the basis for Harris's original November 14 deadline.[2] This law was amended in 1989 to provide that election results may be ignored and board members shall be fined if these deadlines are not met.[3]

But another statute allows any candidate to request a manual recount. This provision states: '[A]ny candidate whose name appeared on the ballot ... or any political party whose candidates' name appeared on the ballot may file a written request with the county canvassing board for a manual recount.'[4] The law provides that the written request may be made prior to the time the board certifies the returns or within 72 hours after the election, whichever occurs later.

The Florida Supreme Court noted that these statutes 'conflict.' The court relied on 'traditional rules of statutory construction'—such as that specific laws prevail over general ones and the more recently enacted law takes precedence over the older one—to conclude that Harris erred in denying the extension of time for the counting. The court also said that 'a statutory provision will not be construed in such a way that renders meaningless or absurd any other statutory provision.' In order to effectuate the law allowing recounts, the court concluded that there must be time for doing so. The court said that the secretary of state's refusal to accept hand recounts after the seven-day deadline was wrong because it negated the statute that expressly provided for those recounts.

On Friday, November 24, the day after Thanksgiving, the Supreme Court of the United States granted certiorari in this case and scheduled oral argument for the following Friday, December 1. In an unprecedented order, the Court permitted the immediate broadcast of the oral argument, a departure from the usual practice of releasing audio recordings at the end of the week of the argument. A few days later, in *Bush v. Palm Beach County Canvassing Board*,[5] the Court remanded the case to the Florida Supreme Court for clarification of

---

2 Fla. Stat. § 102.111.
3 Fla. Stat. § 102.112.
4 Fla. Stat. §102.166(4)(a).
5 531 U.S. 70 (2000).

its earlier decision. In a per curiam opinion, the United States Supreme Court said that it was unclear whether the Florida court's decision was based on its interpretation of the Florida Constitution or Florida statutes. The former apparently would be an impermissible basis for decision, while the latter would be acceptable, based on the United States Supreme Court's interpretation of federal election laws. On Monday, December 4—the day the Florida Supreme Court held oral argument on remand—the court issued a statement saying that its decision was based on its interpretation of Florida statutes, not its constitution.

Meanwhile, on Sunday, November 26, some counties asked for additional time to complete their counting. Palm Beach County asked for two additional hours beyond the 5 p.m. Sunday deadline set by the state supreme court, noting the court had allowed the secretary of state to wait until Monday morning before receiving recount totals. The secretary of state refused all requests for extensions. On Sunday night, November 26, the Florida Elections Canvassing Commission certified the election results: Bush was declared the winner of Florida by 537 votes and thus the winner of Florida's 25 electoral votes.

On Monday, November 27, Gore filed suit in Florida under the Florida law providing for 'contests' of election results.[6] This provision allows a contest based on '[r]eceipt of a number of illegal votes or rejection of a number of legal votes sufficient to change or place in doubt the result of the election'.[7] The statute authorizes a court, if it finds successful grounds for a contest, to 'provide any relief appropriate under such circumstances.'[8]

On Saturday and Sunday, December 2 and 3, a Florida state trial court held a hearing on whether Gore had met the statutory requirements for a successful contest. On Monday, December 4, the Florida trial court held that Gore failed to prove a 'reasonable probability' that the election would have turned out differently if not for problems in counting ballots.

The Florida Supreme Court granted review and scheduled oral arguments for Thursday, December 7. On Friday afternoon, December 8, a 4-to-3 court reversed. It ruled that the trial court had applied the wrong standard in insisting

---

6 Other lawsuits, unrelated to the specific issues in *Bush v. Gore*, were ongoing. For example, voters in Palm Beach County sought a new election based on the so-called butterfly ballot, which they claimed violated Florida law and caused several thousand votes intended for Gore to be mistakenly cast for third-party candidate Pat Buchanan. A Florida trial court concluded that it lacked the constitutional authority to order a new election and the Florida Supreme Court denied review.
7 Fla. Stat. §102.168(3)(c).
8 Fla. Stat. §102.168(8)(3)(c).

that Gore demonstrate a 'reasonable probability' that the election would have been decided differently, where the statute required a showing of '[r]eceipt of a number of illegal votes or rejection of a number of legal votes sufficient to change or place in doubt the result of the election.'[9] The court ordered 'the Supervisor of Elections and the Canvassing Boards, as well as the necessary public officials, in all counties that have not conducted a manual recount or tabulation of the undervotes ... to do so forthwith, said tabulation to take place in the individual counties where the ballots are located.'[10] The court also determined that Palm Beach County and Miami-Dade County had identified net gains of 215 and 168 legal votes for Gore in their earlier recounts and that these should be included in the vote total even though reported after the November 26 deadline.

Just hours after the Florida Supreme Court's decision, on Friday night, December 8, a Florida trial judge ordered that the hand-counting of the uncounted votes commence the next morning and that it be completed by 2 p.m., December 9. The judge retained authority to resolve any disputes.

Counting commenced as ordered on Saturday morning. At the same time, Bush asked the United States Supreme Court to stay the counting and grant certiorari. In the early afternoon that day, the United States Supreme Court, in a 5-to-4 ruling, stayed the counting of votes.[11] Justice Stevens dissented on the grounds that there was not an irreparable injury, a requirement for such a stay.[12] Justice Scalia wrote a short opinion, not joined by any other Justice, in which he said that the requirements for a stay were met. He said that Bush had shown a likelihood of prevailing on the merits and also irreparable injury. Justice Scalia said that there were two such harms: a cloud over the legitimacy of a Bush presidency if the counting showed Gore ahead but the counting was disallowed by the Supreme Court, and degradation of the ballots from their handling, preventing a more accurate counting later if ordered by the Court.[13]

On Monday, December 11, the United States Supreme Court held oral arguments, again broadcast immediately after completion. At approximately 10 p.m. E.S.T. on Tuesday night, December 12, the Court released its opinion in *Bush v. Gore*.

---

9   *Gore v. Harris*, 772 So. 2d 1243 (Fla. 2000).
10 *Ibid.*, 1262.
11 *Bush v. Gore*, 531 U.S. 1046 (2000).
12 *Ibid.*, 1048.
13 *Ibid.*, 1047.

2 The Decision in *Bush v. Gore*

Xavier Cortada depicts two justices standing by an hourglass. But in a per curiam opinion joined by five of the Justices, the Supreme Court held that counting the uncounted ballots without standards denied equal protection and that counting could not continue because Florida wished to choose its electors by December 12. The per curiam opinion was joined by Chief Justice Rehnquist and Justices O'Connor, Scalia, Kennedy, and Thomas. Additionally, Chief Justice Rehnquist wrote an opinion concurring in the judgment, joined by Scalia and Thomas, arguing that the Florida Supreme Court had impermissibly changed Florida's election law in a manner that violated federal law.

The per curiam opinion began by reiterating that the right to vote is a fundamental right and that '[w]hen the state legislature vests the right to vote for President in its people, the right to vote as the legislature has prescribed is fundamental; and one source of its fundamental nature lies in the equal weight accorded to each vote and the equal dignity owed to each voter.'[14] The central problem was that the Supreme Court of Florida ordered the counting of the uncounted ballots but failed to prescribe standards for that counting. 'The problem inheres in absence of specific standards to ensure its equal application. The formulation of uniform rules to determine intent based on these recurring circumstances is practicable and, we conclude, necessary.'[15] The Court said that a recount without explicit standards results in similar ballots being treated differently. The Court also objected to the state's recount procedures:

> In addition to these difficulties the actual process by which the votes were to be counted under the Florida Supreme Court's decision raises further concerns. That order did not specify who would recount the ballots. The county canvassing boards were forced to pull together ad hoc teams comprised of judges from various Circuits who had no previous training in handling and interpreting ballots. Furthermore, while others were permitted to observe, they were prohibited from objecting during the recount.[16]

The Court thus concluded that counting the uncounted ballots pursuant to the order of the Florida Supreme Court would deny equal protection: 'The recount process, in its features here described, is inconsistent with the minimum

---

14 *Bush v. Gore*, 531 U.S. 98, 107 (2000).
15 *Ibid.*
16 *Ibid.*, 110.

procedures necessary to protect the fundamental right of each voter in the special instance of a statewide recount under the authority of a single state judicial officer.'[17] The Court declared that it was deciding only the matter before it, but not setting a general precedent: 'Our consideration is limited to the present circumstances, for the problem of equal protection in election processes generally presents many complexities.'[18]

The Court then confronted the key question: Should the case be remanded to the Florida Supreme Court for it to set standards for the counting or should the Court order an end to the counting process? The per curiam opinion said that Florida indicated that it wished to avail itself of the conclusive federal presumption that a state's electors chosen at least six days before the meeting of the Electoral College[19] would be recognized by Congress.[20] In 2000, the Electors met on December 18, thus the last day for Florida to take advantage of this "safe harbor" was December 12, the day of the Court's decision. The Court thus ordered an end to the counting:

> The Supreme Court of Florida has said that the legislature intended the State's electors to 'participat[e] fully in the federal electoral process', as provided in 3 U.S.C. §5. That statute, in turn, requires that any controversy or contest that is designed to lead to a conclusive selection of electors be completed by December 12. That date is upon us, and there is no recount procedure in place under the State Supreme Court's order that comports with minimal constitutional standards. Because it is evident that any recount seeking to meet the December 12 date will be unconstitutional for the reasons we have discussed, we reverse the judgment of the Supreme Court of Florida ordering a recount to proceed.
>
> Seven Justices of the Court agree that there are constitutional problems with the recount ordered by the Florida Supreme Court that demand a remedy. The only disagreement is as to the remedy. Because the Florida Supreme Court has said that the Florida Legislature intended to obtain the safe-harbor benefits of 3 U.S.C. §5, Justice Breyer's proposed remedy — remanding to the Florida Supreme Court for its ordering of a constitutionally proper contest until December 18 — contemplates action in

---

17 Ibid., 109.
18 Ibid.
19 The Electoral Colleges meets on the first Monday after the second Wednesday in December following the election. 3 U.S.C. § 7.
20 3 U.S.C. § 5.

violation of the Florida election code, and hence could not be part of an "appropriate" order authorized by Fla. Stat. §102.168(8) (2000).[21]

The per curiam ordered an end to vote-counting in Florida based on its interpretation of Florida election law.

Rehnquist's opinion concurring in the judgment focused on §5 and the conclusive presumption that electors chosen under laws enacted prior to election day must be accepted by Congress. Rehnquist argued that this prevented a state from changing its electoral process after the election and that the Supreme Court of Florida had done this by usurping the authority Florida law had vested in the Florida secretary of state and the Florida circuit courts. That court 'significantly departed from the statutory framework in place on November 7, and authorized open-ended further proceedings which could not be completed by December 12, thereby preventing a final determination by that date.'[22]

Each of the four dissenting Justices wrote opinions. Justice Stevens, joined by Justices Ginsburg and Breyer, challenged the per curiam's premise that there had been denial of equal protection. He argued that the procedures created by the Florida Supreme Court, with a trial judge resolving disputes, could prevent unequal treatment of like ballots. 'Admittedly, the use of differing substandards for determining voter intent in different counties employing similar voting systems may raise serious concerns. Those concerns are alleviated—if not eliminated—by the fact that a single impartial magistrate will ultimately adjudicate all objections arising from the recount process.'[23]

Stevens said that if the lack of standards for counting is the problem, the solution is to send the case back to Florida for the creation of standards and subsequent counting. He concluded with powerful language:

> The endorsement of that position by the majority of this court can only lend the credence to the most cynical appraisal of the work of judges throughout the land. It is confidence in the men and women who administer the judicial system that is the true backbone of the rule of law. Time will one day heal the wound to that confidence that will be inflicted by today's decision. One thing, however, is certain. Although we may never know with complete certainty the identity of the winner of this year's Presidential election, the identity of the loser is perfectly clear. It is

---

21 *Ibid.*, 111.
22 *Ibid.*, 122 (Rehnquist, C.J., concurring in the judgment).
23 *Ibid.*, 123 (Stevens, J., dissenting).

the Nation's confidence in the judge as an impartial guardian of the rule of law.[24]

Justice Souter's opinion, joined by the other three dissenters, objected to the Court hearing the case at all. He argued that there were no significant federal issues raised and that the case should have been left to the Florida courts to resolve.[25] Ginsburg's dissent agreed that there was no denial of equal protection and that in any event the appropriate solution was to have the case sent back to Florida for the counting to continue.[26]

Finally, Justice Breyer acknowledged that there were equal protection problems with counting votes without standards, but argued that the Court was wrong to end the counting rather than remand for counting with standards.[27] He stressed that there was nothing magical about the December 12 deadline; states could still choose their electors after that date and could be confident that Congress would recognize them. He ended his opinion forcefully:

> I fear that in order to bring this agonizingly long election process to a definitive conclusion we have not adequately attended to that necessary 'check upon our own exercise of power,' 'our own sense of self-restraint.' Justice Brandeis once said of the Court, 'The most important thing we do is not doing.' What it does today, the Court should have left undone. I would repair the damage done as best we now can, by permitting the Florida recount to continue under uniform standards.[28]

3 What Went Wrong?

Cortada's painting contains two main elements—the hourglass and the two Justices, one red one blue.

3.1 *The False Perception of Crisis*

Cortada's use of an hourglass in his depiction of *Bush v. Gore* conveys the sense that time was running out. Some, such as Judge Richard Posner and John Yoo, have argued that, although its reasoning was flawed, *Bush v. Gore* was justified

---

24   *Ibid.*, 128 (Stevens, J., dissenting).
25   *Ibid.*, 129 (Souter, J., dissenting).
26   *Ibid.*, 136 (Ginsburg, J., dissenting).
27   *Ibid.*, 146 (Breyer, J., dissenting).
28   *Ibid.*, 158 (Breyer, J., dissenting).

to prevent a national crisis.[29] This is an ends-justifies-the-means claim: the goal of preventing a political crisis was sufficiently important to warrant a decision that was wrong as a matter of constitutional doctrine.

This argument is flawed factually and normatively.

Factually, it is wrong to say that a crisis would have occurred had the Supreme Court denied review or upheld the Florida Supreme Court. The additional counting was to be completed by the end of Sunday, December 10, so it would have been completed by that date had the United States Supreme Court not stopped the counting on Saturday, December 9.[30] There were two possibilities at that point: Bush would have remained ahead or Gore would have taken the lead. No one can know which would have occurred. Ironically, media tabulations of ballots showed that Bush would have remained ahead under Gore's preferred approach to counting ballots and Gore would have won Florida under Bush's preferred approach.[31]

Had Bush remained ahead, there obviously would have been no constitutional crisis. Bush would have carried Florida and prevailed in the Electoral College, and no one would have objected. Had Gore gone ahead, it would have been more complicated, but still not a crisis because federal laws provide a basis for resolving disputes about which slate or electoral votes to recognize.[32]

In all likelihood, Florida Governor Jeb Bush would not have changed the ascertainment that he filed in the Electoral College certifying that his brother carried Florida. It also is possible that the Republican-controlled Florida legislature would have enacted a resolution awarding the Florida electors to Bush.

On the other hand, the Florida Supreme Court might have declared that Gore carried the state based on the results of the recount that occurred pursuant to its order. That would have produced two sets of electors from Florida, one for Bush and one for Gore. This has happened before, most recently in Hawaii in the 1960 election between Kennedy and Richard Nixon.[33] Federal law

---

29   Richard Posner, *Breaking the Deadlock: The 2000 Election, the Constitution, and the Courts* (Princeton: Princeton University Press, 2001), 188–89; John C. Yoo, 'In Defense of the Court's Legitimacy' (2001) 68 University of Chicago Law Review 790. For an excellent criticism of Posner's analysis, see H. Jefferson Powell, 'Overcoming Democracy: Richard Posner and *Bush v. Gore*' (2001) 17 Journal of Law & Politics 352.

30   *Gore v. Harris*, 772 So. 2d 1243, 1262 (Fla.) (per curiam), rev'd per curiam sub nom. *Bush v. Gore*, 531 U.S. 98 (2000).

31   E.g., Richard L. Berke, 'Who Won Florida? The Answer Emerges, but Surely Not the Final Word', New York Times, Nov. 12, 2001; 'Recount Would Have Increased Bush Win, Papers Say', Los Angeles Times, Apr. 4, 2001.

32   *See* 3 U.S.C. §§ 1–15 (2000).

33   Jack M. Balkin, '*Bush v. Gore* and the Boundary between Law and Politics' (2001) 110 Yale Law Journal 1421 n.55.

provides that the new Congress meeting in January decides which slate represents the state if the House of Representatives and the Senate agree.[34] Such agreement was highly unlikely here. The new House, which was controlled by Republicans, surely would have voted in favor of the Bush electors. But the new Senate was split evenly between Democrats and Republicans. Under Senate rules, the Vice President breaks a tie. There, of course, is no doubt for whom Vice President Al Gore would have voted. Federal law then provides that if the House and the Senate disagree about which electors to recognize, the governor of the state decides.[35] Obviously, there is no question as to which set of electors Jeb Bush would have chosen to represent Florida.

All of this would have been resolved by early January 2001, well in advance of the January 20 date prescribed for the inauguration of the new President.[36] It would have been dramatic and even entertaining to watch. But a crisis that risked paralyzing the country? No serious risk existed. It is possible to hypothesize legal issues that could have arisen along the way. For example, what if the Florida Supreme Court ordered Jeb Bush to change Florida's ascertainment in the Electoral College and he refused? But any legal issues could have been resolved as they arose and courts, including the Supreme Court of the United States, could have prevented a crisis then. This would have been preferable to acting to forestall a feared crisis that was unlikely to develop.

Normatively, the crisis argument is even more problematic. What exactly is meant by a 'constitutional crisis?' Who decides if one exists? What powers does this bestow on the courts? In early 2017, the federal government shut down because of a budget impasse between the White House and Congress. Would this justify the federal courts stepping in and arbitrarily awarding additional budget power to one side or the other? No one made such a claim even when the federal government was closed for days for lack of funds. During the 1960s and 1970s, the executive branch waged an unpopular war without a formal congressional declaration of war and suits were filed to halt it as unconstitutional. Was this a crisis that justified judicial intervention to stop an unconstitutional war costing thousands of lives and billions of dollars? The Supreme Court never believed so.

Those who advance the 'crisis hypothesis' never explain why averting a crisis justifies changing the usual constitutional rules and doctrines. It is a frightening proposition because the government can claim a variety of crises—fighting the war on terrorism, fighting the war on drugs, stopping communism—and

---

34   3 U.S.C. § 15 (2000).
35   3 U.S.C. § 6.
36   U.S. Const. amend. XX § 1 (1933).

claim that each warrants actions that would otherwise be unconstitutional. Ignoring the Constitution in times of crisis goes against the very core of why there is a Constitution: to ensure that core values and commitments are not sacrificed in difficult times.

3.2 The Court Should Not Have Decided Bush v. Gore

Was *Bush v. Gore* justiciable when the Court decided it on December 12? The Court did not address this issue, perhaps because it was not raised in the briefs. But justiciability is jurisdictional and courts are required to raise jurisdictional issues sua sponte.[37]

There are serious reasons to doubt justiciability. The issues were not ripe for judicial review. The central issue was whether the counting of votes would deny equal protection. There would be a constitutional violation only if similar ballots were treated differently in that counting process. But it could not be known if this would occur until the counting occurred and the trial judge in Florida ruled on all of the challenges. Until then, and at the time the Court decided the case, any problem of similar ballots being treated differently, and thus violating equal protection, was purely speculative.

The per curiam order focused on inequalities that already had occurred, such as differences in the Miami-Dade County and the Palm Beach County countings.[38] But the already-completed counting was not the issue before the Supreme Court.[39] The only issue was whether the counting should continue. Prior experience was not predictive of what would occur because a single judge was overseeing the counting under the Florida Supreme Court's order, hearing all disputes and potentially eliminating any inequalities by applying a uniform standard.

Justice Stevens emphasized this point in his dissent: 'Admittedly, the use of differing substandards for determining voter intent in different counties

---

[37] Erwin Chemerinsky, '*Bush v. Gore* Was Not Justiciable' (2001) 76 Notre Dame Law Review 1098.

[38] *Bush*, 531 U.S. at 107 (per curiam).

[39] The per curiam opinion argued that the past inequalities were relevant. 'That brings the analysis to yet a further equal protection problem. The votes certified by the court included a partial total from one county, Miami-Dade. The Florida Supreme Court's decision thus gives no assurance that the recounts included in the final certification must be complete.' Ibid., 108 (per curiam). But even the Supreme Court's phrasing acknowledges that it was speculative as to whether there would be incompleteness by the time the counting was finished. The existence and extent of this incompleteness could not be known when the Supreme Court decided the case on December 12 precisely because the Court had stayed the counting process.

employing similar voting systems may raise serious concerns. Those concerns are alleviated—if not eliminated—by the fact that a single impartial magistrate will ultimately adjudicate all objections arising from the recount process.'[40] But Stevens did not recognize that his observation showed that the challenge was not ripe for review. Only after the counting was complete could the parties claim that there was inequality and thus a judicially remediable constitutional violation.

Phrased another way, the Supreme Court improperly treated an 'as applied' equal protection challenge as if it were a facial challenge. Bush was not arguing that Florida election law was unconstitutional on its face. Neither in the briefs nor in the oral argument did his lawyers suggest such a facial attack. Rather, Bush argued that counting without uniform standards denied equal protection.[41] This would be an equal protection violation only if, after the counting and the resolution of disputes by the judge, similar ballots were treated differently. But that could not possibly be known until all the ballots were counted.

Bush v. Gore was not ripe for a more basic reason: George W. Bush might well have ended up ahead after the counting. In that event, there would have been no need for the Supreme Court to decide his appeal. The Court repeatedly has held that a case is not ripe when it is unknown whether the injury will be suffered.[42]

Bush v. Gore was not ripe for review when the stay was issued on December 9, when the case was heard on December 11, or when the case was decided on December 12. The case would have been ripe only after all the counting was done if: a) Gore came out ahead in Florida and b) Bush could present evidence of inequalities in how the similar ballots were actually counted. Until and unless these eventualities occurred, the case should have been dismissed.

We also can question whether the Court should have found the case not justiciable as a political question. The most famous defense of the political question doctrine was made by Alexander Bickel.[43] Bickel wrote:

---

40 *Bush*, 531 U.S. at 126 (Stevens, J., dissenting).
41 Pet. for a Writ of Cert. at 20–23, *Bush v. Palm Beach County Canvassing Bd.*, 531 U.S. 70 (2000) (No. 00-836), LEXIS 2000 U.S. Briefs 836.
42 E.g., *O'Shea v. Littleton*, 414 U.S. 488, 495–96 (1974); *Abbott Labs. v. Gardner*, 387 U.S. 136, 148 (1967).
43 Alexander M. Bickel, 'The Supreme Court 1960 Term: Foreward: The Passive Virtues' (1961) 75 Harvard Law Review 46; Alexander M. Bickel, *The Least Dangerous Branch: The Supreme Court at the Bar of Politics* (New Haven: Yale University Press, 1962), 183 ('The culmination of any progression of devices for withholding the ultimate constitutional judgment of the Supreme Court--and in a sense their sum--is the doctrine of political questions.').

> Such is the foundation, in both intellect and instinct, of the political-question doctrine: the Court's sense of lack of capacity, compounded in unequal parts of (a) the strangeness of the issue and its intractability to principled resolution; (b) the sheer momentousness of it, which tends to unbalance judicial judgment; (c) the anxiety, not so much that the judicial judgment will be ignored, as that perhaps it should but will not be; (d) finally ('in a mature democracy'), the inner vulnerability, the self-doubt of an institution which is electorally irresponsible and has no earth to draw strength from.[44]

Although Bickel wrote these words a half century ago, they seem prescient when applied to *Bush v. Gore*. Certainly there is 'strangeness of the issue' and its intractability to a principled resolution. Never had the Supreme Court decided a presidential election. The Court said that counting the ballots without uniform standards would be unequal, but no prior decision had found variations in election practices among counties within one state to be unconstitutional. Nor did the Court explain why this inequality was impermissible while many other inequalities in Florida—such as differences in voting machines, in ballots, and in treatment of minority voters—were constitutional.

Indeed, the Court seemed aware of the problems with applying equal protection to variances among counties and the potential to open the door to challenges to virtually every election because local election officials control the process in every state. The per curiam opinion said: 'Our consideration is limited to the present circumstances, for the problem of equal protection in election processes generally presents many complexities.'[45] This confirms Bickel's concerns about the strangeness of the issue and the lack of principles for resolving it.

Bickel's second factor is even more relevant: 'the sheer momentousness of [the issue], which tends to unbalance judicial judgment.' If any case fits this description, it surely is *Bush v. Gore*. Bickel's latter two criteria point to a concern over what issues should be decided by unelected judges. Bickel's concern was how involvement in political issues could compromise the legitimacy of the Court.

Although I am critical of Bickel's view and of many of the uses of the political question doctrine, *Bush v. Gore* obviously cost the Supreme Court enormous credibility. More than forty-nine million people voted for Al Gore and

---

44 Bickel, *The Least Dangerous Branch*, 184.
45 *Bush*, 531 U.S. at 109 (per curiam).

undoubtedly virtually all of them regarded the Court's decision as a partisan ruling by a Republican majority in favor of the Republican candidate. Few, if any, cases in American history have been more widely perceived as partisan than *Bush v. Gore*.

Why did the Court miss the justiciability issues? I believe it was the time pressure, as reflected in Cortada's hourglass. The petition for certiorari was filed on Saturday, the case was argued on Monday, and the decision was issued on Tuesday night. Without the sense of urgency, the Justices would have had time to pause and see the justiciability problems.

3.3 The Court Was Wrong to Stop the Counting in Florida

Bush v. Gore's treatment of federalism is one of the most important areas to consider. The supreme irony of the case is that the majority was comprised of five Justices who revolutionized constitutional law through their commitment to federalism and states' rights,[46] but here showed no deference to the state court.

The per curiam opinion made two arguments. First, counting the uncounted votes without standards violated equal protection. Second, Florida law prevented the counting from continuing past the safe-harbor date of December 12.[47] This second point is indispensable to the Court's decision to end the counting. Assuming there were inequalities in the counting that violated the Constitution, there were two ways to remedy this situation: count none of the uncounted ballots or count all of the ballots with uniform standards. The latter would require remanding the case to the Florida Supreme Court for development of standards and for such relief as that court deemed appropriate.

It must be emphasized that the Supreme Court did not hold that federal law prevented the counting from continuing. The only reason for not remanding the case—for which Souter and Breyer argued[48]—was the Court's judgment that Florida law prevented this. Two paragraphs near the end of the per curiam opinion explained:

> The Supreme Court of Florida has said that the legislature intended the State's electors to participat[e] fully in the federal electoral process, as

---

46 E.g., *United States v. Morrison*, 529 U.S. 598 (2000) (declaring unconstitutional provision of the Violence Against Women Act as exceeding the scope of Congress's commerce power); *United States v. Lopez*, 514 U.S. 549 (1995) (declaring unconstitutional the federal Gun Free School Zone Act as exceeding the scope of Congress's commerce power).
47 Ibid., 110–111.
48 Ibid., 129 (Souter, J., dissenting); also Ibid., 144 (Breyer, J., dissenting).

provided in 3 U.S.C. §5. ... That statute, in turn, requires that any controversy or contest that is designed to lead to a conclusive selection of electors be completed by December 12. That date is upon us, and there is no recount procedure in place under the State Supreme Court's order that comports with minimal constitutional standards. Because it is evident that any recount seeking to meet the December 12 date will be unconstitutional for the reasons we have discussed, we reverse the judgment of the Supreme Court of Florida ordering a recount to proceed.[49]

The majority responded to Breyer's argument that the case should be remanded to the Florida courts: 'Because the Florida Supreme Court has said that the Florida Legislature intended to obtain the safe-harbor benefits of 3 U.S.C. §5, Justice Breyer's proposed remedy—remanding to the Florida Supreme Court for its ordering of a constitutionally proper contest under December 18—contemplates action in violation of the Florida Election Code, and hence could not be part of an "appropriate" order authorized' by Florida law.[50]

The sole reason the Court ended the counting was its interpretation of Florida law. But no Florida statute stated or implied that the counting had to be done by December 12.

The sole authority for the Supreme Court's conclusion was one statement by the Florida Supreme Court. But the state court made that statement in a very different context and when not faced with the issue created by the Supreme Court's ruling. After the Court decided on December 12 that counting without standards violated equal protection, the issue was the appropriate remedy under Florida law: continue the counting past December 12 or end the counting to meet the December 12 deadline. The United States Supreme Court could not know how the Florida Supreme Court would resolve this issue because it never had occurred before. Prior Florida decisions emphasized the importance of making sure that every vote is accurately counted.[51] The Florida Supreme Court might have relied on this to continue the counting past December 12. Alternatively, it might have ended the counting, treating December 12 as a firm deadline in Florida.

---

49   Ibid., 110–111.
50   Ibid.
51   E.g., *State ex rel. Millinor v. Smith*, 144 So. 333, 335 (Fla. 1932) ('The right to a correct count of the ballots in an election is a substantial right which it is the privilege of every candidate for office to insist on, in every case where there has been a failure to make a proper count.').

Indeed, following *Bush v. Gore*, the Florida Supreme Court dismissed the case.[52] Justice Shaw, in a concurring opinion, declared:

> [I]n my opinion, December 12 was not a 'drop-dead' date under Florida law. In fact, I question whether any date prior to January 6 is a drop-dead date under the Florida election scheme. December 12 was simply a permissive 'safe-harbor' date to which the states could aspire. It certainly was not a mandatory contest deadline under the plain language of the Florida Election Code.[53]

Perhaps a majority of the Florida Supreme Court would have followed this view, perhaps not. The point is that this was a question of Florida law to be decided by the Florida Supreme Court. The United States Supreme Court never allowed it that opportunity.

It is clearly established that state supreme courts get the final word as to the interpretation and meaning of state law. In *Murdock v. City of Memphis*,[54] the Court held that it could review only questions of federal law and that the decisions of a state's highest court are final on questions of state law. The Court explained that the Judiciary Act of 1789 was based on a belief that the Supreme Court must be available to ensure state compliance with the United States Constitution, but that there was no indication that Congress intended the Court to oversee state court decisions as to state law matters.[55] From a federalism perspective, the Court should have remanded the case to the Florida Supreme Court to give it an opportunity to decide under Florida law whether the counting should continue. The Court impermissibly usurped the state court's authority to decide Florida law in this extraordinary case.

Why? Here Cortada got it right: it was all about the Court's perception of time as reflected in that hourglass.

4 Conclusion

Cortada's picture shows one justice seemingly standing with Bush and one with Gore. This subtle depiction of partisanship is important in understanding

---

52 *Gore v. Harris*, 773 So. 2d 524 (Fla.) (per curiam), rev'd per curiam sub nom. 531 U.S. 98 (2000).
53 Ibid., 528–29 (Shaw, J., concurring) (footnotes omitted).
54 *Murdock v. City of Memphis*, 87 U.S. 590 (1874).
55 Ibid., 631–32.

Bush v. Gore. His hourglass, filled with what seem to be ballots, reflects the time pressure that accounts for much of what happened. What is missing from the picture is the decision itself, a 5-4 ruling that made George W. Bush the President of the United States.

Recommended Readings

Bruce Ackerman, *Bush v. Gore: The Question of Legitimacy*. New Haven: Yale University Press, 2002.

Howard Gillman, *The Votes that Counted: How the Court Decided the 2000 Presidential Election*. Chicago: University of Chicago Press, 2001.

Richard Hasen, *The Voting Wars: From Florida 2000 to the Next Election Meltdown*. New Haven: Yale University Press, 2013.

Richard Posner, *Breaking the Deadlock: The 2000 Election, the Constitution and the Courts*. Princeton: Princeton University Press, 2001.

*Stop the Beach Renourishment, Inc.
v. Florida Department of Environmental
Protection,* 560 U.S. 702 (2010)

Xavier Cortada

∴

> This land is your land, this land is my land.
> This land was made for you and me.

Actually, it really belongs to water because it is made by water:

> Water beats and breaks mountains. Grinds them into stone, pebbles. Into grains of sand that rush downstream and are swept out to sea. They toss and turn up and down a water column and with the force of a crashing wave eventually land: One grain of sand multiplied across a shoreline. Until water comes and erodes that shoreline, taking the sand back to sea.

It is an endless dance, seen sharply at the water's edge, even if for a moment, as the water line recedes with the tide. It is most dramatic as it erases shorelines. The dance creates an ever-changing landscape—one that wasn't made for us, but one we want to control so that it best works for us. So the state engages in beach restoration by dredging sand from the deep and adding it to the shoreline.

In Florida, dredging sand to beef up a shoreline may be as futile as any endeavor. Water is always in charge. Dredging sand can be as offensive to the property owners who just lost their waterfront as it is to the littoral creatures who just lost their habitat. But according to the Supreme Court, it is within government's role to do so: Because Florida owns the seabed, there can be no taking.

In the painting for *Stop the Beach Renourishment, Inc. v. Florida Department of Environmental Protection*, there is machinery pumping sand from the deep, displacing water in ways that seem unnatural. There is water chewing away at the shoreline. Boundaries become fluid. In depicting beach restoration, the media I used mattered: I used sand I personally collected at the water's edge to depict the original sea bed in the painting's backdrop. Then, using multi-purpose sand I purchased in a 60-pound bag at Home Depot, I created globs splattering dredged sand from the deep to depict the brutal process of artificially restoring shorelines. As that happens, water drips back in ... Or is it flowing up? Indeed, more than an illustration, the media and composition make the painting a conceptual work: It is impossible to decipher what is up or down. What is land or sky? Water or sand? Where does the property line live? Are you looking at the work as a cross section or from a bird's eye view? It is confusing, disorienting. All remains unresolved, as is our ability to coexist with nature. In time, sea-level rise will resolve all the ambiguity.

FIGURE 12.1 Xavier Cortada, *Stop the Beach Renourishment, Inc. v. Florida Department of Environmental Protection*, 560 U.S. 702 (2010), 48" × 36", acrylic, sand and mixed media on canvas, 2017
PHOTO: ZENAIDA PIRRI, MIAMI, FLORIDA

CHAPTER 12

Stop the Beach Renourishment, Inc. v. Florida Department of Environmental Protection

On Art, Law, and the Power of the Sea

Laura S. Underkuffler

1 Prologue

What is art in human life? When we think of art, it seems at first blush to be just another human endeavor. It is brush strokes of some chosen substance across a piece of canvas or paper. It is the piece of wood or stone left after pieces have been removed by human hands. It is sounds made of a certain pitch and in a certain pattern rather than another.

Yet we know that art is more. It is more than the mechanics of creation or even the materials of which it is comprised. It is more not because of what it is, but because of what it can evoke. Somehow a work of art allows us to access—indeed sometimes forces us to feel—emotions, thoughts, and connections that are buried or denied in everyday life. It allows us or compels us to experience hidden, deeper complexities that humans experience. It is another way of human knowing.

In stark contrast are the processes of law. Law relies on objective facts, syllogistic reasoning, transparent argument, and carefully constructed histories in resolving disputes. Law eschews unarticulated standards and personal or inexplicable emotions. Its processes and products must be express, proven, and knowable by all.

Occasionally, of course, art and law are superficially entwined. Whether a piece of art belongs to this person or that person or to this country or that country is a matter of domestic or international law. Ownership of art, like ownership of all chattels, is determined by legal rules and processes. But the law takes great care to distance itself from the intrinsic properties of the art itself. Even when the identity of the creator of the art, the meaning of the art, or human attachment to the art is important to ownership,[1] the law attempts

---

[1] Consider, for instance, the ownership considerations of cultural property. Rosemary J. Coombe, 'The Properties of Culture and the Politics of Possessing Identity: Native Claims

to restrict inquiries to objectively verifiable standards and criteria. Law determines the structure of interpersonal relations within which a piece of art exists; it does not and—it is believed—cannot be concerned with the inner worlds and emotional powers that art, the subject of the dispute, involves. Law must maintain its integrity. It must strive to stand separate and apart from the emotional, mysterious, and 'degenerate' processes of art.[2]

So we believe. But is it true?

I explore that question in this chapter. The subject of the inquiry is Xavier Cortada's painting depicting the Supreme Court decision in *Stop the Beach Renourishment, Inc. v. Florida Department of Environmental Protection*.[3] This case is famous, dealing with objections by beach-front landowners to government efforts to replenish an eroding strip of beach-front land. The Court's decision, which dealt with important 'takings' issues,[4] is presented in careful, factual, and objective terms. The painting, which appears at the beginning of this chapter, is another matter. It is a mélange of streaks of vivid and clashing colors; it presents a dissection of a piece of coastline, with a swath of dark brown land, an equally vivid swath of orange for dry-sand beach, and an intrusive red line separating both from what appears to be the roiling sea. A bluish-black pipe stretches along the bottom of the painting, curved and snake-like. The pipe spews darkly colored matter that crosses the red line separating water and beach and spreads across the existing sand. The picture is not of the natural beauty of the place or even of human experience or desire for the sea. It portrays division and violent collision, with spaces and forces that cannot be reconciled.

The contrast between the painting and the Court's decision is stark. It tends at first glance to reinforce the separation of law and art. Whatever the painting is meant to convey, it is both fortunate and necessary—we immediately believe—that the law did not consider those dark and twisting forces. The law must maintain its focus and refrain from sinking into the abyss of conflicts such as this. To do so would be to risk the integrity of the law, the objective

---

in the Cultural Appropriation Controversy' in *After Identity: A Reader in Law and Cultures*, eds Dan Danielson and Karen Engle (Abingdon: Routledge, 1995), 251–272.

2 Laura S. Underkuffler, *Captured by Evil: The Idea of Corruption in Law* (New Haven: Yale University Press, 2013), 1–2 ('The contemporary Western ideology of law assumes that law must operate within a universe of knowable and articulable standards, logical and demystified.') Ways of knowing that defy these standards are deemed to be 'degenerate' or 'incommensurable,' as something which the dominant theory cannot explain.

3 560 U.S. 702 (2010).

4 U.S. Const. amend. V ('[N]or shall private property be taken for public use, without just compensation.').

standards and methods of the law, which (we believe) are essential if law is to succeed.

2   A Deeper Assessment: *Stop the Beach Renourishment*

Stop the Beach Renourishment[5] deals with property, government, and individual expectations. It also deals with the relationship of humans with each other and with the sea.

The case arose from a decision by local Florida authorities to restore a 6.9-mile stretch of beach that had been severely eroded by several hurricanes.[6] This project, undertaken under the authority of the Florida Beach and Shore Preservation Act,[7] involved dredging sand from the floor of the ocean and adding it to the diminished beach. As designed, the project would add approximately seventy-five feet of dry sand to the beach, seaward of the existing mean high-tide line.[8]

Under other provisions of Florida law, title to private littoral property—beach-front land—extended from the uplands of the property to the mean high-tide line. The mean high-tide line marked the usual boundary between private beachfront property and state-owned land. The private owner possessed the dry-sand area. But the State owned, in trust for the public, the area of the beach that was exposed at low tide and the land that was permanently submerged beneath the sea.[9]

Ocean shorelines are ever-changing. Over time, sand is deposited and eroded by the sea. Under Florida law, accretions to shoreline land—additions to the dry-sand beach that occurred gradually and imperceptibly over time—inured to the benefit of the owner of the private land. A sudden change in the shoreline—termed an avulsion—was handled differently. In this case, the seaward boundary of the private beachfront land remained what it was: the high-tide line before the avulsion occurred. Newly added land became the property of the owner of the seabed, which in the case of the ocean was the State.[10]

Of course, what the ocean giveth, it also taketh away. Beaches that are the recipients of sand from the sea can also be the victims of the taking of sand

---

5 560 U.S. at 702.
6 Ibid., 711.
7 Beach and Shore Preservation Act, Fla. Stat. Ann. §§161.011–161.45 (West 2006).
8 *Stop the Beach*, 560 U.S. at 711.
9 Ibid., 707–08.
10 Ibid.,708–09.

from opposite tidal forces. Just as the owners of private ocean-front property could gain land by natural accretion, they could lose land by natural erosion. Under Florida law, if the shoreline eroded, mean high- and low-tide lines moved landward and beachfront owners lost the land that was now seaward of the mean high-tide line.[11]

Beach-renourishment projects—by which seabed sediment is artificially added to the beach—introduce a new dimension to this process. Such government projects can add hundreds or thousands of cubic yards of sand to beaches and are intended to be permanent. When such a project was undertaken, the Beach and Shore Preservation Act required that a new boundary between private beachfront property and State-owned land be established. The State—which held title to the seabed—was required to set a new and fixed 'erosion control line' to replace the fluctuating mean high-tide line as the boundary between public and private property. Once the new line was recorded it became permanent, and neither accretion to nor erosion from the (newly created) public beach affected the private property owner's boundaries. In *Stop the Beach*, the erosion control line was fixed at the location of the pre-existing mean high-tide line.[12] Upward of that line, the private owners owned dry-sand beach and uplands. Below that line were the State's new dry-sand beach, the wet-sand area, and the ocean floor.

Although the renourishment project benefitted the private owners by saving their property from erosive dangers, they nonetheless sued the State. They claimed that the project and the law authorizing it deprived them of vested property rights without just compensation. Those rights were to receive accretions to their property and to have their property in contact with the ocean's waters.[13]

In the course of state-court litigation, a question was certified to the Supreme Court of Florida: whether the Beach and Shore Preservation Act unconstitutionally deprived the upland owners of littoral rights without compensation.[14] That court answered the question in the negative. It held that the right to own future accretions was a future contingent interest, not a vested property right, and that private owners had no littoral right to contact with the water.[15]

---

11   Ibid.
12   Ibid., 711.
13   *Save Our Beaches, Inc. v. Florida Dept. of Environmental Protection*, 27 So.3d 48, 57 (Fla. 2006).
14   *Stop the Beach*, 560 U.S. at 1105.
15   Ibid., 1112, 1119–1120.

The owners obtained review in the Supreme Court of the United States. They argued that the Florida Supreme Court's decision changed Florida law and effected a taking of the owners' rights in violation of the Fifth and Fourteenth Amendments.[16] The Fifth Amendment, which is applied to the states through the Fourteenth, provides that private property cannot be taken for public use without the payment of just compensation.

The landowners' case raised a previously latent but potentially far-reaching claim, not yet addressed in Supreme Court jurisprudence. All prior takings claims adjudicated by the Court had involved challenges to legislative or executive action. *Stop the Beach* raised a new question: whether a state judicial decision that 'changed' the law—through clarification, interpretation, or new policy—constituted a taking of property in violation of the federal Constitution.[17]

The far-reaching implications of this abstract issue cannot be overstated. Takings law in the United States serves what many would argue to be an outsized function: in both the law and the popular mind, it is believed to define the boundary between individual vested rights and the exercise of government power.[18] This purported role is largely mythical—political, cultural, practical, and other constraints on the actions of government are far more powerful as a practical matter than the threat of takings lawsuits. Nevertheless, takings claims and their prospect remain a powerful tool in the maintenance of the existing private/public detente. Any wholesale extension of their purview to an entirely new class of government actions would upend that balance.

In addition, the idea of extending takings claims to state court decisions was an analytical Achilles' heel in takings jurisprudence. The Supreme Court

---

16   U.S. Const. amend. v.
17   *Stop the Beach*, 560 U.S. at 707.
18   As I have previously written, '[t]he American preoccupation with constitutional cases—in particular, takings cases—as the battleground for determining the meaning of rights of private property has been a subject of some mystification to observers abroad. Clearly, issues about the nature, scope, and legitimacy of private property claims occur in contexts far more varied than simply that of constitutional constraints on government action. Indeed, most government issues, and all disputes between private citizens, do not involve constitutional questions at all.' Nonetheless, it is the constitutional context 'that has fired the American debate about the meaning of rights in private property. In particular, the Takings Clause has provided the contemporary stage for real and symbolic struggles among different visions of individual prerogative and state power.' Laura S. Underkuffler, *The Idea of Property: Its Meaning and Power* (Oxford: Oxford University Press, 2003), 37–38 (footnotes omitted).

has repeatedly stated that federal takings law does not define the private interests that are protected; that is the province of state law.[19] The '[s]everal [s]tates [are] possessed of residual authority ... to define "property" in the first instance.'[20] This black-letter statement, repeated in virtually every Supreme Court takings decision in the past forty years,[21] contains an internal and analytically fatal contradiction. If states can define—indeed definitively define—the individual interests protected by the Takings Clause, how can a state's undertaking of that act—in any manner—be deemed unconstitutional? Put another way, if an individual's protected expectations are determined by state law, how can an individual have protected expectations that 'conflict' with the law that determines them? 'If "property" for Fifth Amendment purposes is a creature of state law, created with complete authority by the organs of state government, why cannot states interpret it, change it, or eliminate it—by judicial, legislative, or executive means—as they see fit?'[22] The idea that states have the power to determine property rights is incompatible with the notion that, when they exercise that definitional function, they unconstitutionally destroy those rights. If property is a creature of state law, it is not something that exists apart from that law. Either states can determine what property is or they cannot determine what property is; it cannot be both.

Some members of the Court had attempted to limit this problem by dividing state law into two kinds: legislative and executive acts, which are subject to constitutional challenge, and 'background' principles of state law—such as statements of the common law by courts—which are not.[23] If challengeable actions include state court decisions, this distinction crumbles. If any state court's clarification, interpretation, or recognized evolution of state law can be challenged in a takings case, the idea that there is any realm in which the state can independently determine property law and protected individual interests under that law vanishes. Instead, we move into a realm in which any change in

---

19 *Phillips v. Washington Legal Foundation,* 524 U.S. 156, 164 (1998); accord, *Stop the Beach,* 560 U.S. at 707.
20 *Pruneyard Shopping Center v. Robins,* 447 U.S. 74, 84 (1980).
21 E.g., *Stop the Beach,* 560 U.S. at 707; *Palazzolo v. Rhode Island,* 533 U.S. 606, 630 (2001); *Phillips v. Wash. Legal Found.,* 524 U.S. 156, 164 (1998); *Lucas v. S.C. Coastal Council,* 505 U.S. 1003, 1027–1230 (1992).
22 Laura S. Underkuffler, 'Judicial Takings: A Medley of Misconceptions' (2011) 61 Syracuse Law Review 203, 206.
23 E.g., *Palazzolo,* 533 U.S. at 630; *Lucas,* 505 U.S. at 1016, 1027–30. This distinction is a dubious one. Presumably it is rooted in some idea that the legislative and executive branches—universally, the elected branches of government—are more likely to take radical action or ignore legitimate individual expectations than are courts.

any state law that harms any individual interest becomes a potentially unconstitutional taking of property.

A plurality of the *Stope the Beach* Court attempted to defend the idea of judicial takings with the following argument. Property is a creature of state law. But the state remains constrained in an important way. Once a property right has been established, the usually legitimate exercise of state power ends.[24] 'If a legislature *or a court* declares that what was once an established right of private property no longer exists, it has [unconstitutionally] taken that property.'[25]

The idea of constitutionally protecting (only) established rights has a certain appeal, but it has serious problems. In particular, when is there an 'established' right and what is its 'elimination?' Consider the following examples, selected at random from a recent legal publication:

An appellate court held that a party to a loan contract could pursue a class action against the lender, despite an arbitration clause and class-waiver provision in the loan agreement. Under Supreme Court precedent, the appellate court's decision appeared to be contrary to the lender's rights.[26] Has the appellate court deprived the lender of a previously established property right?

A state supreme court engrafted a new requirement onto its prior interpretation of an 1867-era statute dealing with rights to church property by breakaway congregations, jeopardizing the claims of the plaintiff breakaway congregation to disputed church property.[27] If this additional rule is factually held on remand to bar the plaintiff's property claims, has the plaintiff lost a previously established property right?

A state's bulk sale of driver's license data to third parties and the resale of these data to other parties were upheld by an appellate court, despite what appeared to be clear statutory law to the contrary.[28] Did this decision eliminate the individuals' previously established property interests in their personal information?

An appellate court overruled its prior decisions in an area of law on the ground that they were ill-advised and rejected by other courts.[29] Has the

---

24   *Stop the Beach*, 560 U.S. at 715 (plurality opinion).
25   Ibid. (emphasis in original).
26   *Fensterstock v. Educ. Fin. Partners*, 611 F.3d 124, 127 (2d Cir. 2010).
27   *Protestant Episcopal Church in the Diocese of Va. v. Truro Church*, 694 S.E.2d 555, 558 n.3, 559 (Va. 2010).
28   *Staylor v. Acxiom Corp.*, 612 F.3d 325, 340 (5th Cir. 2010).
29   *S Jeld-Wen, Inc. v. Van Brunt (In re Grossman's Inc.)*, 607 F.3d 114, 120, 121 (3d Cir. 2010) (en banc).

plaintiff, who lost a valuable monetary claim as the result of the court's action, been deprived of a previously established property right?

In short, the unworkability of the plurality's division of state law into 'established' and 'non-established' rights, with the first protected and the latter not, is obvious. Presumably every judicial decision that a court issues will 'establish' law and thereby 'establish' individual rights. Unless a court simply and woodenly repeats what it previously held, with no modification whatsoever, there will be a 'change' from 'prior law' that adversely affects some individual's 'previously established' property right. It is a court's task to declare the law. Its duty is to interpret and to apply the law under new or uncertain circumstances. Under the plurality's view, there is no allowance for this function. A potential takings claim arises in the course of every exercise of this basic judicial power.

Against this swirling background, the Court avoided these issues and decided the case on other grounds. All eight justices[30] agreed that the landowners should lose on the ground that under prior Florida law, they had in fact lost nothing.[31] Neither of the legal rights claimed by the landowners was ever a 'right' under State law, thus the decision by the Supreme Court of Florida deprived them of nothing. A landowner's right to accretions long had been subordinate to the doctrine of evulsion, which was what the beach-restoration project triggered.[32] In addition, there was no right under Florida law that guaranteed a private beach-front owner contact with the sea.[33] Because the state supreme court's decision did not change the law, the question of any 'judicial taking' was eliminated. As for the future theoretical viability of such claims, the Court splintered.[34]

One can breathe a sigh of relief that the Court did not go down another hopeless ('judicial') takings path and into the doctrinal morass that would have come with it.[35] If 'non-determination' is 'determination,' then the Court might have resolved the critical issue in the case. The difficult and overwhelmingly important question of 'judicial takings'—and with it the question of what 'rights' individuals can claim in the legal status quo—was left in the judicial dustbin.

---

30   Justice Stevens took no part in the decision of the case.
31   *Stop the Beach*, 560 U.S. at 729–33.
32   Ibid., 730–33.
33   Ibid., 732–33.
34   Ibid., 713–28 (Kennedy, J., concurring in part and concurring in the judgment), 734–45 (Breyer, J., concurring in part and concurring the judgment).
35   Underkuffler, 'Judicial Takings,' 203.

Other frustrations with the Court's decision remain, however. The legal question of judicial takings did not arise in just any context. The case would not have raised such widespread passions among observers if the challenged judicial 'change' had been in a zoning law, an OSHA safety standard, or an agricultural regulation. There was, in fact, far more involved in the case than the Justices acknowledged.

3   Cortada's Painting

The remaining question is what else *Stop the Beach* involved and whether that 'else' was important to the case. For these questions, we turn to Cortada's painting.

At first glance, the painting has little to do with the case that it portrays. The colors are vivid, clashing, harsh, and stark. It seems to portray a piece of coast. A dark brown color, uniformly heavy in its tone, demarcates the upland area that the claimants own. Beneath this area is a straight black line, depicting an unwavering and implacable boundary between this land and sand. Next is an area of sand, lighter and slightly more variable in color, but drawn with the same severity. A thick red line—incongruous in color—separates this area from the sea.

The ocean is next, a roiling mass of cobalt blue and black. A snake-like pipe looms along the bottom, large and grotesque, a brooding and threatening presence in the sea. The pipe expels an avalanche of matter, bursting upward and outward, polluting the water and obliterating the beach and its red boundary line. This pipe is 'renourishing' the beach. There is nothing tentative or delicate, integrated or harmonious, about what this painting depicts. The feeling is one of cold and colliding forces upon a starkly outlined division of land and sea.

At first, the violence that this painting evokes seems to be too much. We think of the beach as a place of serenity and beauty, happiness and sharing. Our image of it has nothing of the restless forces that this painting portrays.

But more of the facts behind *Stop the Beach* might help us to understand this painting. In an essay entitled 'A Stake in the Sand,'[36] *New York Times* writer Andrew Rice captured the history of the place where the case arose:

> The sands found Destin first. They started off eons ago, from the Appalachian Mountains, washing their way down the rivers that flow into the

---

36   Andrew Rice, 'A Stake in the Sand,' New York Times, Mar. 19, 2010.

ON ART, LAW, AND THE POWER OF THE SEA 223

> Gulf of Mexico. Winnowed to pure, hardy quartz, the sediment moved with the gulf's currents and gathered into the necklace of narrow barrier islands that buffer Florida's panhandle. Time and tides refined the sand into a soft, sun-bleached powder. By the 1830s, when a Yankee sea captain named Leonard Destin sailed down to the wilderness of the Florida Territory, he discovered beaches as dazzling and white as a fresh blanket of snow. The sight evidently impressed the captain, for his reaction—like that of so many migrants who followed—was to claim a piece of the shore. ...
>
> For a long time after that, very little changed in the community of Destin. Well into the 1970s, the town still had fewer than 2,000 full-time residents. ... But then word got out about its emerald green waters, its mountainous dunes and, most of all, the sugary sand.
>
> Beachgoers arrived, followed by developers, who swiftly set about bulldozing Destin's pine barrens to build condominiums, amusement parks, golf resorts and luxury outlet malls.[37]

Beneath this apparently stable picture, however, the threatening forces of nature loomed. '[A]ll along the coast beaches were growing wider and more alluring,' Rice wrote. '[O]nly a few longtime residents remained wary of the folly of staking out [the] shifting sands.'[38]

Later, Destin's tides—and fortunes—changed. 'Both human interventions ... and natural phenomena ... have dire consequences for the world's coastlines, the vast majority of which are currently slipping out to sea.'[39] In Destin's case, catastrophe hit in 1995, when Hurricane Opal destroyed the shoreline's twenty-foot dunes and critically eroded the structure of the beach.[40] The human response was to do what the case describes: to pump the ocean floor upon the beach, in a mechanical and (many scientists believe) ultimately doomed effort to thwart the power of the sea.

The painting depicts this struggle. Age-old natural processes threatened what the humans valued in this case, and the humans battled back with violence. The painting's portrayal of the human project as a dark, threatening, snake-like creature invokes the project's environmental dangers. Material was dredged from the ocean's bottom—a mixture of sediment and creatures—and spewed onto the dwindling beach's sand. This was indeed a place of violently

---

37   Ibid.
38   Ibid.
39   Ibid.
40   Ibid.

conflicting forces, with unknown costs in the attempted imposition of human will on the ancient processes of the sea and land.

The collision, however, between human 'renourishment' efforts and natural processes is not the only arrogance of human will of which the painting tells. Dividing the painting into artificial zones of upland, beach, and the ocean's depths tells of more. Humans conflicted with humans, struggling to protect what they had prior to the ravages of the sea.

To appreciate this, we must begin with one of the case's central mysteries. Why would beachfront owners—whose land was saved by the beach-renourishment project—so bitterly oppose it? Why would owners, who understood that this battle with nature was the only way to save their land, go to court to stop it? The answer can be found in a fact that was not a part of their formal legal claims: that the creation of a 'renourished' State-owned beach bordering their land would force them to share with the public their connection to the sea.

Rice described this fear in his essay about the case. The renourishment project, officials initially believed, would be a win-win for everyone. The town would save its shoreline and the owners would save their land. It was a surprise, therefore, when opposition to the plan arose. As Rice observed, '[g]enerally, people protest when they're losing something, not regaining [it]. ... [W]hy would a beachfront property owner oppose ... renourishment?'[41] The answer lay in the ownership of sand.

> 'Private Beach,' the sign warned, with a big red stop signal. 'No Trespassing.' On a stormy morning, unusually high waves crashed almost to the base of the wooden signpost at the edge of Linda Cherry's property. 'The bottom line,' Cherry was saying, 'is you've got to leave Mother Nature alone.' As the wind whipped the thin strip of beach that separates the gulf from her three-story Destin vacation home, Cherry tried to explain how she'd become a leader in the fight against Florida's efforts to counter erosion. ... [T]he root justification was simple: [the desire] to be left alone. ...
>
> 'They add 100 feet of sand,' Cherry said. 'So you no longer own waterfront property, you own public beachfront property.' ... Cherry would rather see the beach wash away than cede an inch of it to ... masses [of strangers].[42]

---

41 Ibid.
42 Ibid.

Cherry and a neighbor, Mike Wright, described their historical problem with trespassers. 'Cherry pulled out a digital camera to show ... pictures of sunny days, [with] beached watercraft and multicolored umbrellas' on what was then her private beach. These owners 'believe they've paid handsomely for their privacy.' The loss of their control was worse than the prospect of their beaches' loss.[43]

Perhaps most inexplicable to these owners was their discovery that members of the public believed they had an inherent right to occupy private beachfront land. The owners described how, when confronted, members of the public were incredulous that there could be a 'private beach' under existing legal rules and regulations, into which they were forbidden entry. Just 'as the homeowners ... believe they've paid handsomely for their privacy, ... the public feels viscerally entitled to the shore.'[44] After the beach-renourishment program, any possible private claim would be gone. There would be a new, large, dry-sand area which the public could occupy between the owners' private properties and the sea.

The painting captures these issues and emotions roiling beneath the surface of the case. Human efforts to divide and control the beach are represented by harsh, heavy black and red lines that separate 'zone' from 'zone' and 'claim' from 'claim.' This is not an area of natural land in which humans share and on which they lightly tread; it is one of ownership claims, conflict, division, and exclusion. Although we tend to think (as humans) that boundaries are magical, predestined, or the products of nature, the painting's vivid and incongruous colors separating human zones of claimed control remind us that they are not. Nature will neither respect nor reify such boundaries, and they will be resisted by the land we parcel out.

Reflecting on all of this, the Court's opinion suddenly seems strangled and flat. Here we are, in the nation's highest court, with a case presenting the deepest struggles of human against nature and human against human. In fact, we feel these conflicts over every inch of coastline that divides dry land from the sea. The painting is right in its unmasking of stark claims, violence, and the collision of spaces and forces. Yet the Court's opinion mentions none of these. It is a detached presentation of contextless arguments, an analytical chess match on the courtroom floor. It does not recognize the bitter and futile struggle with nature that beachfront renourishment involves. It does not recognize

---

43 Ibid.
44 Ibid.

the bitter conflicts over access and privacy—of human against human—that every private beachfront case presents.

It is undeniable that the painting illuminates other, darker, more complex dimensions of the case. All of the impressions and questions raised by the painting might be true in some emotional or other realm and might be valuable in that space. But do they have anything to do with law? Should a case that turned on a narrow legal issue be represented by a painting that depicts a 'renourishment' pipe as a large, threatening, snake-like apparatus, or that portrays human and natural conflicts in vivid and clashing colors, with a bright red line (blood red line?) dividing dry land and sea?

4 Law, Art, and the Art of Law

Cortada's painting and the law share one important legal truth. Property conflicts have winners and losers. If my claim to fence this land, to clear this timber, or to control this beach is upheld, your claim to access or to control the same is denied. The very nature of these resources and of property claims to them means that property rights in one person inevitably deny the same rights in others. At its most fundamental level, any court judgment—or the vindication of any other claim to land by force—is necessarily and unavoidably an allocative act.[45]

In considering the parties' conflicting claims in *Stop the Beach,* the Court implicitly recognizes this truth. There is no suggestion that both claims might be honored or that the Court should establish some other form of sharing. The landowners with their claims, and the members of the public (represented by government) with theirs, were locked in a struggle for control. There could be but one winner. Both the Court's decision and the violence of Cortada's painting recognize this truth.

Beyond this basic truth, the Court's decision avoids any mention of the tale of turbulence that the Cortada painting tells. It does not discuss the relentless forces of ocean and shore which created the crisis and which continue today. It does not discuss the nourishment project's violence and its threat to plant and animal life or the ultimate futility that such projects involve. There is no sense of the passions that the human parties felt or of the ultimate arbitrariness of the artificial boundaries that they struggled to draw in the shifting sand. All

---

45   Underkuffler, *The Idea of Property,* 140–41.

that mattered to the Court was what the Florida courts previously had decided the parameters of State law to be.

As a strictly 'legal' matter—as we think of the law—the Supreme Court's approach was undoubtedly correct. The core question presented by the case was whether federal constitutional takings claims could be extended to decisions by courts. This question would have been presented, and the same abstract inquiry pursued, no matter where or how the underlying case arose. If a state court had changed entitlements under banking laws or marital-property division laws or land-use laws, the legal issue would have been the same. The passions, violence, and futilities involved in the underlying facts in *Stop the Beach* had no bearing on the case.

If that is true, why does Cortada's painting continue to haunt us? Is there some reason, in this case, why we cannot so easily separate law and art?

In *The Humane Imagination*,[46] constitutional-law scholar and artist Charles Black explored 'law as ... art.' By law, he meant 'the whole set of methods of viewing law'—the construction of statements, the historical insights, the legal anthropology that we unconsciously use. These methods and approaches, he wrote, 'partake in ... [an] artistic quality.' 'Even as mathematics and the physical sciences proceed by intuition, by creative leap, to their most significant results,' so we come to our greatest legal insights. Law as art is 'a set of possibilities.' It is a process of human choice, 'using the materials at hand,' to produce results that affect us all. Despite its protestations, law is 'within the range' of human creation, 'from painting to medicine, to which we commonly give the name of art.'[47]

Cortada's painting haunts us. And it haunts the processes of law because it forces us to see the smallness of the world that law is often deemed to be. Although the Supreme Court's ruminations and decision in *Stop the Beach* are 'controlled,' 'cerebral,' and reflect what we expect a court to say, the painting subtly and powerfully indicts the smallness of these processes. There is nothing controlled, limited, or cerebral about this painting. It depicts, and forces us to confront, the larger realities of the case. We feel the relentless processes of nature and the arrogance of human attempts to interfere with them. We feel the artificiality of our red and black boundary lines and the dangers inherent in our belief that our machines will protect our exclusive realms of privacy and control. No matter how much we try to tell ourselves that the issues in the case stand apart from these, in the deep recesses of our minds we doubt it. After our

---

46   Charles L. Black, Jr., *The Humane Imagination* (Woodbridge: Ox Bow Press, 1986).
47   Ibid., 18–21.

encounter with the painting, our way of viewing—our *way of knowing*—the case has changed.

Should we celebrate this new disquiet or condemn it? There is an argument for the latter. As I have previously written, there are powers and dangers in the admission of 'degenerate' concepts and ways of knowing into the processes of law. For instance, in a criminal case 'invitations to decision makers to implement subjective ideas of evil are arguably invitations toward standardlessness, emotionally driven prosecutions, and other violations of basic guarantees of the rule of law.'[48] These are ways of knowing that invite us 'to indulge our disgust, to express our outrage, to feel our anger and desire for retribution against the accused.'[49] Such dangers might be more acute in a criminal case, when the life of an individual 'deviant' is at stake, than in a civil case. Emotions, however, can unpredictably and unfairly warp the decision in any case. There are potential costs in letting emotions of this sort influence our decisions and police our social boundaries.[50]

Against this cost we must consider other factors. The Cortada painting haunts us, disturbs us, and influences us because of the truth that it conveys. We know that the dispute in *Stop the Beach* involves exactly what the painting portrays. We know that these messages are important. In addition, we know that emotions are part of all social institutions to some degree and that they act in concert with cognition to convince us of fact. How this knowledge is achieved often seems quite secondary to the truth that it conveys.

Finally, law as we construct it is not the detached enterprise that the strictly 'objective' and 'neutral' conception pretends. Is how we resolve this case only a matter of history and reason, with no connection to the integrity of nature and human needs? Does the result of the Supreme Court's decision lack any connection to human blindness to natural processes, the violence of man-made 'restorative' efforts, and the human need for connection with the sea? We can tell ourselves that the Court's decision has only abstract legal-doctrinal effect, but we know this is untrue. A decision of any kind—for what it says and for what it does not say—is part of the building of an edifice of power. By acting we decide. By closing our eyes, we also decide. Willful blindness will not change the nature of the contending forces that the case presents and the fact that our act—or failure to act—will make an effective choice among them.

In *The Immense Journey,* the great naturalist and evolutionist Loren Eiseley ruminated on the connection that human beings feel to the ocean's waters.

---

48   Underkuffler, *Captured by Evil*, 106.
49   Ibid., 108.
50   Ibid., 108–113.

The connection is deep and powerful; it is atavistic and material. It is rooted in the lime in our bones, which persists from the historical time when we emerged as creatures from the sea. '[W]e are all castaways,' with historical roots, memories, and desires that we cannot possibly understand. 'No utilitarian philosophy explains a snow crystal, no doctrine of use or disuse. ... There is no logical reason for the existence of a snowflake, any more than there is for [our] evolution [from the sea]. It is an apparition from that mysterious shadow world beyond nature, that final world which contains—if anything contains—the explanation of men and catfish and green leaves.'[51]

Recommended Reading

Black, Charles L., Jr. *The Humane Imagination*. Woodbridge: Ox Bow Press, 1986.

Coombe, Rosemary J. 'The Properties of Culture and the Politics of Possessing Identity: Native Claims in the Cultural Appropriation Controversy.' In *After Identity: A Reader in Law and Culture*, edited by Dan Danielson and Karen Engle, 251–270. New York: Routledge, 1995.

Eiseley, Loren. *The Immense Journey: An Imaginative Naturalist Explores the Mysteries of Man and Nature*. New York: Random House, 1957.

Rice, Andrew. 'A Stake in the Sand.' *New York Times*. Mar. 19, 2010.

Underkuffler, Laura S. *Captured by Evil: The Idea of Corruption in Law*. New Haven: Yale University Press, 2013.

Underkuffler, Laura S. *The Idea of Property: Its Meaning and Power*. Oxford: Oxford University Press, 2003.

Underkuffler, Laura S. 'Judicial Takings: A Medley of Misconceptions.' *Syracuse Law Review* 16 (2011): 203–12.

---

51 Loren Eiseley, *The Immense Journey: An Imaginative Naturalist Explores the Mysteries of Man and Nature* (New York City: Random House, 1975), 6, 14, 27.

Florida v. Jardines, 569 U.S. 1 (2013)

Xavier Cortada

∴

This is a picture of what lies inside a house, what you find when you walk across the front door of a private home. The texture is rich, as is the information stored therein: The molecules swirling as odor in the air and residue on a wall are all the crumbs of evidence left behind. They capture what is happening or has happened inside that home. It is evidence ready for taking, if you can access it.

Human-made technology allows us to collect that information with a swab, place in a plastic cup, and analyze at the lab—but only with a search warrant. That requirement even applies to searches that would allow law enforcement to use technologies that could collect that information from the front porch, without having to step inside.

Through breeding and training, humans have actually developed that kind of technology. It's called a dog.

In the painting, I've depicted the information a search dog 'sees' with its nose from the other side of a locked door. A dog's ability to 'see' what is inside using different neurons—olfactory neurons—is astonishing. It is so effective that it is tantamount to being able to use a dog's nose to bust open a door and see what's inside.

That is why in the painting I have depicted the animal as all nose. It is its strongest asset.

But there's also another dimension to this depiction. We coevolved with this animal and think of it as a companion. It is a species that we domesticated. Brought into our homes and our lives. Pets that lick us, sleep in our bedrooms, chew on our toys.

Like so much in nature, we've also molded this species to fit our own interests: We've bred them into pets (wagging tails), guard dogs (all teeth), racing dogs (all feet), police dogs (all nose). Most of us know better than to try to pet a dog from the K-9 unit. And a community knows all too well that seeing a police officer bring a dog to sniff your front door is an altogether different visual than having your neighbor walk his dog on your front lawn. They are two different animals: One requires a pooper scooper, the other probable cause.

The police officers failed get a search warrant for the dog they brought to Jardines's front porch. The Supreme Court told them they were wrong in not doing so: Bad dog.

FIGURE 13.1 Xavier Cortada, *Florida v. Jardines*, 569 U.S. 1 (2013), 48" × 36", acrylic on canvas, 2017.
PHOTO: ZENAIDA PIRRI, MIAMI, FLORIDA

CHAPTER 13

Florida v. Jardines
The Distortions of Implied Artistic License

Andrew Guthrie Ferguson

1   Introduction

Painting begins on a blank canvas—a white space for the creative mind. Judicial writing begins with a similarly blank page. But unlike painters, judges sketch within a framework of rules, precedent, and shared understandings to provide implicit and explicit guideposts for the outcome. A good legal opinion is built on a solid and clearly visible foundation of logic, factual reasoning, and persuasive evidentiary support. A bad legal opinion is more impressionistic, emotive, and ultimately unconvincing.

Florida v. Jardines[1] is a bad legal opinion—an unpersuasive, scattershot decision more memorable for its vivid writing than for any lasting coherent argument. Yet in its bold claims about social customs, nosy neighbors, and Girl Scouts selling cookies, the story of 'Franky,' the drug-sniffing dog invading Joelis Jardines's home, will remain forever memorable. The opinion, like its author Justice Antonin Scalia, offers a colorful, vivid, and arrogantly untethered answer to a long-standing criminal procedure question—what Fourth Amendment protection can citizens expect in and around their homes.

The Fourth Amendment protects against unreasonable searches and seizures:

> The right of the people to be secure in their persons, houses, papers, and effects, against unreasonable searches and seizures, shall not be violated, and no Warrants shall issue, but upon probable cause, supported by Oath or affirmation, and particularly describing the place to be searched, and the persons or things to be seized.[2]

---

1   *Florida. v. Jardines*, 569 U.S. 1 (2013).
2   U.S. Const. amend. IV.

Jardines asked whether it is Fourth Amendment "search" for police investigators to bring a trained drug-detection dog to the front door of a home to uncover evidence of illegal drug possession.

Xavier Cortada's painting inspired by *Jardines* mirrors this sense of creative license. Colorful, vibrant, and memorable, the painting distills the central emotion that animates Scalia's majority opinion—a physical intrusion into the home violates a sense of security, property, and order. Bursting through the frame is Franky's canine nose, as scents swirl in a chaos of un-centered movement. It reveals the constitutional harm by juxtaposing size and structure into the center of a protected home. The painting reflects a Fourth Amendment doctrine in flux and Scalia's largely unsuccessful effort to paint over doctrinal gaps with vigorous assertions that blur and confuse upon close examination.

This chapter explores the concepts of 'constitutional distortion,' 'implicit license,' and 'intrusion' as connecting themes of the *Jardines* opinion and Cortada's painting. Both formerly blank canvases accurately capture the emotional impact of a Fourth Amendment violation, even if in the end they are both better thought of as creative works of creative thinkers—a result generally more acceptable for visual artists than Supreme Court Justices.

The chapter begins by setting forth the colorful facts of *Jardines*, then situates these facts amid the larger constitutional fault lines that undergird the choices made by Scalia and the concurring and dissenting Justices. *Jardines* both clarified and confused Fourth Amendment doctrine and its rationale has had a significant effect on protections around the home. Finally, the chapter looks at the meaning of *Jardines* in the context of the Fourth Amendment. The lens for this legal examination is Cortada's painting that accurately and cleverly captures the chaotic spirit and quirkiness of modern Fourth Amendment theory.

2 Coloring the Facts

Picture the hot sun of Florida, blue sky, colorful houses, a bright landscape of greens and yellows, blues and whites. Interrupting this brightness is a big brown spot—a dog's nose. The dog's name is Franky and Franky works for the Miami-Dade Police Department. His handler, Detective Douglas Bartelt, described Franky in court as 'wild,' 'energetic,' and 'erratic.'[3] But Franky is a

---

3 *Jardines*, 569 U.S. at 4.

professional with one job to do: sniff. His job is to detect the scent of marijuana, cocaine, heroin, and other drugs.

Franky is on the scene because the police are following up on an unverified tip that Joelis Jardines was growing marijuana in his home. Franky's job is to get close enough to the house to determine whether or not the scent of marijuana can be detected coming from inside the home.

A path leads up to Jardines's front door. On a six foot leash, Franky tugs Detective Bartelt toward the area just outside the home called the 'curtilage.'[4] An old-fashioned legal term, curtilage is the area right around the home where the intimate activities of the home extend and are protected by the Fourth Amendment.[5] Officers watch Franky to see if the dog 'alerts' to any suspicious airborne scents. As Franky begins approaching the front door, he starts 'bracketing,' pacing back and forth looking for the odor's strongest source. Franky sniffs at the base of the front door and sits down, an established signal alerting police that illegal narcotics might be present. With suspicions confirmed, detectives leave the scene and apply for a search warrant using the evidence from Franky's snout. This search warrant leads to a full search of Mr. Jardines's house and the eventual recovery of marijuana.[6]

Jardines was charged with trafficking in cannabis. Prior to trial, he sought to exclude the plants from evidence by challenging the use of the drug-sniffing dog as violating the Fourth Amendment. The constitutional question turned on whether Detective Bartelt and Franky coming onto Jardines's property constituted a 'search' for Fourth Amendment purposes. If the sniffs were a search, then the evidence would be suppressed because they were done without a proper search warrant (or any applicable exception to the warrant requirement). If the sniffs were not a search, then the resulting evidence (obtained with a search warrant) would be admissible in court and could justify his conviction.

In short, the entire case turned on Franky's sniff—whether a police dog's sniff outside a person's home should be considered a search for constitutional purposes. As depicted in Cortada's painting, two aggressive nostrils intruding into the frame shape Fourth Amendment freedoms.

---

4 *United States v. Dunn*, 480 U.S. 294, 300 (1987); *Oliver v. United States*, 466 U.S. 170, 182 n.12 (1984).

5 Andrew Guthrie Ferguson, 'Personal Curtilage: Fourth Amendment Security in Public' (2014) 55 William & Mary Law Review 1283–1364.

6 *Jardines*, 569 U.S. at 5.

3   Background: Constitutional Distortion

If one were going to paint the Fourth Amendment, an artist could do worse than visualizing it as an untidy swirl of color with perspectives that push against each other in waves of confused lines. The Fourth Amendment is not a Mondrian grid or a Vermeer windowpane. Nor is it a purposefully distorted Picasso figure. Instead, it is an internally inconsistent mess—the result of colorful cases and hard lines drawn somewhat haphazardly between values of security and privacy, order and autonomy. It is as if a series of talented sketch artists tried to trace an outline over and over, blurring each line and creating distortions in the name of clarity.

Cortada's use of color and structure mirrors this chaotic Fourth Amendment reality. We see a painting born of real life, not of realism. We see colors as scents. We see vibrant confusion. We see a distorted frame that tells a story but remains unclear.

And this distortion is a perfect representation of the state of the Fourth Amendment leading up to *Jardines*, which presented not merely the narrow question of the constitutionality of drug-sniffing dogs, but broader questions over the proper way to interpret the Fourth Amendment. For criminal justice scholars, *Jardines* was a test case about the future path of the Fourth Amendment on the meaning of 'search.' That simple question defied a simple answer.

Law, like any discipline, has developed its own technical language. Terms of art retain specialized meanings based on prior judicial interpretations and legal decisions. The Fourth Amendment is notorious for taking ordinary English words and distorting them. 'Search' comes from the text of the Fourth Amendment that prohibits 'unreasonable searches and seizures' of 'persons, houses, papers, or effects.'[7] But what search means or what constitutes a search is not so clear. Common usage offers one answer. If asked whether police searched Jardines's property for evidence of drug use, most people would say 'of course.' How else would you explain why police detectives brought a trained narcotics dog to the front door? They were searching for evidence using a dog and their own senses.

But Fourth Amendment jurisprudence does not define a search in ordinary terms. Instead, the Supreme Court has redefined the test with a series of doctrinal rules.

For much of the early twentieth century, a search involved a physical intrusion into a constitutionally protected space. Courts interpreted the physical

---

7   U.S. Const. amend. IV.

nature literally. As a result, a microphone used to eavesdrop on a home was not a search because the microphone did not trespass on the boundaries of the home.[8] But once a microphone touched the inner wall of the house to listen to the same conversation, the action became a search.[9] The only difference between the cases was that one involved the physical touching of the microphone to a constitutionally protected space (the home) and the other remained physically outside the home. Such a parsimonious definition left much private human activity unprotected from law enforcement surveillance and drew significant scholarly criticism.

This understanding changed in 1967 when the Supreme Court introduced a new legal distortion in *United States v. Katz*.[10] *Katz* involved the wiretapping of a public phone booth by FBI agents investigating Charlie Katz for gambling. The police placed a listening device on a public telephone booth and recorded incriminating statements. Under a narrow traditional definition, this action was not a Fourth Amendment search because Katz could claim no property interest in the public telephone booth and there had been no physical intrusion into a constitutionally protected space. But Katz argued that this government action violated his Fourth Amendment rights to have a private, confidential conversation. The Supreme Court agreed, rejecting the old property-based rules as ill-suited for 'new' surveillance technologies and crafting a new test emphasizing the reasonable expectation of privacy.[11]

Post-*Katz*, whether there is a Fourth Amendment search turned on whether one had 'an expectation of privacy' that was both subjectively and objectively reasonable.[12] One might have a subjectively and objectively reasonable expectation of privacy of what one does in the bedroom, but not what one does on Main Street. One might have a subjectively and objectively reasonable expectation of privacy in what one writes in a diary, but not what one publishes in the newspaper. A search occurs when the government intrudes upon this reasonable expectation of privacy (goes into a home or reads a diary); if a search occurs, it is permissible only if government has a warrant or if some exception to the warrant requirement applies. In Charlie Katz's case, the Court held he had a reasonable expectation of privacy in his phone conversation because he had paid his 'toll' to use the phone and closed the phone booth door behind

---

8   *Goldman v. United States*, 316 U.S. 129, 135 (1942), *overruled in part by Katz v. United States*, 389 U.S. 347 (1967).
9   *Silverman v. United States*, 365 U.S. 505, 507 (1961).
10   *Katz v. United States*, 389 U.S. 347 (1967).
11   Ibid., 359.
12   Ibid., 361 (Harlan, J. concurring).

him. Due to the important role telephones played in society, the Court wanted to protect this type of private communication. Katz thus had a subjective expectation of privacy in his call that society would deem objectively reasonable.

If the reasonable expectation of privacy test sounds fuzzy, it is, being both circular in logic and unpredictable in application. Expectations of privacy can be influenced by judges' own expectations and remain frustratingly unclear until decided by those same judges. Expectations of privacy have been found in hotel rooms, pockets, briefcases, urine, and diaries, but not in trash, backyards, barns, and discarded genetic material (DNA). Scholars and some Justices have complained about the indeterminate nature of the test that seems to turn on what five (or more) Justices think is reasonable. Scalia long criticized *Katz* as both ungrounded in Fourth Amendment text and unhelpful in Fourth Amendment practice, and he tried to do something about it; *Jardines* presented an opportunity to build on his earlier criticism.[13]

To understand *Jardines*, one must take a little detour back to *United States v. Jones*, one of the most significant Fourth Amendment cases of this century. *Jones* set the stage for the legal debate occurring behind the scenes in *Jardines*. This is why what initially appears to be a minor battle about dogs is really a major battle about doctrine and the dominant Fourth Amendment analysis.

In *Jones*, police investigators placed an electronic GPS device on Antoine Jones's car and tracked his whereabouts for 28 days.[14] The device provided a detailed digital mosaic of his travel patterns that helped law enforcement connect Jones to a large-scale drug-distribution conspiracy. Jones's car was close enough to various drug stash houses to be good evidence of his criminal involvement. The problem for the government was they conducted this long-term tracking without a valid warrant. (The original warrant had expired and only authorized the investigation in a different state). Jones challenged the use of the device as an unconstitutional search conducted without a proper warrant.[15]

Jones tested how the Supreme Court would grapple with new surveillance technologies. After all, if no judicial warrant was required to track Jones, police could track any car for any reason without judicial approval. Or, in Fourth Amendment terms, the definition of a 'search' opened or closed the door for mass warrantless surveillance via GPS tracking devices.

The Court agreed that a search occurred, but divided as to why. Writing for a five-Justice majority, Scalia held that the police conduct a search through the

---

13   *United States v. Jones*, 565 U.S. 400 (2012).
14   Ibid., 402.
15   Ibid.

act of 'physically occupy[ing] private property for the purpose of obtaining information.'[16] Ignoring the privacy harm of 28 days of warrantless tracking and the legal reality that if no warrant was required police could track anyone for any reason, Scalia returned to a physical-based trespass test. Because police touched Jones's car, his constitutionally protected 'effect,' and did so to investigate criminal activity, this intrusion was a search that was unlawful without a warrant.

Four Justices, in an opinion by fellow conservative Justice Samuel Alito, found a search under the traditional *Katz* reasonable expectation of privacy framework.[17] Alito chided the majority for applying an eighteenth-century tort law principle of trespass to a twenty-first-century surveillance problem. The concurring Justices argued that the *Katz* test adequately resolved the constitutional question and that the majority was wrong to revert to a pre-*Katz*, property-focused Fourth Amendment analysis.

Justice Sonia Sotomayor further confused matters. She joined Scalia's majority opinion, providing the fifth vote for the conclusion that the placement of the tracking device was a trespass search. But she wrote a concurring opinion in which she agreed with Alito that the long-term surveillance violated an expectation of privacy.

Scalia's reversion to property-based search concepts surprised most Court watchers. For decades since 1967, criminal procedure professors had been teaching that the property-focused trespass theory of the Fourth Amendment was dead and buried. *Katz* was the law. And while confusing and unsettled, at least courts knew which test to apply. *Jones* upended that certainty by providing another possible test. Now there were two tests to apply in every case: (1) a trespass-physical intrusion test from *Jones* and (2) the reasonable expectation of privacy test from *Katz*. No one knew which test would prevail. Lawyers and commentators awaited the next case that would give the Justices the opportunity to clarify the rules. *Jardines* was that case.

Again writing for a five-Justice majority, Scalia doubled down on *Jones*, holding that Franky's presence on the curtilage of the home meant he physically invaded (trespassed upon) Jardines's property. If physically placing a GPS device on a car was a search, then physically placing a police dog on a front porch to sniff a home was a search. Both involved physical intrusion into constitutionally protected spaces (effects or homes) with the intent to gain incriminating information.

---

16   Ibid., 404.
17   Ibid., 414 (Sotomayor, J. concurring).

THE DISTORTIONS OF IMPLIED ARTISTIC LICENSE 241

Scalia boldly and disingenuously tried to paint a direct line from *Jones* all the way back to the pre-*Katz* era for his holding, claiming that this was a simple case reflecting longstanding views about private property:

> The [Fourth] Amendment establishes a simple baseline, one that for much of our history formed the exclusive basis for its protections: When the Government obtains information by physically intruding on persons, houses, papers, or effects, a 'search' within the original meaning of the Fourth Amendment has undoubtedly occurred. By reason of our decision in *Katz v. United States*, property rights are not the sole measure of Fourth Amendment violations,—but though *Katz* may add to the baseline, it does not subtract anything from the Amendment's protections when the Government does engage in a physical intrusion of a constitutionally protected area.[18]

As applied, the case turned on whether police had physically intruded into this constitutionally protected space. Scalia continued:

> That principle renders this case a straightforward one. The officers were gathering information in an area belonging to Jardines and immediately surrounding his house—in the curtilage of the house, which we have held enjoys protection as part of the home itself. And, they gathered that information by physically entering and occupying the area to engage in conduct not explicitly or implicitly permitted by the homeowner.[19]

The problem is that this line is neither direct nor clear and had largely been painted over by *Katz*. It was for this reason that Justices Elena Kagan, Ruth Bader Ginsburg, and Sotomayor joined Scalia's majority opinion, but argued in a concurring opinion that *Katz* should control the outcome.[20] Whether Jardines's property interests were violated, clearly his privacy interests were infringed by a dog sniffing under his door. Perhaps equally powerfully, the four-Justice dissent argued that Scalia's attempt to claim a direct line to a traditional understanding of the Fourth Amendment was largely imaginary and did not hold up under scrutiny.[21]

---

18   *Florida v. Jardines*, 569 U.S. 1, 5 (2013).
19   Ibid., 6.
20   Ibid., 14 (Kagan, J. concurring).
21   Ibid., 1–17 (Alito, J. dissenting).

In the end, *Jardines* neither clarified the Fourth Amendment nor unified the Justices. While offering an opportunity to expose different theories of the search doctrine, the decision instead confused them, providing new inconsistencies and new distortions. Post-*Jardines*, the doctrinal forces continue to swirl against each other, looking to the next case for clarity.

Cortada's painting captures this swirl of confusion. This is not a case (or a painting) that offers clarity, but one that obscures with overlapping lines. Chaotic, impressionistic walls mask a carpet of scents, all off-kilter in non-linear space. The color blends and mixes; dots, curves, swirls all bump against each other. The space is busy with action, senses, and visual noise. The confusion is the point—which, again, is probably more appropriate for a painting than a legal decision.

4   Style: Implicit Realism

What is it that we see when we examine a painting? How do we make sense of what we see?

Walk past Cortada's *Jardines* painting in the halls of a law school and what would be revealed? A door? A window? A light? A dog's nose? We see a colorful room, but why the nostrils of an animal? We might surmise that the dog smells something because of the vapors entering his nostrils, but what could that mean? The story we might tell ourselves comes from inferences, implicit clues that ground and frame an invented story but do not control it.

Law is not supposed to work that way. While courts infer facts and draw conclusions, judges are not supposed to create stories out of whole cloth. But Scalia's Fourth Amendment reasoning in *Jardines* is not far from this fiction. He determined that Franky's quick walk up to the front porch invaded Jardines's property interest because it violated an 'implied license' we all share about access to our homes:

> [T]he question before the court is precisely whether the officer's conduct was an objectively reasonable search. As we have described, that depends upon *whether* the officers had an implied license to enter the porch, which in turn depends upon the purpose for which they entered. Here, their behavior objectively reveals a purpose to conduct a search, which is not what anyone would think he had license to do.[22]

---

22   Ibid., 10.

Who is 'anyone' in that last sentence? What is this 'implied license' that Scalia so readily sees? What does it mean for Jardines's home or for our homes? Lawyers cannot really say because 'implied license' had no Fourth Amendment meaning before *Jardines*. In fact, it had no independent or established legal meaning up to the moment Scalia created it and wielded it to control the outcome of the case.

But a few questions might arise even for non-lawyers. Aren't front porches and doors meant to be visited? The obvious answer is yes. Before *Jardines*, the Court had ruled that police and other people were allowed to come up to your house and talk to you. This is how Girl Scouts sell cookies, how peddlers sell their wares, and how Jehovah's Witnesses proselytize. Absent a 'no soliciting' sign, people are invited to your door and it is not a trespass or some implicit violation. This holds for police, who not only can approach your home to sell you tickets to the Policeman's Ball but also to gather information (a tactic called 'knock and talk').

If police can walk to your door and knock, why can't they bring a dog with them to sniff? The mere presence of a dog cannot be the problem because neighbors could walk up to the door with their dogs and knock. Are only police dogs prohibited and, if so, why are police dogs different? Does the dog's drug-sniffing capabilities provide the crucial distinction? Scalia does not answer, simply asserting that civil society would not take kindly to such actions because the conduct violates that accepted implied license. We might be okay with Girl Scouts and aluminum-siding salespeople arriving at the front door, but not drug-sniffing police dogs.

How do we know when implied license exists? We do not, another big problem with *Jardines*. Where does this license come from? Again, we do not know. Scalia begins painting his own Fourth Amendment protection of the home:

> As it is undisputed that the detectives had all four of their feet and all four of their companion's firmly planted on the constitutionally protected extension of Jardines' home, the only question is whether he had given his leave (even implicitly) for them to do so. He had not.
>
> 'A license may be implied from the habits of the country,' notwithstanding the 'strict rule of the English common law as to entry upon a close.' ... We have accordingly recognized that 'the knocker on the front door is treated as an invitation or license to attempt an entry, justifying ingress to the home by solicitors, hawkers and peddlers of all kinds.' ... This implicit license typically permits the visitor to approach the home by the front path, knock promptly, wait briefly to be received, and then (absent invitation to linger longer) leave. Complying with the terms of

that traditional invitation does not require fine-grained legal knowledge; it is generally managed without incident by the Nation's Girl Scouts and trick-or-treaters.

But introducing a trained police dog to explore the area around the home in hopes of discovering incriminating evidence is something else. There is no customary invitation to do *that*. An invitation to engage in canine forensic investigation assuredly does not inhere in the very act of hanging a knocker.

To find a visitor knocking on the door is routine (even if sometimes unwelcome); to spot that same visitor exploring the front path with a metal detector, or marching his bloodhound into the garden before saying hello and asking permission, would inspire most of us to—well, call the police. The scope of a license—express or implied—is limited not only to a particular area but also to a specific purpose. Consent at a traffic stop to an officer's checking out an anonymous tip that there is a body in the trunk does not permit the officer to rummage through the trunk for narcotics. Here, the background social norms that invite a visitor to the front door do not invite him there to conduct a search.[23]

From this reasoning—largely around how one interprets 'hanging a knocker' on the front door—it appears that we know what is permissible and what is not by some shared implicit understanding that controls Fourth Amendment protections around the home. Confused? Join the club who finds an analysis of implicit license an odd way to determine Fourth Amendment protections.

Is a Fourth Amendment built around implicit license made up—the legal equivalent of painting the illusion of three-dimensional space? Yes. But is it normatively wrong? Probably not. Scalia tried to shape an impressionistic understanding of what police can and cannot do that is recognizable from Fourth Amendment principles, even if not clear from those principles. He drafted an explicit legal rule from implicit assumptions of social norms. There is a difference between a Girl Scout selling cookies and a detective investigating a crime. There is a recognizable principle, even if we cannot draw clear lines or paint a coherent theory. Implicit social norms control much in our lives, and Scalia draws a line around the home for added protection from police investigation.

This is why Xavier Cortada's painting is so appropriate for the reality of *Jardines*. We must make sense of implicit clues from fixed structures, windows, lights, frames. We get a sense of that structure even if we cannot (without full

---

23   Ibid., 8–9.

context) make sense of the whole picture. We are forced to invent a theory to make sense of our imagined reality. And while our invented story may not be completely convincing, it is persuasive and reasonable enough. So it is with art. So it is with law.

5 Meaning: The Harm of Intrusion

If the precise reasoning of *Jardines* leaves room for criticism, the major point of the opinion does not. A police dog invading the sanctity of one's home requires Fourth Amendment protection. It is an invasion. The dog—thus the government—is intruding on your personal property and privacies of life.

Again, Cortada's painting captures this sense of invasion. The nose pushes into the visual frame, larger than life, inside the home, half the size of the door, and into the observer's memory. The overhead light illuminates its centrality. The nose anchors the image, forceful, violent, present without eyes or body. A dark instrument of sensory collection, it crashes through the closed red door. In doing so, it releases waves of colors and scents to the outside world. The private space of the home is left exposed to the intrusive presence of a clearly unwanted snout.

Were one to paint the history that led to the adoption of the Fourth Amendment, a similar thematic imaging might emerge. The Supreme Court has long described the violent, arbitrary, and intrusive invasions of colonial era customs agents whose zeal for searching necessitated a constitutional amendment. In *Riley v. California*,[24] the Supreme Court summarized the Founders' fears of physical intrusion into their homes and lives:

> Our cases have recognized that the Fourth Amendment was the founding generation's response to the reviled 'general warrants' and 'writs of assistance' of the colonial era, which allowed British officers to rummage through homes in an unrestrained search for evidence of criminal activity. Opposition to such searches was in fact one of the driving forces behind the Revolution itself. In 1761, the patriot James Otis delivered a speech in Boston denouncing the use of writs of assistance. A young John Adams was there, and he would later write that '[e]very man of a crowded audience appeared to me to go away, as I did, ready to take arms against writs of assistance.'[25]

---

24   134 S. Ct. 2473 (2014).
25   Ibid., 2494.

The harm was the officers' home invasion; the Fourth Amendment was drafted to respond to this frightening intrusion. As Alito explained in *Carpenter v. United States*,[26] the violation was one of social norms, exposing intimate family details and undermining a sense of security:

> Searches generally begin with the officers, 'mak[ing] non consensual entries into areas not open to the public.' Once there, officers are necessarily in a position to observe private spaces generally shielded from the public and discernible only with the owner's consent. Private area after private area becomes exposed to the officers' eyes as they rummage through the owner's property in their hunt for the object or objects of the search. If they are searching for documents, officers may additionally have to rifle through many other papers—potentially filled with the most intimate details of a person's thoughts and life—before they find the specific information they are seeking.[27]

Scalia's opinion in *Jardines* mirrored these foundational themes. He connected the Fourth Amendment to the home. '[W]hen it comes to the Fourth Amendment, the home is the first among equals. At the Amendment's very core stands the right of a man to retreat into his own home and there be free from unreasonable governmental intrusion.'[28] What is exposed is not merely the scent of marijuana, but the security of the home.

The concurring justices in *Jardines* evoke this shared theme of intrusion, but with a different emphasis. In her concurring opinion for three, Kagan locates this harm in violations of privacy rather than property. What is being intruded upon was not the curtilage line of the porch, but the private information coming from our homes.

> The Court today treats this case under a property rubric; I write separately to note that I could just as happily have decided it by looking to Jardines' privacy interests. A decision along those lines would have looked ... well, much like this one. It would have talked about ' "the right of a man to retreat into his own home and there be free from unreasonable governmental intrusion." ' ... It would have insisted on maintaining the 'practical value' of that right by preventing police officers from standing in an adjacent space and 'trawl[ing] for evidence with impunity.' ... It would have

---

26 138 S. Ct. 2206 (2018).
27 Ibid., 2251 (Alito, J. dissenting).
28 *Jardines*, 569 U.S. at 6.

explained that '"privacy expectations are most heightened"' in the home and the surrounding area. ... And it would have determined that police officers invade those shared expectations when they use trained canine assistants to reveal within the confines of a home what they could not otherwise have found there.[29]

Cortada's painting reflects this privacy-protective sentiment. The invading nose is not a threat merely because it crosses the threshold of the home, but because of how and why it is present. Franky's foregrounded nose sticks inside our private space. The harm is clear from the exaggerated size and aggressive breaking of the frame. As a physical and psychological matter, private space has dissolved into colorful chaos. Whoever lives in that home has lost an expectation of privacy and has been revealed as vulnerable and insecure. The meaning is clear because the visual intrusion reflects the privacy intrusion.

6 Conclusion: Memorable Images

At its core, Scalia's opinion in *Florida v. Jardines* is about what we understand to be true without proof—a shared implied understanding that falls apart on examination—not unlike how we evaluate art. The resulting artistic creation is not properly judged by rules or logic, but by feeling—by the emotional and intellectual impact of the work. Great art can be formalistic or impressionistic. Great artists can be technical perfectionists or radical interpreters. The ultimate goal is a painting's visceral effect on our thinking about the world around us. The difference between good art and bad art is that one moves us and one does not.

Cortada's visual and visceral canine search moves us to see the invasion, the confusion, and the harm. The painting works because it simplifies the harm to the security of the home. The intrusion is Franky. Franky's nose remains present, signifying and signaling an unwanted invasion which captures this violation of property and privacy. The painting also works because the centered harm is placed within a chaos of color. Just as the law at issue in *Jardines* was fluid, moving, and uncertain, so too is Cortada's painting.

Unfortunately, the same charitable embrace of chaos and visceral imagery cannot be granted to the *Jardines* opinion itself. Scalia's strategic approach, while cementing his physical invasion (trespass-like) theory of Fourth

---

29   Ibid., 13 (Kagan, J. concurring).

Amendment searches, did not clarify the doctrine; worse, it created a host of new issues to examine around the concept of license. What do we mean by implied license in other cases? Or at homes without door knockers? Or apartments? Or mobile homes? Can a homeowner change an implied license by explicitly posting signs revoking any license to enter?[30] What if instead of a police dog, police brought a mechanical chemical sniffer to the door? These and other questions remain unanswered, awaiting the next case (or cases) to resolve.

Stare at Xavier Cortada's painting long enough and one can almost imagine the curling scents around Franky's nose turning into floating question marks—a fitting symbolism for Scalia's *Jardines* opinion and the future of the Fourth Amendment. How we see the law (and art) is always subject to questioning.

Recommended Reading

Blitz, Marc Jonathan. 'The Fourth Amendment Future of Public Surveillance: Remote Recording and Other Searches in Public Space.' *American University Law Review* 63 (2013): 21–86.

Clancy, Thomas K., *The Fourth Amendment Its History and Interpretation*. Durham: Carolina Academic Press, 2008.

Clancy, Thomas K. 'What Does the Fourth Amendment Protect: Property, Privacy, or Security?' *Wake Forest Law Review* 33 (1998): 307–370.

Ferguson, Andrew Guthrie. 'Personal Curtilage: Fourth Amendment Security in Public.' *William & Mary Law Review* 55 (2014): 1283–1364.

Hancock, Catherine. 'Justice Powell's Garden: The Ciraolo Dissent and Fourth Amendment Protection for Curtilage-Home Privacy.' *San Diego Law Review* 44 (2007): 551–571.

Henderson, Stephen E. and Andrew Guthrie Ferguson. 'LAWn Signs: A Fourth Amendment for Constitutional Curmudgeons.' *Ohio State Journal of Criminal Law* 13 (2016): 487–502.

Maclin, Tracey. 'The Complexity of the Fourth Amendment: A Historical Review.' *Boston University Law Review* 77 (1997): 960–65.

Sklansky, David A. 'The Fourth Amendment and Common Law.' *Columbia Law Review* 100 (2000): 1739–1814.

---

30   Andrew Guthrie Ferguson and Stephen E. Henderson, 'LAWn Signs: A Fourth Amendment for Constitutional Curmudgeons' (2016) 13 Ohio State Journal of Criminal Law 491.

Stern, Stephanie M. 'The Inviolate Home: Housing Exceptionalism in the Fourth Amendment.' *Cornell Law Review* 95 (2010): 906–908.

Taslitz, Andrew E. *Reconstructing the Fourth Amendment: A History of Search and Seizure*. New York: New York University Press, 2006.

Index

Abela, Eduardo 28
Adams, John 245
Adams-Onís Treaty 176
A Fight for Jenny 136
AIDS 29
Alaska 185
Alciato, Andrea 16
Alexander, Gregory 20
Alito, Samuel 159–160, 164, 240, 246
American Civil Liberties Union (ACLU) 129–130
American Law Institute (ALI) 102
American Revolution 23
Ancestral Journeys 27, 41–42
animal sacrifice 6, 142, 144–148, 152–159, 161, 165
Arizona 101
Articles of Confederation 172–174, 186
Astrid 41
AT&T 87
Axum Stele 19

Babalú-Ayé 35, 144–145, 156, 162
Bacon, Francis 28, 36, 96, 99, 108–110, 113–114, 116
bank craps 178
Barron, Jerome 79, 81–82, 85–86, 88, 92
Bartelt, Douglas 235–236
Beasley, James 78–79, 81–82, 84
Becker-Moelands, Margariet 10
Beckham, Ethel 80
Bickel, Alexander 204–205
Bilchick, Shay 30
Bill of Rights 48
bingo 7, 177–178
Biscayne Bay 40–41
Black, Charles 227
Black Lives Matter 68
blackjack 178
Blackmun, Harry 85, 155, 163
Blackstone, William 182
Boehme-Neßler, Volker 20
Brennan, William 98, 111, 161
Breyer, Stephen 101n17, 198–200, 206–207
Bridging the Gap 27, 29

Broward County 193
Bruegel, Pieter 15
Buchanan, Pat 8, 195n6
Buck, Morison 122, 125–136
Burger, Warren 85–86, 122, 133, 136
Bush, George W. 8, 29, 37, 190, 192–193, 195–196, 201, 204, 208
Bush, Jeb 201–202
butterfly ballot 8, 37, 190, 195n6

California 101, 131, 178
Cambyses 11, 15
cannabis 236, 246
Capital Jury Project (CJP) 103–106
capital punishment 1, 16, 96, 98, 103, 104, 112–113n72, 115
CERN 42
chads 22, 37, 190
Cherokee 176
Cherry, Linda 224–225
Chiles, Jackie 48
Chiles, Lawton 180
civil rights 5, 68–70, 129–130, 158
Civil War 177
Classroom Teachers Association (CTA) 79–80
Confederacy 173, 177
Constitution of Cádiz 19
Court of Chancery 182
Cuba 23, 27–28, 32–33, 76, 144, 146–147
Cubism 29
Curtis, Dennis 10, 18
Cutler Fossil Site 41

Damhouder, Joos de 16
Dar es Saalam, Tanzania 29
Davis, Allen Lee 111
death penalty 36, 39, 96, 98–108, 110–116
Declaration of Independence 172
Deering Estate 41
Destin, Leonard 223
Diatom Fountain 43
Dicey, A.V. 182
discrimination 33, 89, 91, 98, 120, 122, 128, 137, 153, 161

Disney World   23
DNA   41–42, 239
dog   22, 35, 38, 142, 144, 156, 157, 232, 234–237, 239–245, 248
Douglas, William   98
Douzinas, Costas   18
Dubuffet, Jean   38
Due Process Clause   49
duFresne, Elizabeth   81

Earls, Leigh   130
Edgerton, Samuel   10
Eighth Amendment   101n17, 111n60
Eiseley, Loren   228
Electoral College   198, 201–202
electric chair   35, 96, 98, 111–112
Eleventh Amendment   35, 168, 170–171, 179, 180–181, 183–186
Enríquez, Carlos   28
equal protection   130, 197–200, 203–207
Everglades   6, 43

Facebook   87, 92
Fairness Doctrine   83, 87, 92
Fauvism   29
Fifth Amendment   49, 218–219
Finch, Atticus   48
First Amendment   4, 34, 76, 78, 81–88, 91–92, 145, 148–152, 154, 157–159, 161
  Free Exercise Clause   145, 149, 151–153, 155, 160–162
  Press Clause   34, 84, 88, 91 *See also* freedom of the press
  Speech Clause   88, 91 *See also* freedom of speech
Five Action Steps to Stop Sea Level Rise   42
Fleming, Francis   177
Florida Beach and Shore Preservation Act   216–217
Florida Elections Canvassing Commission   195
Florida Man   2, 8
Florida Today   127
Flower Force   42
Flynn, Billy   48
Fonda, Henry   3, 56
Foreign Sovereign Immunity Act   184
Fortas, Abe   3
Fourth Amendment   38, 234–248

Fourteenth Amendment   49, 180, 218
Franky   234–236, 240, 242, 247–248
freedom of speech   83–85, 87–88, 91, 149
freedom of the press   1, 21, 34, 84–85, 87–88, 90–92
Freetown, Sierra Leone   29
Fries, Hans   12

gaming   7, 168, 170–171, 177–178
Gambini, Vincent   48
García Valdés, Victor Manuel   28
Gattorno, Antonio   28
German Imperial Court   10
George III, King   172, 182
Georgia   1, 173, 176, 181–183
Gideon, Clarence Earl   3, 32, 39, 46, 48–51, 54–57
Gideon's Trumpet   3, 56
Ginsburg, Ruth Bader   101n17, 199–200, 241
Goetsbloets, Pierre   18
González-Torres, Félix   20
Goodman, Saul   48
Goodrich, Peter   17–18
Google   87
Gore, Al   8, 37, 190, 192–193, 195–196, 201, 204–205, 208
Gorsuch, Neil   164
GPS   239–240
Granma   76

hanging chads   37, 190
Hand to Hand   29
Harris, Katherine   8, 193–194
Harrison, Crutcher   80
Hawtrey, John   131–132
Hialeah, Florida   6, 35, 142, 144, 147, 152–159, 161–163
Hillsborough County, Florida   122, 124
Hogarth, William   18
Holder, Eric   50
Hubrich, Ann-Kathrin   13
hurricanes   23, 216
Hutz, Lionel   48

implied license   242–244, 248
Indian Commerce Clause   171, 174–175, 179
Indian Gaming Regulatory Act (IGRA)   168, 170, 178, 180, 184–185, 186

Indian Trade and Intercourse Act   175
internet   2, 87, 90–92
Iredell, James   183

Jackson, Andrew   171, 176
Jay, John   182
Jefferson, Thomas   176
Jet   132
Jeter, Mildred   124
Jim Crow   5, 23, 177
Johannesburg, South Africa   29
Judiciary Act of 1789   208
juror diversity   69–71

Kagan, Elena   101n17, 241, 246
Katz, Charlie   238
Kavanaugh, Brett   164
Kelly, Ellesworth   20
Kennedy, Anthony   152–153, 157–158, 197
Kennedy, John F.   192, 201
Kennedy, Robert F.   32, 46, 50, 56
Kentucky   133
Key Biscayne, Florida   142
Key West, Florida   23
King, Martin Luther Jr.   31
Knox, Henry   173, 175
Kooning, Willem de   28

Lady Justice   11, 15
Lam, Wifredo   28, 32
Langbein, John   10
Last Judgment   12, 14
Leadville, Colorado   29
legal realism   22
lethal injection   36, 96, 112–113, 115
Lerner, Renée Lettow   11
LGBTQ   134, 137
Lincoln, Abraham   192
Long, Huey   89
Los Angeles, California   146
Louisiana   89, 127
Louisiana Purchase   176
Loving, Richard   124

Madison, James   174
Madrid, Spain   29
Make America Great Again   70
Maldonado, Solangel   137

Manchester, A. H.   10, 17
mangrove   39–40
Marijuana, *see* Cannabis
Marshall, John   175, 192
Marshall, Thurgood   128, 132
Martinez, Mel   30
Martyn, Georges   16
Mauldin, Bill   192
McMurdo Station   40
Medina, Pedro   111
Menendez, Manuel   134–135
metoo   68
Miami, Florida   1, 23, 27–28, 40–43, 78–79, 81, 142, 147
Miami Beach, Florida   40
Miami Dade County   6, 39–40, 79–80, 93, 193, 196, 203
Miami Dade Police Department   235
Milano, Gary   40
Mississippi   5, 176
Model Penal Code   102
Modigliani, Amedeo   28
Mondrian, Piet   237
Mulberry, Florida   129

National Association for the Advancement of Colored People (NAACP)   129
Narváez, José Ramón   19
National Organization for Women (NOW)   129
Native American   168, 170, 172–173, 176, 183–184
Native American Church   151
Nead, Lynda   18
Necessary-and-Proper Clause   175
New York   27, 146
New York Times   128, 222
new federalism   179
Nixon, Richard   3, 201
Northwest Ordinance   174

O'Connor, Sandra Day   155, 163, 197
Oklahoma   127, 171, 176
Ol' Sparky   111
Otis, James   245

Palm Beach County   8, 193, 195, 195n6, 203
Palmore Jr., Clarence   32, 122–123, 125–126, 132, 134–137

Panama City, Florida 49
Paul, Dan 81, 85
Paumen, Vanessa 14
Peace Palace, The Hague 19
Peel, Joseph A. Jr. 3
Peláez, Amelia 28, 32–33
peremptory strikes 69, 71–72
Phillip and Patricia Frost Museum of Science 40
Picasso, Pablo 28, 237
Pichardo, Ernesto 146–147, 163, 164–165
Pittman, Craig 2–3, 6, 8
poker 178
Pointillism 38
Ponce, Fidelio 28
Port Louis, Mauritius 29
Porterfield, Ernest 127
Posner, Richard 200
Proclamation Line of 1763 173
Protecting America's Children: A National Message Mural 27, 30

racism 6, 22, 110, 120
racial discrimination 98, 122, 128
Reclamation Project 27, 39–42
Rehnquist, William 153, 179, 197, 199
Religious Freedom Restoration Act (RFRA) 161–162
Religious Land Use and Institutionalized Persons Act (RLUIPA) 162
Resnik, Judith 10, 18
Reynolds, George 150
Rice, Andrew 222–224
right-of-reply 4, 81–84, 89–90
right to counsel 21, 32, 46, 48–54, 57
Robert Rauschenberg Foundation 43
Roberts, John 160, 164

Saint Augustine, Florida 19, 23
Saint Lazarus 35, 142, 144
Santería 6, 35, 142, 144–149, 153–159, 161–165
scales of justice 66
Scalia, Antonin 153, 157, 196–197, 234–235, 239–244, 246–248
search warrant 232, 236, 238–240
Seminole 6, 35, 168, 170–171, 176–177, 180, 187

Seminole Tribe of Florida 6, 35, 168, 170–171, 176–178, 180
Seminole Tribe of Oklahoma 177
Seventh-day Adventist 150
Shapiro, Robert 129, 131
Shaw, Leander J. 208
Sherwin, Richard 18
Sidoti, Anthony 122–123, 125, 128, 132, 134–137
Sidoti Palmore, Linda 32, 122–129, 131–137
Simon, Tobias 79, 81–82
Sixth Amendment 39, 48–51, 53, 62–63
slavery 23, 144, 176–177
slot machines 35, 168, 170, 178, 186
Smith, Bruce 11
social media 92
Solomon 11
Solórzano Pereira, Juan 17
Sotomayor, Sonia 101n17, 240–241
Souter, David 183, 200, 206
South Carolina 150–151, 181
sovereign immunity 1, 7, 170–171, 179, 180–186
Spain 17, 23, 29, 42, 173, 175–176
Stamp Act 89
Steiker, Carol 103n23, 115
Steiker, Jordan 103n23, 115
Stepping into the American Dream 27, 29
Stevens, John Paul 196, 199, 203–204
Stewart, Potter 99
Supreme Court of Florida 1, 31, 50, 84, 90, 193, 198–199, 201–208, 217, 221
Surrealism 28, 33

Takings Clause 218–219, 218n18
Tallahassee, Florida 80
Tamiami Trail 6
Tampa, Florida 122, 126, 132
Tampa College 125
Tennessee 176
Texas 123, 129, 132, 134–136
The Markers (South Pole) 27, 40, 42
Thomas, Clarence 54, 160, 164, 197
Tomrys 15
Tornillo, Pasquale 'Pat' 4, 33, 78–85, 92–93
Twitter 92

United Teachers of Dade 4, 79, 92–93
University of Miami 27

INDEX

Velázquez, Diego   36, 110
Verizon   87
Vermeer, Johannes   237
Victor Manuel, *see* García Valdés, Victor Manuel
Volusia County   193

Wainwright, Louis L.   3
Wallace, George   85
Warren Court   3
Washington, George   174
Weisberg, Robert   107
Well, Spencer   41
Widener, Mike   12

Williams, Johnny   62–63, 66–67, 74
Williams, Patricia   110
Wilson, James   181–182
wiretapping   238
women   29, 34, 42, 63, 69–71, 127, 129, 199
Wright, Mike   225
writs of assistance   245

Yoo, John   200
Young, Alison   18

Zaleucus   15
Zuckerberg, Mark   69

Printed in the United States
By Bookmasters